The Unitary Executive Theory

The Unitary Executive Theory

A Danger to
Constitutional Government

Jeffrey Crouch, Mark J. Rozell, and
Mitchel A. Sollenberger

University Press of Kansas

Published by the University Press of Kansas (Lawrence, Kansas 66045),
which was organized by the Kansas Board of Regents and is operated and
funded by Emporia State University, Fort Hays State University, Kansas State
University, Pittsburg State University, the University of Kansas, and Wichita
State University.

Library of Congress Cataloging-in-Publication Data

Names: Crouch, Jeffrey, author. | Rozell, Mark J., author. |
Sollenberger, Mitchel A., author.
Title: The unitary executive theory : a danger to constitutional government
/ Jeffrey Crouch, Mark J. Rozell, and Mitchel A. Sollenberger.
Description: Lawrence : University Press of Kansas, 2020. | Includes index.
Identifiers: LCCN 2020011788
ISBN 9780700630035 (Cloth)
ISBN 9780700630042 (Paperback)
ISBN 9780700630059 (ePub)
Subjects: LCSH: Executive power—United States. | Constitutional
law—United States.
Classification: LCC KF5050 .C76 2020 | DDC 342.73/062—dc23
LC record available at https://lccn.loc.gov/2020011788.

British Library Cataloguing-in-Publication Data is available.

Printed in the United States of America

10 9 8 7 6 5 4 3 2 1

The paper used in this publication is acid free and meets the minimum
requirements of the American National Standard for Permanence of Paper
for Printed Library Materials Z39.48-1992.

To Louis Fisher: scholar, mentor, friend.
JC, MJR, and MAS

Contents

Acknowledgments   ix

Introduction. A Flawed Theory with Dangerous Consequences   1
    SANCTUARY CITIES   4
    TRAVEL BAN   5
    CHINA TRADE POLICY   7
    THE UNITARY EXECUTIVE THEORY: OVERVIEW   10

CHAPTER 1. Presidential Power and the Unitary Executive
Theory   14
    LITERALIST THEORY   14
    PRESIDENTIAL PREROGATIVE: "LIFE AND LIMB" THEORY   15
    STEWARDSHIP THEORY   17
    ORIGINS OF THE UNITARY EXECUTIVE THEORY   18
    WEAK VERSUS STRONG THEORIES   22
    TEXTUAL ELEMENTS OF THE UNITARY EXECUTIVE THEORY   23
    UNITARY EXECUTIVE ADVOCATES VERSUS CRITICS   26

CHAPTER 2. Domestic Powers: Part I   28
    DISCRETIONARY AND MINISTERIAL DUTIES   30
    DISCRETIONARY DUTIES AND THE LIMITS OF PRESIDENTIAL CONTROL   34
    PRESIDENTIAL POWER: DEPARTMENTS AND BUREAUS   36
    EXECUTIVE ORDERS   40
    SIGNING STATEMENTS   44
    FEDERAL EXECUTIVE CLEMENCY: THE PRESIDENT'S POWER TO
      PARDON   49
    CONCLUSION   51

CHAPTER 3. Domestic Powers: Part II   53
APPOINTMENTS   53
MYERS V. UNITED STATES: REMOVALS AND STATUTORY
    QUALIFICATIONS   61
INDEPENDENT COUNSEL AND THE REMOVAL POWER   66
CONCLUSION   74

CHAPTER 4. Domestic Powers: Part III   76
THE LEGISLATIVE VETO   76
PRESIDENTS AND AGENCY-LEVEL RULEMAKING   82
REINING IN THE PRESIDENT'S CZARS   87
EXECUTIVE PRIVILEGE: CONSTITUTIONAL, YET LIMITED   95
CONCLUSION   102

CHAPTER 5. Foreign Affairs Powers: Part I   103
THE UNITARY EXECUTIVE AND THE COMMANDER-IN-CHIEF CLAUSE   106
THE DECLARE WAR CLAUSE: A HOLLOW LEGISLATIVE POWER?   109
LEGAL OBFUSCATION TO TAKE UNITARY ACTION   112
AN EMERGENCY PRESIDENTIAL POWER?   115
"SOLE ORGAN" DOCTRINE   122
CONCLUSION   125

CHAPTER 6. Foreign Affairs Powers: Part II   127
MILITARY COMMISSIONS AND HABEAS CORPUS   128
FOREIGN AND DOMESTIC SURVEILLANCE   134
TORTURE   138
EXTRAORDINARY RENDITION   140
STATE SECRETS PRIVILEGE   144
CONCLUSION   147

Conclusion   150
DOMESTIC POWERS   153
FOREIGN AFFAIRS POWERS   157
OUR MODEL: HOW GOVERNMENT SHOULD FUNCTION   159
GOING FORWARD   161

Notes   165
Index   203

Acknowledgments

We gratefully acknowledge those who provided assistance in making this book possible. At the University Press of Kansas, Acquisitions Editor David Congdon believed in this project at the outset, and he guided it through to publication. Graham Dodds and an anonymous reviewer provided very helpful feedback on an earlier draft of the manuscript. Hannah Lutz and Aaron Stuvland, both graduate students in the George Mason University Schar School of Policy and Government, provided research assistance. Special thanks to Editor George C. Edwards III and *Presidential Studies Quarterly* for publishing our cowritten articles on Barack Obama's use of signing statements in 2013, and Donald J. Trump and the unitary executive theory in 2017, two sources from which we drew material for this book. American University generously provided a Faculty Research Support Grant for Jeff Crouch to work on this project. He appreciates the backing of his program's deans, Carola Weil and Jill Klein, and the Center for Congressional and Presidential Studies (CCPS), and offers special thanks to his colleagues CCPS Founding Director Jim Thurber and CCPS Director David Barker.

Louis Fisher, to whom we dedicate this book, supported this project through its early stages. Over the years he also has critiqued many of the earlier manuscripts that each of us has written for this press and others. The influence of his scholarly work on each of us is evident in this volume.

Introduction

A Flawed Theory with Dangerous Consequences

When the president does it, that means it is not illegal.
—Richard M. Nixon, 1977

I have the right to do whatever I want as president.
—Donald J. Trump, 2019

On December 18, 2019, the House of Representatives approved two articles of impeachment against President Donald J. Trump. The first article, approved by a vote of 230 to 197, charged that President Trump abused his powers by soliciting the interference of a foreign government in the 2020 presidential election. The second article, approved by a vote of 229 to 198, declared that Trump obstructed Congress in directing "the unprecedented, categorical, and indiscriminate defiance of subpoenas issued by the House of Representatives."[1] At the core of Trump's impeachment is the abuse of power for personal gain in that the president and his allies attempted to leverage government resources in the form of appropriated military aid to Ukraine in exchange for the Ukraine government investigating Hunter Biden, the son of the 2020 Democratic presidential nominee, former vice president Joe Biden.

Although the Senate ultimately voted to acquit President Trump on nearly party-line votes, the two impeachment resolutions highlight some of the more troubling aspects of the modern presidency, particularly the adoption—either explicitly or implicitly—by nearly all

1

modern occupants of the White House of elements of the unitary executive theory, which ultimately values unilateral executive power over constitutional constraints. That theory posits that the president of the United States controls the entire executive branch of the government and that he occupies a position of primacy in our constitutional system of separated powers and thus may exercise vast unilateral powers for the public good. This book is a critical response to the increasingly influential theory that has inflicted serious damage on core constitutional principles.

Presidents understandably want to have as much freedom to act as possible. However, presidents often are frustrated that our Constitution's system of separated powers and checks and balances delays or even derails their plans. Pro-executive political theorists have, over time, developed the unitary executive theory as a way not only to explain how presidents work around these constitutional constraints but also to justify such actions. In that way, the unitary executive theory is a normative view of the presidency used not only to describe presidential behavior but also to justify it.

The first impeachment resolution sits at the core of the fundamental principle of the unitary executive theory, which is that the president alone controls the powers of the executive branch. In the case of using government resources for personal benefit, the very act is but a logical extension of the unitary executive theory. To be sure, some advocates of the unitary executive theory claim that they are agnostic to the question of the scope of presidential power, or they declare that there are some limits to its use (albeit qualified ones). However, the overarching theory advanced provides the necessary framework for presidents not only to use power aggressively but also to attempt to wall themselves off from the traditional institutional checks provided in the Constitution and laws. The latter point is perfectly represented in the second impeachment resolution, which charged that President Trump obstructed Congress's attempts to investigate the potential abuses of power in the executive branch.

The impeachment of President Trump underscores the serious consequences of legitimizing the unitary executive theory. Presidents may run amok and believe they can do just about anything and get away with it. President Trump appeared genuinely shocked that he had been impeached for what he has called "perfect" conduct in office. He and his supporters thus dismissed the charges against him as a partisan-motivated "witch hunt" without substance.

The fundamental tenets of the unitary executive theory are not supported by core, constitutional principles of separation of powers and checks and balances. Nor is it a theory for which supporters can marshal empirical evidence that the American government currently, or ever, has adopted it as a working model that advances republican principles. Despite these realities, the unitary executive theory has increasingly become an influential tool for shaping presidential behavior and has paved the way for presidents such as Donald J. Trump to take aggressive unilateral actions. In the case of this presidency, the aggressive use of the unitary executive theory aided in Trump's impeachment by a Congress, albeit along purely partisan lines, willing to stand for its own constitutional prerogatives to check executive power and conduct investigations of alleged wrongdoing. Trump's first response: refuse to even acknowledge the legitimacy of Congress's authority to act—behavior that would have no legitimacy itself, and would not be taken seriously by anyone, without an underlying theory of presidential primacy to justify it.

Throughout US history, numerous presidents of course have taken aggressive or unilateral actions. Consider the presidencies of Abraham Lincoln, Theodore Roosevelt, Woodrow Wilson, and Franklin D. Roosevelt—all generally revered as "strong" or even "great" presidents. Mostly these and other presidents who acted unilaterally did so under emergency circumstances (i.e., Civil War, Great Depression, and world wars) and never claimed that their extraordinary exercises of powers were permanent features of our governing system to be used any time a president decides to do so. The unitary executive theory is different than the claim of temporary emergency powers belonging to presidents. The theory strikes at the very core of the ongoing operations of our delicately balanced system of powers among the branches of the national government.

The unitary executive theory only came into use in the 1980s during the presidency of Ronald Reagan. It then burst onto the public scene in a much more aggressive manner two decades later when George W. Bush was at the helm of the ship of state. His administration vigorously defended executive power and, in the post-9/11 world, enjoyed some success in doing so. Bush's successor, Barack Obama, initially expressed a more modest view of presidential power than his predecessor, but over time he, too, drew on the actions of prior presidents to claim authority to circumvent Congress in several policy areas, particularly the deployment of US military forces overseas.

Donald J. Trump assumed the presidency without a record of public service, but with decades of experience as the owner and CEO of a business enterprise (and star of a reality television program based on his life as a corporate CEO). Not surprisingly, his approach to governing has drawn on his prior management experience. A common thread between businessman Trump and many of his politician predecessors: shared frustration with the Madisonian system of shared and overlapping powers. President Trump has openly blamed our system of government under the Constitution for some of the difficulties he has experienced in getting his preferred policies enacted. In a *Fox News* interview marking the first hundred days of his presidency, Trump lamented: "It's a very rough system." Going further, he offered, "It's an archaic system. . . . It's really a bad thing for the country."[2]

A brief review of some of President Trump's early presidential decisions demonstrates that presidents continue to act in ways consistent with the major tenets of the unitary executive theory. These examples also highlight why we believe it is important to analyze and critique the unitary executive theory, which is the main goal of this book. The legitimization of the unitary executive theory, along with the rise of a CEO as president, created the "perfect storm" of circumstances giving rise to the need to thoroughly challenge the claims of unitary executive theory proponents. Beyond the impeachment episode, other actions of the Trump presidency point to a disturbing growing, trend in the use of unilateral presidential powers and challenges to constraints on the executive. Consider, for example, how Jay Sekulow, President Trump's personal attorney, asked the Supreme Court to provide a "temporary presidential immunity" from criminal prosecutions.[3] President Trump indeed attacks not just the legislative power but even the authority of the federal courts.

SANCTUARY CITIES

In 2017, the Donald J. Trump administration stepped up federal deportation activities against undocumented immigrants located in the United States. In response, several cities declared that they were "sanctuary cities"—the term used to describe those municipalities that pledged to protect undocumented immigrants from being identified and then possibly deported by federal authorities. Frustrated by their defiance of his authority, the president declared that he would withhold federal law enforcement grant money that had been allocated by Congress from any city or state that defied executive enforcement of deportation powers. The Trump Department of Justice (DOJ) then issued conditions that specifically mandated that local and state law enforcement authorities alert federal officials when an undocumented immigrant is to be released from custody in order to allow federal agents time to interview that person while he or she is still being held.

A federal court challenge yielded a judicial determination that the Trump DOJ action was unconstitutional and that the administration could not compel local authorities to act on behalf of the federal government as a condition for receiving local law enforcement grants. The federal judge for the US District Court for the Southern District of New York determined that local authorities alone have the power to respond to local public safety needs and that the president could not force local entities to act as the tools of federal powers.[4]

This judicial ruling laid bare the limits of unilateral presidential powers. The president claimed that he alone could block the delivery of federal funds that had already been allocated by imposing presidential conditions for receiving grant money. By threatening to unilaterally withhold such funding, the president was in effect declaring that his authority extended to overriding congressional lawmaking and funding authority. This claim threatens Congress's Article I powers and, indeed, the very foundations of our constitutional system of separated powers and checks and balances. As the judge declared: "The separation of powers acts as a check on tyranny and the concentration of power." Continuing, the judge noted: "If the Executive Branch can determine policy, and then use the power of the purse to mandate compliance with that policy by the state and local governments, all without the authorization or even acquiescence of elected legislators, that check against tyranny is forsaken."[5]

TRAVEL BAN

One of President Trump's most controversial unilateral actions to date was Executive Order 13769, which imposed a three-month travel ban on immigrants from Iraq, Iran, Syria, Yemen, Libya, Somalia, and Sudan, all Muslim-majority countries, and also stopped refugees from entering the United States for four months.[6] This move both surprised and stunned the world.[7] A federal court noted: "The impact of the Executive Order was immediate and widespread. It was reported that thousands of visas were immediately canceled, hundreds of travelers with such visas were prevented from boarding airplanes bound for the United States or denied entry on arrival, and some travelers were detained."[8]

As the *Economist* pointed out, "When a president's executive order crosses into the realm of policymaking or violates the law, lawsuits pop up."[9] This is precisely what happened. The states of Washington and Minnesota successfully sued for a temporary restraining order to stop the executive order travel ban from taking effect.[10] Upset with the decision, Trump lashed out on Twitter, deriding US district judge James Robart (a George W. Bush appointee) as a "so-called judge" and characterizing the decision as "ridiculous."[11]

On February 9, a three-judge panel of the Ninth Circuit Court of Appeals considered whether to leave in place the temporary restraining order that had stopped Trump's executive order from going into effect.[12] The Trump administration argued that its actions were "unreviewable" by the federal courts and asked not only for the restraining order to be lifted but also for the case to be dismissed.[13] The Ninth Circuit rejected the administration's request, declaring that "there is no precedent to support this claimed unreviewability, which runs contrary to the fundamental structure of our constitutional democracy."[14] The panel upheld the lower court's temporary restraining order.

President Trump's initial reaction came in the form of a tweet after the decision was handed down: "SEE YOU IN COURT, THE SECURITY OF OUR NATION IS AT STAKE!"[15] The Trump administration's emphasis on national security is nothing new, as numerous presidents have relied on national security concerns to advance their powers and overcome both congressional and judicial checks.

On March 6, President Trump issued Executive Order 13780, which revoked his previous executive order.[16] The new order suspended the US Refugee Admissions Program for 120 days and restricted admissions to, and denied new visa applications for, citizens from Iran, Libya, Somalia, Sudan, Syria, and Yemen for a period of 90 days. It also provided for entry restrictions into the United States after the 90-day period. Although Executive Order 13780 was aimed at addressing some of the shortcomings of the earlier order, the Hawaii and Maryland district courts almost immediately issued temporary restraining orders blocking enforcement of key provisions of the new order.[17]

The Trump administration eventually won Supreme Court approval for a version of its travel ban in *Trump v. Hawaii*.[18] However, the travel ban example is worth highlighting because it represents a classic case of the unitary executive mind-set. The Trump administration not only claimed singular authority in the realm of national security but also argued that a court was unable to review the constitutionality of the president's action. Such broad claims of executive powers are antithetical to the constitutional system of checks and balances.

Even pro–executive power scholar John Yoo is offended by Trump's wide-ranging understanding of his own presidential capabilities. Yoo is an academic and a unitary executive advocate who famously wrote the so-called torture memos defending the legality of waterboarding under President George W. Bush. His many contributions to the unitary executive theory will be discussed later in this book. For now, it is important to note that he wrote a *New York Times* editorial entitled "Executive Power Run Amok" that cited Trump's immigration order as one reason why, perhaps surprisingly, "even I have grave concerns about Mr. Trump's uses of presidential power."[19]

The travel ban executive order is, by itself, concerning enough in that it shows how President Trump is acting consistent with a unitary executive mind-set. But more disturbing still is the fact that, since settling into office, the president developed a habit of using broad, unilateral action to govern without congressional involvement.

CHINA TRADE POLICY

President Trump's attempts to restrict immigration into the United States attracted the lion's share of American media and public attention, but other important stories also merit discussion. One example is the Trump administration's National Security Strategy report in December 2017 that established the framework for its highly aggressive trade actions toward China.[20] Remarkably, the president claimed national security and emergency powers both to restrict direct foreign investment in the United States and to enact export controls for regulating outward investment and technology transactions.

President Trump's reliance on national security concerns to justify aggressive trade actions is overly broad. He claimed authority to act from Section 232 of the Trade Expansion Act and argued that, among other trade restrictions, national security concerns require high tariffs on steel and aluminum imports. Briefly noted, Section 232 does allow the president to impose trade tariffs to address national security threats.[21]

The president had claimed that Congress had already delegated to him the power he requires to act unilaterally on trade. He appears to be counting on the legislative branch's ready acquiescence to his recent moves and does not seem hesitant to call Congress's bluff, if needed. Indeed, given the Republican-heavy membership of the legislative branch at the time of these actions, President Trump may have believed he had little reason to worry about Congress mounting an effective challenge or even offering its own counterinterpretation.[22] But the 2018 elections likely changed the calculation, as control of the House of Representatives switched to the Democratic Party, and even some Republicans began to question the president's claims of unilateral trade powers. Most notably, the Senate Finance Committee chair Chuck Grassley (R-IA) has proposed that Congress pass legislation that would limit the president's Section 232 powers. As Grassley aptly put it: "Maybe the definition of national security or maybe the conditions under which national security could be used as an excuse is a little wide."[23] Short of legislative action limiting the president, the federal court system is the only remaining control on the president. But here, too, the president apparently believes he has little cause for concern: federal courts tend to offer substantial deference to presidents when it comes to emergency powers or national security questions.

And in early 2019, the US Court of International Trade did just that when it upheld President Trump's reliance on Section 232 of the Trade Expansion Act against a challenge that Congress's delegation of trade policy power to the president was too broad and therefore unconstitutional.[24] In upholding the president's authority, the Court even admitted that it lacked the ability to properly review questions of impermissible delegation under the act: "One might argue that the statute allows for a gray area where the President could invoke the statute to act in a manner constitutionally reserved for Congress but not objectively outside the President's statutory authority, and the scope of review would preclude the uncovering of such a truth. Nevertheless, such concerns are beyond this court's power to address, given the Supreme Court's decision in *Algonquin*."[25]

The US Court of International Trade ruling should not be surprising. No federal court has refused to uphold the "non-delegation doctrine" in decades. The courts instead have generally agreed that the president should have broad discretionary powers in this arena. Indeed, multiple presidential administrations have successfully resorted to claiming national security needs as a basis for unilateral action. In the case upholding Trump's travel ban mentioned earlier, the Supreme Court majority deferred to the president's authority to act unilaterally and refused to inquire beyond the broad statutory language and the administration's claimed reliance on national security concerns for its actions. Indeed, the Court completely ignored the president's own past statements advocating that Muslims be banned from entering the United States.[26] The president may now be emboldened to act alone if he believes that neither Congress nor the courts will object to his policies. This is especially likely since he has also shown little inclination to defer to any international bodies whose judgments might clash with his own interpretation of US national interests.

The president's unilateral actions on trade and on international agreements, more specifically, have been far-reaching. To date, he has withdrawn the United States from the Trans-Pacific Partnership, the Paris Climate Accord, the Iran nuclear deal, and the United Nations Human Rights Council. He also has threatened to withdraw the country from the WTO. Moreover, he has threatened allies in the European Union, Canada, and South Korea over tariff issues, including threatening to exclude Canada from the renegotiated North America Free Trade Agreement (NAFTA). At one point in the NAFTA talks Trump even threatened to "terminate NAFTA entirely" if Congress interfered.[27] Notably, the president has made these major decisions based solely on his own unilateral authority. But again, Trump's unilateral actions here are not a completely new development. In fact, unilateral presidential actions by Trump's predecessors had committed the United States to several of these key international agreements in the first place—most recently, in President Barack Obama's agreement with Iran on nuclear weapons.

The unitary executive theory mind-set is alive and well in the Trump administration, just as it has been present in other presidential administrations. In the chapters to follow, we explore how this phenomenon appears across a broad array of presidential powers and responsibilities, both domestic and foreign. For now we describe how the unitary executive theory differs from more commonly recognized models of presidential power. We begin with an overview of the unitary executive theory.

THE UNITARY EXECUTIVE THEORY: OVERVIEW

The unitary executive theory is more complex than it might initially seem. In fact, several leading scholars and practitioners have each developed their own definition of the concept.[28] Still, the most popular definitions of the unitary executive theory share common characteristics. The first shared feature is an abiding belief in the existence of a strong, vigorous presidency endowed with various unilateral powers. Unitary executive scholars also agree that the president controls any and all constitutional executive functions. This belief is based on the structural design of the chief executive position whereby the Constitution bestows executive power on a single individual.[29] Unitary executive scholars argue that a president can exert control over all decisions made by departments, agencies, and commissions.[30] They also believe that presidents are entitled to use, and should use, powers derived from inherent constitutional authority.[31] Finally, they maintain that Congress cannot check the president when he is exercising executive powers.[32]

This definition of presidential power simply does not conform to the Constitution. The governing document as written by the framers provides for only express and implied (not inherent) powers and is designed to specify and confine the reach of the federal government to protect the people from tyranny. As constitutional scholar Louis Fisher explained, "Express powers are explicitly provided for in the Constitution; implied powers are those that can be reasonably drawn from express powers." Inherent powers, however, cannot be found in the Constitution, nor can they reasonably be "implied from express powers."[33] When presidents claim inherent powers, they are operating outside the Constitution and are not restrained by it. In this scenario, the president would enjoy a tremendous amount of power at the expense of Congress and the courts.

Moreover, inherent powers cannot be exercised in a limited manner. Whether used regularly or hardly at all, inherent powers undermine the Constitution because the White House sees its control and authority strengthened at the expense of the other branches of government. Unitary executive proponents who support even a "limited" inherent power would still be effectively stripping away any constitutional legitimacy, and therefore controls, from the unitary executive theory.

For a time, President George W. Bush's administration relied heavily on claims to inherent presidential powers. This approach provoked significant opposition and eventually led to the widespread unpopularity of inherent power claims. Even unitary executive proponents felt the need to walk back some of the more controversial elements of the theory. Constitutional law scholars Steven Calabresi and Christopher Yoo wrote a leading book on the unitary executive theory based in part on the question of presidential power. After dedicating roughly five hundred pages to explaining how presidents from George Washington to George W. Bush gained power and confronted the other two branches of government, they somewhat perplexingly concluded that "the theory of the unitary executive is ultimately agnostic about the question of the scope of executive power."[34] Even liberal constitutional law professor Cass Sunstein defended a weaker view of the unitary executive. "Those who believe in a unitary executive need not think that the president can defy the will of Congress, or torture people, or make war on his own," he argued. Instead, Sunstein believed that "the principle of a 'unitary' executive involves only one thing: The president's hierarchical control over implementation ('execution') of federal law."[35] Ilya Somin, a libertarian legal scholar, supported Sunstein's view and noted that it "is perfectly consistent with simultaneously believing that the scope of executive power is relatively narrow, and that the president has no authority to ignore laws enacted by Congress, including those that constrain many military and foreign policy decisions."[36] Finally, Supreme Court justice Samuel Alito said at his confirmation hearing that the "question of the unitary Executive . . . does not concern the scope of Executive powers, it concerns who controls whatever power the Executive has. You could have an Executive with very narrow powers and still have a unitary Executive."[37]

Each of these statements is based on a narrow or even revisionist understanding of the unitary executive theory. These scholarly theories do not match up well with models favored in practice by the presidential administrations of Ronald Reagan and George W. Bush. In fact, all modern presidents have adopted a position that not only does their control of a power matter but also the extent to which they can wield such power. Generally, presidents are not content to merely claim that they have power. Instead, through the course of modern history we have countless cases of presidents pushing the limits of their exercise of power while attempting to limit or eliminate the traditional checks provided by Congress, the courts and the public. The aggressive nature of the modern presidency has significant and, we believe, serious implications for public policy, which have been so clearly seen during the Trump presidency. If the unitary executive theorists truly believe that their model is not concerned with the extent of presidential power, then that in itself is a serious flaw and one that should cause great concern for its adoption.

As a result, we argue that the debate over the unitary executive is very much about the extent of presidential power. The danger presented by the unitary executive theory is that presidents will cite it as justification for becoming an "imperial presidency" and claiming greater power vis-à-vis Congress and the courts, and in doing so may go beyond the acceptable bounds of separated powers. As Andrew Rudalevige wrote, "Presidents have regained freedom of unilateral action in a variety of areas, from executive privilege to war powers to covert operations to campaign spending." Yet, this development, as he explained, was not just dependent on George W. Bush and "would have endured even had President Bush failed of reelection in 2004." The result has been that the "default position between presidents and Congress has moved toward the presidential end of the interbranch spectrum—and irreversibly so."[38]

The George W. Bush administration demonstrated the type of threat that the unitary executive theory can present to democratic governance. Barack Obama initially expressed a more limited view of presidential powers than that held by members of the Bush administration, but he, too, ultimately followed a very similar path once in the White House. President Donald Trump fell into this pattern as well. Once precedents have been established for presidents to exercise expansive presidential powers with little pushback, future chief executives will be less likely to feel responsible for dialing them back.

The ultimate danger of the unitary executive theory is that it may embolden a president to use expanded and concentrated executive power in a risky manner that could harm the nation. Of course, a president who operates under a unitary conception is not necessarily a danger, provided he understands that there are limits to his powers. However, the very nature of the unitary executive theory requires that power unmistakably drifts toward the president. We believe that this theory is based on a flawed understanding of the nation's governing structure and does not conform to the text of the Constitution, the founders' intent, or much historical practice.

The unitary executive theory is a misguided model for understanding presidential power. In its place, we suggest that the controlling framework should be the familiar arrangement of a republican government featuring structural safeguards, including the principles of separation of powers and checks and balances. These principles, which are rooted in the Constitution, are the democratic controls that guide government actions.[39]

We counter claims that presidents should use the unitary executive theory to manage the executive branch and exercise power. The chapters are organized into discussions of groups of both domestic and foreign affairs powers. We provide a comprehensive analysis that addresses the theoretical components and historical arguments used by others to advance the belief that presidents enjoy unchecked plenary powers. It will become apparent that the unitary executive theory—particularly the "strong" version of it—is not solidly grounded. We believe this to be true whether one is considering the disparate parts of the theory or the complete model as a prism through which to view presidential behavior.

CHAPTER 1

Presidential Power and the Unitary Executive Theory

The unitary executive theory should not be considered in isolation. It is not the first theory of presidential behavior, and it will certainly not be the last. Well before the unitary executive theory's emergence in the 1980s, chief executives had provided other models of how to understand presidential behavior. These models include William Howard Taft's "literalist" theory, "presidential prerogative" (or "life and limb" theory) as expressed by Abraham Lincoln, and Theodore Roosevelt's "stewardship" theory. We organize these theories in order of the degree to which each model attempts to justify aggressive, unilateral presidential action, not in chronological order.

LITERALIST THEORY

William Howard Taft is the exemplar for a limited view of the presidency, which holds that only those powers expressly provided in the Constitution may be exercised.[1] Taft's view has been implicitly (and sometimes explicitly) derided by both academics and some twentieth-century presidents. For example, in his book *The Chief Executive*, Louis Koenig wrote that the "Taft-like President makes little use of his independent powers or prerogative." Koenig argues that the literalist approach is "inadequate for the necessities of the contemporary presidency."[2] The literalist theory as expressed by Taft himself included the following key concepts:

that the President can exercise no power which cannot be fairly and reasonably traced to some specific grant of power or justly implied and included within such express grant as proper and necessary to its exercise. Such specific grant must be either in the Federal Constitution or in an act of Congress passed in pursuance thereof. There is no undefined residuum of power which he can exercise because it seems to him to be in the public interest, and there is nothing in the Neagle case and its definition of a law of the United States, or in other precedents, warranting such an inference.[3]

Taft pays attention here to the constitutional roots of presidential power, but he does not interpret executive power in such a way that unnecessarily limits the president's capabilities. At the same time, the literalist theory accommodates implied powers but argues against an "undefined residuum of power." Seen in this light, Taft's model of the presidency fits well into a system of government that values both checks and balances and the rule of law.

PRESIDENTIAL PREROGATIVE: "LIFE AND LIMB" THEORY

Taft had emulated a model of presidential behavior that dated back to George Washington and nearly all nineteenth-century presidents, including, for a time, Abraham Lincoln. But Lincoln eventually became the father of another model: "prerogative power," or "life and limb" theory, which is often cited by executive power advocates as a prime example of presidents exercising powers not expressly or implicitly granted by the Constitution.

Citing an extraordinary emergency as justification, Lincoln exercised both executive and legislative powers during the Civil War, but—crucially—he later sought congressional approval for doing so.[4] Specifically, Lincoln summoned the militia to put down a rebellion by seven Southern states. Then, he ordered that the ports of seceded states should be blockaded. He added 23,000 men to the army and 18,000 to the navy and ordered the Treasury to appropriate emergency funding. Finally, and perhaps most significantly, Lincoln suspended the writ of habeas corpus.[5]

In taking these actions, Lincoln claimed what is often referred to as "prerogative power"—the authority to act outside the boundaries of the Constitution, and even against it, in extraordinary circumstances. Claiming prerogative power is controversial, as shown by the academic literature on the topic. But Lincoln provides a concrete example of this theory in action, and President Franklin D. Roosevelt provides a second: in the period leading up to World War II, FDR circumvented some of the legislative restrictions imposed by Congress in the neutrality acts. Scholars have generally accepted these moves by both Lincoln and Roosevelt as necessary and even legitimate under the circumstances. Importantly, neither man claimed to be creating a precedent for his successors to cite so they might also wield prerogative powers.

Lincoln's actions in the context of the Civil War would later underlie Theodore Roosevelt's "stewardship" theory—the understanding that a president could use any executive powers that were not expressly forbidden by the Constitution. However, a key point neglected by many who favor an expansive reading of presidential powers is how Lincoln acknowledged that the system of separated powers restrained his ability to act even during a grave national crisis.

The Lincoln administration defended its actions in arguments before the Supreme Court. In doing so, it did not advocate for the concept that presidents are the ultimate authority over matters of war. Instead, the administration merely contended that President Lincoln needed to be able to act during a civil war. As it stated in its brief to the Supreme Court, the administration argued that in "case of civil war, the President may, in the absence of any Act of Congress on the subject, meet the war by the exercise of belligerent maritime capture."[6] This is a much more qualified and limited position than arguing that the president has the unilateral prerogative to go to war.

Lincoln never claimed that the powers he assumed in an emergency were drawn from Article II of the Constitution. To be sure, he issued his orders while Congress was out of session, and he did not seek approval until July 4, when he finally summoned Congress back to Washington, DC, for a special session.[7] Once reassembled, however, Congress enacted a statute that stated "all the acts, proclamations, and orders of the President respecting the army and navy of the United States . . . are hereby approved and in all respects made valid . . . as if they had been issued and done under the previous express authority and direction of the Congress of the United States."[8] For years, Congress continued to ratify Lincoln's measures. In 1862, Congress retroactively approved Lincoln's censoring of telegraph lines and passed the Militia Act to allow the president to draft more troops. In

1863, Congress passed a law approving Lincoln's action to suspend the writ of habeas corpus and approved a draft law that legitimized the president's earlier unilateral issuance of the draft.[9]

Congress had at its disposal a vast arsenal of constitutional weapons, including outright disapproval of Lincoln's actions, the ability to end appropriations for future war-related activities, and even the power to impeach and remove the president from office. The fact that Congress opted instead to approve Lincoln's actions says much about the circumstances he faced. Congress accepted the fact that Lincoln needed considerable leeway to preserve the Union.

The Supreme Court was also sympathetic to the president's plight. When Lincoln's power to block the ports of southern states was challenged in the *Prize Cases,* the blockade was upheld, and the Court even endorsed Lincoln's actions, declaring that the president fulfilled his duty to put down the rebellion by using whatever force was necessary to do so, even if he acted before Congress could approve.[10] The *Prize* majority ruled that Lincoln's actions before July 13, 1861, the date that the justices all agreed was the official beginning of the "state of war," were not beyond his authority; even if they were, Congress's subsequent approval was sufficient to vindicate Lincoln.[11]

The *Prize* decision may seem to have approved vast executive power in general, but instead it only authorized an action that was in keeping with the Constitution, as Lincoln "had not initiated a war, but had taken measures to resist a war that was thrust upon the Government."[12] Had Lincoln initiated war, or had there been precedent established for him to follow, the Court may very well have been less deferential. Furthermore, after Lincoln's death, the Court checked Lincoln's use of prerogative powers. In *Ex parte Milligan,* the Court ruled that Lincoln exceeded his authority in subjecting nonmilitary prisoners to military commissions if the civil courts in the area were operating.[13]

STEWARDSHIP THEORY

The stewardship theory is a vision of the presidency and Constitution first articulated by President Theodore Roosevelt. Presidents serving before Roosevelt would generally have been shocked by the stewardship theory's wide-ranging claim of executive powers for the president. Roosevelt championed an aggressive model of the presidency in which the chief executive became "a steward of the people bound actively and affirmatively to do all he could do for the people." He explained that the president has not only a right but also a "duty to do anything that the needs of the Nation demanded unless such action was forbidden by the Constitution or by the laws."[14] As a result, Roosevelt reasoned that "the action of the executive offers the only means by which the people can get the legislation they demand and ought to have."[15] He even suggested that if the legislative branch failed to govern, its power might need to be exercised elsewhere: "As in any nation which amounts to anything, those in the end must govern who are willing actually to do the work of governing; and insofar as the Senate becomes a merely obstructionist body it will run the risk of seeing its power pass into other hands."[16] Although Roosevelt did not elaborate on where an "obstructionist" Senate's power would ultimately reside, it is reasonable to assume he believed that the president would be the beneficiary.

Unitary executive advocates have cited the prerogative power and stewardship theory as sources for staking their claim to even more expansive presidential powers. However, a close reading of those theories, together with even a cursory review of presidential history, reveals the fundamental flaw in their attempts to ground the unitary executive theory in the past: the principles underlying Taft's "literalist" theory comprised the dominant model of presidential behavior in the nineteenth century, and were directly contrary to the unitary executive theory. We will explore the origins of the unitary executive theory in the next section.

ORIGINS OF THE UNITARY EXECUTIVE THEORY

Unitary executive proponents contend that the unitary executive theory has long-standing roots in theory and practice, much like the other theories of presidential power discussed earlier in this chapter. Legal scholars Steven Calabresi and Christopher Yoo argue that the unitary executive theory can be traced back to the dawn of the presidency, as "all of our nation's presidents have believed in the theory of the unitary executive."[17] We argue that the unitary executive theory is a recent invention, and we see its advocates as less concerned about mere hierarchical control of the executive branch (though the two do have a connection, as we will discuss later) and instead focused more on the extent of presidential power.

In our view, the theory's origin as expressed by Calabresi and Yoo runs counter to the general consensus of presidency scholars. Most scholars cite Theodore Roosevelt as the first president to advance a rationale for a more robust and aggressive model of the presidency. Other presidents, notably Woodrow Wilson, advocated for a similar understanding of presidential power, seeing the president as "predominant and the 'center' of national leadership and representation."[18] Wilson famously said, "The President is at liberty, both in law and conscience, to be as big a man as he can."[19] Presidential leadership of public opinion is the key: As Gary Gregg observes, Wilson believed that "with a direct link to this public opinion that the other institutions of government lack, the presidency is able to dominate the government in the name of 'the nation as a whole.' "[20]

Political science scholars eventually moved from opposing to accepting a more assertive view of presidential power. Consider an early 1940s dispute between Congress and President Franklin D. Roosevelt. In one of his most aggressive attempts at using the bully pulpit, Roosevelt attacked Congress for its inaction regarding his desire to repeal a provision of the Emergency Price Control Act. In doing so, Roosevelt stated, Congress's refusal to act "will leave me with an inescapable responsibility to the people of this country to see to it that the war effort is no longer imperiled by threat of economic chaos." He then declared: "In the event that the Congress should fail to act, and act adequately, I shall accept the responsibility, and I will act."[21] Edward Corwin was so alarmed by these remarks that he wrote they could "only be interpreted as a claim of power on the part of the President to suspend the Constitution in a situation deemed by him to make such a step necessary."[22]

Corwin's view as described here was the general consensus of the political science discipline during the first half of the twentieth century. Since then, Richard Neustadt's widely read book *Presidential Power* (1960) has become the bellwether for the discipline's newfound acceptance of broader claims of presidential power. In his book, Neustadt argued that the office of the chief executive is essentially divorced from the Constitution and that "presidential *power* is the power to persuade."[23] He believed that Corwin's narrower view did not adequately appreciate the many dimensions of presidential power in action.

Richard M. Nixon's presidency spurred some presidential scholars to rethink the Neustadtian model. For example, Arthur Schlesinger Jr. argued in his book *The Imperial Presidency* (1973) that the executive office had acquired more power than the Constitution actually supports.

But even while criticizing increased executive power, Schlesinger noted: "The answer to the runaway Presidency is not the messenger-boy Presidency. . . . We need a strong Presidency—but a strong Presidency *within the Constitution*."[24] Schlesinger intended to push back against what he viewed as an imperial presidency, but in doing so he opened a path for justifying presidential power that would later be followed by unitary executive advocates.

Less than ten years after Schlesinger's book was published, Ronald Reagan was elected president. The new president and his staff had plans to restore the executive branch to what they saw as its proper role in the federal government.[25] To Reagan and his supporters, the post-Watergate presidency faced unprecedented scrutiny from the public and the mass media, and Congress had passed a series of misguided laws intended to check presidential power, including the Congressional Budget and Impoundment Control Act, the Ethics in Government Act, and the War Powers Resolution.[26] The restrained leadership styles of Gerald Ford and Jimmy Carter likely added to the sense of a decline in the presidency.[27]

These federal laws aimed at restraining presidential power were triggered by the excesses of the Nixon administration and the resulting congressional and public pushback that supported legislative restrictions. The laws temporarily bottled up the emerging trend toward increased independent presidential powers and vastly expanded authority for chief executives, but even they ultimately ended up as merely temporary dams before the rising tide of presidential power. The unitary executive theory emerged in this context. With the presidency secured, Reagan and his supporters could now effectively push back against Congress and what they saw as illegitimate interference with the president's constitutional responsibilities and powers.[28]

Many of the fathers of the unitary executive theory were presidential power advocates who worked in Reagan's Department of Justice. They shared the goal of restoring what they viewed as a weakened presidency to its central place in government. Attorney General Edwin Meese, along with staff lawyers Steven Calabresi and Samuel Alito, helped to shape the core tenets of the unitary executive theory under Reagan. Unlike their pro–presidential power predecessors, they largely rejected a governing system based on coequal branches of government that could check one another. As Charlie Savage explained: "The team [within the Reagan Justice Department] rejected the mainstream view that the Constitution creates three separate institutions and then gives them overlapping authority over the government as a means of preventing the tyranny of concentrated power. Instead, they said, the Founders cleanly divided the powers of government, assigning to each institution the exclusive control of its own universe."[29]

Savage argues that the heart of the unitary executive theory is the idea that the president controls the entire executive branch simply by possessing "the executive power" as entrusted to the president in Article II of the Constitution. Accordingly, all executive officers, whether housed within the White House itself or occupying a tiny office somewhere halfway around the world, are subordinate to the president and therefore subject to his views of policy, laws, and the Constitution. In the end, executive branch officers must follow the president or risk being removed at his discretion. Except in clear cases where presidential power is limited by the Constitution, the unitary executive theory also contends that the president's control of the executive branch is not subject to limitations imposed by Congress or the courts. At the time, the unitary executive debates usually played out in the domestic arena and featured increased presidential involvement and control over the regulatory process. Notably, the Reagan administration used the newly created Office of Information and Regulatory Affairs (OIRA) within the Office of Management and Budget (OMB) to dictate presidential policy through regulations.[30]

Somewhat surprisingly, scholarly commentary from the end of Reagan's presidency was not necessarily bullish on the future strength of the chief executive vis-à-vis Congress. In their edited book *The Fettered Presidency* (1989), L. Gordon Crovitz and Jeremy Rabkin highlighted the various "legal constraints" placed on the presidency that pose "risks and dangers" to public policy.[31] The foreword, written by former solicitor general Robert Bork, noted that the book demonstrated "that the office of the president of the United States has been significantly weakened in recent years and that Congress is largely, but not entirely, responsible." He continued, "Some recent presidents have failed to defend their office's prerogatives, allowing Congress to establish easements across the constitutional powers of the presidency that time and use may make permanent."[32] That same year, Gordon Jones and John Marini invoked Schlesinger's famous work in their book *The Imperial Congress*, in which they argued that "congressional failure to observe traditional limits on its power" has resulted in the "arrogation of power."[33] Their solution was an assertive president who would reclaim control over the executive branch and take an

aggressive approach to interacting with Congress as a way to restore
the balance of power between these two branches.

Previous presidents had tried to articulate a more robust view of
presidential power, but the Reagan administration successfully advanced the modern presidency past the traditional notions of a representative democracy: adherence to the rule of law and checks and
balances. Since Reagan, all presidents have adopted, either in practice
or at least in theory, the central tenets of the unitary executive theory.[34]

WEAK VERSUS STRONG THEORIES

Despite its revolutionary nature, the Reagan administration's view
of presidential power is now considered to be the "weak theory" of
the unitary executive.[35] The most well-known supporters of the weak
theory are Steven Calabresi and Christopher Yoo, who wrote that the
"Constitution gives presidents the power to control their subordinates
by vesting all of the executive power in one, and only one, person:
the president of the United States. All subordinate nonlegislative and
nonjudicial officials exercise executive power, and they do so only by
implicit or explicit delegation from the president."[36]

A much more aggressive version of the unitary executive theory
emerged during the George W. Bush administration.[37] Its supporters
included Vice President Dick Cheney and Berkeley law professor and
former Justice Department attorney John Yoo. In their view, the president has the power to direct executive branch officials, *and* Congress
has no right to limit the president's executive powers. Moreover,
Cheney, Yoo, and others believe that the president can invoke an
inherent power that is not drawn from traditional sources of constitutional authority. President George W. Bush put this wide-ranging
version of the unitary executive theory into action when he authorized
the National Security Agency to wiretap phone calls without judicial
controls; established military commissions; identified US citizens as
"enemy combatants"; detained US and foreign citizens indefinitely
without charging them with a crime; and undertook an "extraordinary rendition" program that transported US-held terrorist suspects
to foreign countries for aggressive questioning and potentially torture.[38] As John Yoo wrote, "In the exercise of his plenary power to
use military force, the President's decisions are for him alone and are
unreviewable."[39]

Even proponents of the "weak" version of the unitary executive theory defended President George W. Bush's claim to robust presidential power. For example, Calabresi explained that Bush "pushed an overly vigorous view of presidential power that expanded far beyond the logical boundaries of the unitary executive," but then praised Bush for "his determination to defend the prerogatives of the executive branch."[40] In fact, in their book, Calabresi and Yoo seem to accept the validity of the strong version of the unitary executive theory in their claim that a president could easily adopt "a limited view of inherent executive power."[41]

TEXTUAL ELEMENTS OF THE UNITARY EXECUTIVE THEORY

Advocates of both the weak and strong versions of the unitary executive theory rely on three crucial constitutional provisions: the Vesting, Oath, and Take Care Clauses.[42] The Reagan administration repeatedly cited these three clauses as a way to provide a constitutional source for a theory of presidential power that was in fact only recently created within the Department of Justice.[43] Later unitary executive advocates would go further, developing novel legal theories and selectively citing historical events to establish what they viewed as a firmer intellectual foundation for the theory.[44]

The Vesting Clause is usually read expansively by unitary executive supporters as a general grant of "executive power" to the president. This phrase is interpreted broadly to justify presidential authority over the entire executive branch. As justification for this interpretation, unitary executive supporters lean heavily on an observation made in the Pacificus-Helvidius debates by Alexander Hamilton in which he explained differences in the grants of power described in Article I and Article II of the Constitution.[45]

Article I of the Constitution contains the following language: "All legislative powers herein granted shall be vested in a Congress of the United States." In Article II, power is granted without the "herein granted" language: "The executive power shall be vested in a President of the United States." Hamilton remarked on this difference that

> it would not consist with the rules of sound construction to consider this enumeration of particular authorities as derogating from the more comprehensive grant contained in the general clause, further than as it may be coupled with express restrictions or qualifications; as in regard to the cooperation of the Senate in

the appointment of officers, and the making of treaties; which are plainly qualifications of the general executive powers of appointing officers and making treaties.[46]

Unitary executive advocates maintain that Hamilton's argument from 1793 advancing expanded presidential power should be considered the definitive interpretation for an expansive reading of the Vesting Clause. Indeed, Calabresi and Yoo wrote approvingly: "That Hamilton would write such a powerful defense of the constitutional construction that underlies the theory of the unitary executive and of presidential removal power is especially telling."[47] But if Calabresi and Yoo intend to rely on Hamilton's words here, they must also confront a major flaw in Hamilton's argument: not all powers listed were merely "qualifications of the general executive powers." Article II also provides other specific executive powers to the president. As James Pfiffner noted, "That the framers took care to make the authority explicit in Article II is a strong indication that they had not, by the vesting clause, already given the president extensive executive powers not specified in the Constitution."[48]

Despite conflicting evidence of the Vesting Clause's utility in this context, unitary executive advocates still almost universally claim it as a primary defense against perceived encroachments on presidential power. Consider, for example, Justice Antonin Scalia's now-classic dissent in *Morrison v. Olson*: "'The executive Power shall be vested in a President of the United States'. . . . This does not mean *some of* the executive power, but *all* of the executive power."[49] One might interpret Scalia's assertation here as a reasonable construction. However, it is important to keep in mind the context in which the framers decided to add "the executive power" to the Constitution in the first place. Edward Corwin famously argued that the framers only included that clause "to settle the question whether the executive branch should be plural or single and to give the executive a title."[50] To Corwin, the framers did not intend to provide the president with the ability to wield whatever powers he believed may be necessary to achieve his policy goals.

The key point of contention over the Vesting Clause is the question of whether Congress or the president may expand on the list of powers included in the Constitution. Unitary executive advocates argue that the president has always been able to expand his influence. We do not believe that the president has *always* had the ability to expand his executive powers. In a later chapter, we explore *Little v. Barreme,* where the Supreme Court held that the president did not have the authority to expand executive powers provided by a statutory provision. Similarly, we point out the inability of President Harry Truman to expand his constitutional or legal authority in *Youngstown Sheet & Tube Company v. Sawyer.*

We do not contend that the president should be powerless, of course. Rather, we do not believe that the Vesting Clause should be understood as an automatic source of new powers. The presidency is not unlimited, a fact seemingly acknowledged by Steven Calabresi, who has admitted that the Vesting Clause is not as expansive as some may hope. He recognized in his own study of the Vesting Clause that it "confers on the President a grant of 'executive power' *not* a grant of 'regal' or of 'imperial' power."[51] Another unitary executive supporter, Saikrishna Prakash, also admitted that the "clause was qualified by relatively defined limits and was incapable of legitimating anything and everything the president might wish to do."[52]

We turn our attention now to the Oath Clause—another constitutional provision relied on by unitary executive supporters. The Oath Clause requires individuals to take an oath or affirmation to "solemnly swear (or affirm) that I will faithfully execute the Office of President of the United States, and will to the best of my Ability, preserve, protect and defend the Constitution of the United States." To unitary executive supporters, the Oath Clause provides the president with his own ability to evaluate a law's constitutionality by deciding whether or not to enforce it.[53] For example, President Reagan and his successors have advanced the position that they can make substantial changes to laws through presidential signing statements. We analyze and ultimately reject this particular interpretation of the unitary executive theory in a later chapter.

The third and final constitutional clause relevant to this discussion is the Take Care Clause, which provides that the president "shall take Care that the Laws be faithfully executed." Here, unitary executive supporters contend that the president is responsible to the nation for the implementation of the laws and therefore must have total control over his subordinates in the executive branch.[54] This interpretation would have a profound effect on the way the president manages and provides direction to executive branch officials. In its most extreme form, the Take Care argument completely separates the executive branch from statutory direction and legislative oversight. However, as we will address in a later chapter, people in the eighteenth century would generally have had a very different understanding of executive power than many twenty-first-century Americans.

UNITARY EXECUTIVE ADVOCATES VERSUS CRITICS

In the chapters to come, we will highlight the various textual, historical, and constitutional weaknesses of the unitary executive theory. At times, even the most well-known unitary executive theory advocates have acknowledged the model's inconsistencies. For example, President Ronald Reagan's solicitor general Charles Fried—the first person to advance unitary executive arguments in court—admitted that the unitary executive "vision I offer is not literally required by the words of the Constitution. Nor did the framers' intent compel this view." Instead, Fried contended that one needed to look at the "structure" of the Constitution "as a whole" to see clearly how the unitary executive model fits in.[55]

As we noted earlier, Alexander Hamilton is one of the guiding lights for unitary executive advocates. In *Federalist* No. 70, he wrote: "That unity is conducive to energy will not be disputed. Decision, activity, secrecy, and dispatch will generally characterize the proceedings of one man in a much more eminent degree than the proceedings of any greater number; and in proportion as the number is increased, these qualities will be diminished." Unitary executive advocates, such as Steven Calabresi, take Hamilton's "energy" thesis and run with it: "Hamilton clearly stated that a single strong leader is vital to protect both the property and 'the steady administration of the laws' from efforts by ambitious individuals or seditious classes to get their own way at the public's expense."[56]

Critics of the unitary executive theory take issue with the concept because of its origin, rationale, and use, and the danger it represents to governmental openness and transparency. The version of the unitary executive theory supported by proponents is actually very different from what the framers discussed more than two hundred years ago. To the framers, the "unitary executive" was a preference for a structural arrangement: having one person in charge instead of many. Niels Bjerre-Poulsen argues that Hamilton's reference to "the unity of the executive" in *Federalist* No. 70 was not related to the "relative strength of the executive branch: He is simply speaking in favor of having one person rather than several lead the executive branch."[57]

And "energy in the executive," as Hamilton mentions, "connotes unity only in the sense of a single manager, as opposed to plural managers."[58] There is no indication that Hamilton meant anything else by "unitary executive" apart from expressing the framers' desire to have a single president, not many, and one who is not shackled to an executive council.[59]

Unitary executive advocates invoke Hamilton for support, although we find their interpretations of his writings unpersuasive. They also ignore other textual elements in the Constitution that provide powers to Congress. Article I of the Constitution vests in the legislature the ability to make laws; appropriate money; declare war; regulate the armed forces; and exercise other powers inferred from the Necessary and Proper Clause. Indeed, many of the most important federal powers are listed in the legislative article of the Constitution.

Moreover, unitary executive supporters often overlook constitutional clauses that would simply not make sense if, as they argue, the president enjoys plenary power over all aspects of the executive branch. For example, why would the framers have included an Opinions Clause, which gives the president the power to demand opinions from the various department heads, if he already possessed the ability to command or even remove them from their positions? As Cass Sunstein has noted, the "notion that the President must specifically be given the power to demand opinions in writing seems to me very strong textual evidence against the Unitary Executive concept."[60]

We now turn to focusing on domestic powers and addressing one of the fundamental tenets of the unitary executive theory: that the president controls all executive branch officials.

CHAPTER 2

Domestic Powers

Part I

One of the core tenets of the unitary executive theory is that all executive officials are under the direct control and command of the president of the United States. The theory contends that these officials must take, and then follow, all orders from the president. In their book on the unitary executive theory, Steven Calabresi and Christopher Yoo explain that "the Constitution creates a unitary executive to ensure energetic enforcement of the law and to promote accountability by making it crystal clear who is to blame for maladministration" and note that the execution of the law will be done "in a consistent manner and in accordance with the president's wishes."[1] Continuing, they write that the "Constitution gives presidents the power to control their subordinates by vesting all of the executive power in one, and only one, person: the president of the United States. All subordinate nonlegislative and nonjudicial officials exercise executive power, and they do so only by implicit or explicit delegation from the president. They are thus all subject to the president's powers of direction and control."[2]

The Constitution indeed created a singular presidency and not the plural one that was debated at the Constitutional Convention. However, the document is silent as to where direction, control, and even accountability, ultimately lie. Moreover, the Constitution did not implicitly or explicitly delegate to executive branch officials all of the president's executive power, so there is no complete subjection of direction and control despite what unitary executive supporters would lead one to believe.

28

This point is crucial. Unitary executive theorists contend that a model of the presidency that "gives presidents the power to control their subordinates" also presumes that executive branch officials cannot, or have not, functioned independently of the president or taken direction from others. Admittedly, some support for this view comes from Alexander Hamilton, who wrote in *Federalist* No. 72:

> The persons, therefore, to whose immediate management these different matters [of the administration of government] are committed, ought to be considered as the assistants or deputies of the chief magistrate, and on this account, they ought to derive their offices from his appointment, at least from his nomination, and ought to be subject to his superintendence. This view of the subject will at once suggest to us the intimate connection between the duration of the executive magistrate in office and the stability of the system of administration.

But as scholar Donald Brand noted, "Hamilton's description . . . was not intended to preclude congressional supervision of administration through the lawmaking (and budgetary) process."[3] In fact, the framers understood administrative powers much differently than unitary executive supporters. For the framers, the central concern of administrative functions was not the command and exercise of powers, but rather to safeguard against abuse and allow for subordinates to effectively undertake their assigned responsibilities. To them, administrative powers were geared toward the protection of individual freedoms and liberty against possible oppressive government action. They did not concern themselves with whether the president had complete command of all executive branch officials, but instead focused on whether those officials were properly performing their duties.

As administrative law scholar Leonard White explained, because administrative powers "affect the private citizen, they have always been the subject of solicitude by representative bodies and courts. The opposition of the colonists to imperial officials and the great debates that led to armed resistance and independence had caused Americans to cherish personal freedom and liberty, and to look with suspicion upon official authority. Personal rights, not public power, were consequently the principal concern of legislative bodies and courts."[4] The framers were concerned with both the exercise of authority and the need to check power. One of the initial ways the First Congress

ensured that officials performed their duties as prescribed by law was
to require them to take oaths "to perform well the duties of the office
in question."[5]

These duties were prescribed in law then, and still are today.
Federal laws passed by Congress and signed by the president provide
the structure, powers, and policy direction for the various departments, agencies, commissions, and other federal entities. Speaking
during the First Congress, James Madison declared that the "legislature creates the office, defines the powers, limits its duration, and
annexes a compensation."[6] In 1819, Chief Justice John Marshall explained in *McCulloch v. Maryland* that Congress has the ability through
the Necessary and Proper Clause to create government structures that
"shall be necessary and proper for carrying into Execution" its express
powers.[7] Four years later, Attorney General William Wirt wrote that
"the Constitution assigns to Congress the power of designating the
duties of particular officers."[8] Finally, Chief Justice William Howard
Taft, a former president himself, explained in *Myers v. United States*:
"To Congress under its legislative power is given the establishment of
offices, the determination of their functions and jurisdiction, the prescribing of reasonable and relevant qualifications and rules of eligibility of appointees, and the fixing of the term for which they are to be
appointed, and their compensation—all except as otherwise provided
by the Constitution."[9]

DISCRETIONARY AND MINISTERIAL DUTIES

When discussing the impact of various laws on executive branch officials, it is important to understand the differences between discretionary and ministerial duties. Discretionary duties involve the exercise of
choice and judgment and—depending on the type of official[10]—are
subject to the president's control. These types of duties often occur
when the law is not precise and officials enjoy the latitude to decide
for themselves. For example, the secretary of the interior has the discretion to appoint an assistant secretary. Ministerial duties, in contrast, require no judgment, as the law is specific about the actions that
must be taken. Here, the office is only executing the law as prescribed.
For example, officials within the Social Security Administration are
legally required to disburse payments to those listed as beneficiaries
of the Social Security system.

Early in the nation's history, the Supreme Court weighed in on the difference between a department head exercising either discretionary or ministerial duties. In the case of *Marbury v. Madison*, a key fact was the delivery of a commission by the secretary of state as the final step in making an appointment. Chief Justice John Marshall noted that after a commission has been signed by the president "the subsequent duty of the Secretary of State is prescribed by law, and not to be guided by the will of the President."[11] Marshall proceeded to articulate the general principle of administrative duties by noting that the president

> is invested with certain important political powers, in the exercise of which he is to use his own discretion, and is accountable only to his country in his political character and to his own conscience. To aid him in the performance of these duties, he is authorized to appoint certain officers, who act by his authority and in conformity with his orders. In such cases, their acts are his acts; and whatever opinion may be entertained of the manner in which executive discretion may be used, still there exists, and can exist, no power to control that discretion. The subjects are political.[12]

As a result, officials can be subject to the discretion and control of the president. But, as Marshall explained, there are other administrative duties that are outside the supervision of the president and belong only to that particular official: "When the Legislature proceeds to impose on that officer other duties; when he is directed peremptorily to perform certain acts; when the rights of individuals are dependent on the performance of those acts; he is so far the officer of the law, is amenable to the laws for his conduct, and cannot at his discretion, sport away the vested rights of others."[13]

The concepts of discretionary and ministerial duties arose again in *Kendall v. United States*—a case addressing the refusal of Postmaster General Amos Kendall to pay the legally required amount of money to a mail contractor. As Marshall had done earlier, Justice Smith Thompson articulated the responsibilities that officials owe when exercising their duties and explained that, although the Constitution does vest the executive power in the president, "it by no means follows that every officer in every branch of that department is under the exclusive direction of the President."[14] In fact, Thompson declared, "It would be an alarming doctrine that Congress cannot impose upon any executive officer any duty they may think proper which is not repugnant to any rights secured and protected by the Constitution, and, in such cases, the duty and responsibility grow out of and are subject to the control of the law, and not to the direction of the President."[15]

After holding that Kendall must make the specified payment to the mail contractor, Thompson noted that it "was urged at the bar that the Postmaster General was alone subject to the direction and control of the President with respect to the execution of the duty imposed upon him by this law, and this right of the President is claimed as growing out of the obligation imposed upon him by the Constitution to take care that the laws be faithfully executed."[16] Such a doctrine, Thompson stated, "cannot receive the sanction of this court." He also noted that the concept has no "support in any part of the Constitution" and if given sanction "would be clothing the President with a power entirely to control the legislation of Congress and paralyze the administration of justice." Finally, Thompson declared, "To contend that the obligation imposed on the President to see the laws faithfully executed implies a power to forbid their execution is a novel construction of the Constitution, and entirely inadmissible."[17]

The Supreme Court's interpretation of the Constitution and application of administrative law received the repeated endorsements of various US attorneys general. For example, writing in 1854, Attorney General Caleb Cushing argued that when laws "define what is to be done by a given head of department, and how he is to do it, there the President's discretion stops; but if the law require an executive act to be performed, without saying how or by whom, it must be for him to supply the direction." Cushing concluded that his view on the subject "has been followed, uniformly, in the practical administration of the Government."[18] Writing in 1905, Attorney General William Moody told the secretary of the interior that under the provision of a 1903 law, "the duty imposed upon you to draw warrants is purely ministerial and you have no discretion in the matter."[19]

Shortly after leaving the presidency, William Howard Taft wrote that the executive and legislative branches are independent from one another, at least in theory. However, he admitted that it is difficult to "draw the line and to say where Legislative control and discretion to the Executive must cease, and where his independent discretion begins." Continuing, Taft noted that executive officials are subordinate to the president, "yet Congress can undoubtedly pass laws definitely limiting their discretion and commanding a certain course by them which is not within the power of the Executive to vary." Because of this situation, he admitted that one of Congress's "chief functions" is "fixing the method in which Executive power shall be exercised." By passing laws, Congress provides the executive with "a duty" to act and details "how that duty is to be carried out"; put another way, the laws in effect provide guardrails or, in Taft's words, "restrictions that the Executive is bound to observe." Taft ended his assessment of legislative direction and command by noting that Congress may place discretion in executive officials "which the President may not himself control."[20]

It is important to keep in mind Taft's statement that "the President may not himself control" the duties and responsibilities of executive officials, as assigned by Congress, when one considers the consequences of discretionary and ministerial duties and their relationship to a president's direct command. Writing in 1941, administrative law scholar Robert Cushman concluded that "Congress may constitutionally give to an officer a practical sort of independence from Presidential control by specifying in elaborate detail the nature and scope of his duties and the methods to be followed in performing them."[21] A unitary executive advocate who accepted this division of duties and then argued that executive officials who exercise discretionary responsibilities are *still* subject to absolute presidential control would simply be incorrect and on the wrong side of history and actual practice.

A key example of an executive branch position possessing discretionary powers that were not subject to the control of the president or a department head was the comptroller of the Treasury, established by Congress in 1789 within the Department of the Treasury.[22] The comptroller had the responsibility to decide whether to countersign warrants signed by the secretary of the Treasury. No less an executive power supporter than Alexander Hamilton explained that, in exercising such power, "the comptroller is a check upon the Secretary."[23] Congress also charged the comptroller to be the final arbiter of appeals on government accounts from decisions of the auditor.

Speaking during the debate over the creation of the comptroller position, James Madison argued that the nature of the job is "not purely of an executive nature" and, instead, is more of a "judiciary quality as well as executive; perhaps the latter obtains in the greatest degree." This assessment led Madison to conclude that "there may be strong reasons why an officer of this kind should not hold his office at the pleasure of the executive branch of the Government."[24]

With the comptroller of the Treasury, the First Congress established a position within the executive branch whose occupant had discretionary powers that were intended to provide independent judgment and a "check" on the head of the Treasury Department. Speaking to whether a president could review cases settled by the comptroller, Attorney General Wirt noted that doing so "would be a usurpation on the part of the President which the accounting officers would not be bound to respect."[25] The example of the comptroller of the Treasury shows that, despite what unitary executive advocates may believe, presidents do not have complete control to provide direction and command.

DISCRETIONARY DUTIES AND THE LIMITS OF PRESIDENTIAL CONTROL

Whether the president has the capacity to give "direction and control" to executive officials in practice is not a question not often discussed by unitary executive advocates. They do not seem to view critical to their theory the fact that the president may not actually be able to exercise absolute control over the entire executive branch. We believe it is a helpful question to examine because it highlights the futility of heralding the "unitary executive" as an actual working model for presidential behavior.

Along these lines, Attorney General Wirt argued that the president is unable to interfere with the decisions of the comptroller of the Treasury. He noted that doing so would require the president "to perform an impossibility himself" and would be "a construction too absurd to be seriously contended for."[26] Writing to President James Polk in 1846, Attorney General John Mason also noted that, considering "the high constitutional duties of the President, which occupy his whole time, it requires no argument to show that he could not acquit himself, by their adequate performance, if he were to undertake to review the decisions of subordinates on the weight or effect of evidence in cases appropriately belonging to them."[27]

More important, even in the early nineteenth century, executive branch officials were required to perform various functions to implement public policies enacted by Congress as part of an increasingly complex administrative system. As Leonard White has argued, presidents therefore "were prisoners of the administrative system." He noted that their "freedom of action was limited by the collective habit and weight of momentum of the machine itself and by the comparative feebleness of their own means of action. Law and practice had already created an elaborate body of precedent."[28] The difficult political reality faced by antebellum presidents runs counter to the notion that they could simply direct any and all executive branch officials without (or despite) congressional interference.[29]

By the 1860s, more than sixty years of laws, procedures, and practices had built up and established a complex federal government. Regardless of whether the president had been bestowed "executive power" by the Constitution, the executive branch was not easily managed or controlled by a single person or office. Writing about public administration in the late nineteenth century, White noted that "the executive branch was tacitly understood to be a cluster of department heads, each asking for appropriations and legislation to meet the needs of his agency, each directly responsible to the proper committee of Congress, and each bowing to the decision of the people at the biennial elections in case of a stubborn dispute with Congress." The reality, according to White, was that the president during this time period "was a mere onlooker."[30]

White's verdict here is probably a bit too harsh. The fact is, well before the late nineteenth century Congress passed several laws to give the president and various executive branch officials a significant amount of regulatory and administrative authority.[31] But White's point is still a valid one, as presidents did not enjoy the unitary command over the executive branch that unitary executive theorists contend they did. Indeed, public administration scholar William Willoughby wrote in 1927 that the "administrative function, that is, the function of direction, supervision, and control of the administrative activities of the government, resides in the legislative branch." He went on to declare, "Congress is the source of all administrative authority."[32]

By the late 1930s, the president's ability to provide direction and control to the executive branch had not greatly improved. In response, President Franklin D. Roosevelt established the Brownlow Committee to investigate and recommend changes to the administrative management of the executive branch, noting, "The President must be given direct control over and be charged with immediate responsibility for the great managerial functions of the Government."[33] The Brownlow Committee's findings highlighted in general terms the numerous laws and practices that often restricted and even dictated the actions of the president and various executive branch officials.

If the president had always had the power to directly control executive branch subordinates, as Calabresi and Yoo contend, why would

Roosevelt need a presidential commission to make such a request? In reality, the president was not able to provide direction and control, and the Brownlow Committee even noted that Congress imposes "upon the Executive in too great detail minute requirements for the organization and operation of the administrative machinery."[34] The presidency as it actually existed under FDR hardly seemed free to provide "unitary" direction to the executive branch.

The same criticism expressed by the Brownlow Committee resurfaced a decade later in the First Hoover Commission reports. Writing in 1949, the Hoover Commission—led by former president Herbert Hoover—described a president's lack of administrative control over the executive branch. "It is not any one of these factors alone but, like the Lilliputian threads that bound Gulliver," the report noted, "it is the total complex of these restrictions—lack of organization authority; grants of independent executive powers to subordinate officials; restrictive controls over personnel; divided controls over accounting and preaudit of expenditures; diffusion of the spending power of appropriations; overly detailed legislation—that weakens the powers of management in the executive branch and makes it difficult if not impossible to fix responsibility."[35] Fifteen years later, another presidential commission made similar—albeit more forceful—declarations that such restrictions were, in fact, "diluting the President's power to control the Executive Branch."[36] A more accurate assertion would have been that the president has never actually held such sway over the executive branch.

PRESIDENTIAL POWER: DEPARTMENTS AND BUREAUS

Starting with George Washington's presidency, one can immediately see a variety of practical challenges to executing the "unitary executive" model at the department level. Washington's secretary of the Treasury, Alexander Hamilton, did not oversee all aspects of the Treasury Department, and Secretary of State Timothy Pickering had no top-down command authority over the various US attorneys trying to enforce federal statutes such as the Sedition Act, even though it was one of the most important laws to the Federalist Party at the time.[37]

By the mid-nineteenth century, department-level business had devolved into separate "bureaus" that, for all intents and purposes, functioned as independent departments of government.[38] In debating the creation of the Interior Department in 1849, Senator John

Niles stated that the reality was that bureaus were "substantially independent of the departments" and that "the ordinary business of the bureau may be considered as independent of the department."[39] In 1903, Senator Porter McCumber, speaking about the bill to create the Department of Commerce and Labor, articulated the common turn-of-the-century understanding of administrative control within departments: "What power, what control, what authority has the new Secretary of Commerce over any of these bureaus which are to be placed under him and subordinate to that particular Department? I can not see that he has any such power."[40] The Hoover Commission expressed a similar view, noting that the "line of authority from departmental heads through subordinates is often abridged by independent authorities granted to bureau or division heads" and that "bureau autonomy undermines the authority of both the President and the department head."[41]

Decentralized departments persist even today and have simply been a fact of life for all modern chief executives. Presidential scholar Richard Neustadt wrote in his 1960 classic *Presidential Power* that "the executive establishment consists of separated institutions sharing powers" and noted how "below the department level, virtually independent bureau chiefs head many more."[42] In his proposal to Congress to reorganize the executive branch, President Richard M. Nixon expressed how the various offices and bureaus "behave like a series of fragmented fiefdoms—unable to focus Federal resources or energies in a way which produces any concentrated impact."[43] Nixon's assessment was supported a decade later by Harold Seidman and Robert Gilmour, who called secretaries "highly ornamental figureheads" unless they had the "loyalty, or at least neutrality, of their principal bureau chiefs."[44] Even as recently as 2002, presidential scholar Andrew Rudalevige remarked "that bureaus have their own independent standing; they are created by statute, with mandates and missions assigned by law."[45]

Congress's continuing delegation of powers to the president has not substantially changed these decentralized dynamics. To be sure, Congress acted on the Brownlow Committee's claim that the president "needs help" by giving chief executives the statutory authority to hire presidential aides, creating an Executive Office of the President, unifying budget authority, and providing other institutional powers. As Herbert Kaufman explained, however, bureau chiefs "still seem to find Congress more important for their own and their bureaus' survival and success. The concessions by Congress did not diminish its influence (which may be why it was willing to make them)."[46] In fact, the Constitution gives Congress significant authority to provide direction and administrative management of the executive branch. Aside from its ability to actually create the very structures of government, Congress also codifies the policy direction of the various departments and bureaus and provides annual appropriations. This is an impressive list of congressional responsibilities even before one reaches the oversight hearings held by congressional committees and the less well-known agency- and committee-level staff interactions regarding spending and general policy direction.[47]

The evidence we have been reviewing so far suggests that unitary executive supporters who assert that the president has complete control over the executive branch are incorrect. Furthermore, the president's inability to provide unilateral direction and control of the executive branch is not actually a shortcoming in our system of government. Rather, it is a deliberate design feature intended to prevent one person from accumulating too much power. The president certainly possesses a *qualified* authority under the Constitution to manage or provide some level of direction to other executive branch officials, and we acknowledge the existence of a limited form of presidential management. However, we take issue with the claim of unitary executive theorists who argue that a president enjoys unfettered power to provide direction and command over all executive officials. This type of argument attempts to wall off the president from the checks and balances of our constitutional system of government. It is a danger that constitutional scholar Louis Fisher has identified as well: "More threatening is executive activity cut loose from legislative moorings and constitutional restrictions—presidential action no longer tethered by law."[48] Presidential activity not limited by any legal constraints can place the entire system at risk.

Unitary executive supporters understand the executive branch to be a single body or institution with a shared mission and authority base. In many ways, the unitary executive theory advances the idea that the executive branch functions hierarchically, with authority flowing downward from the president. In reality, this is not how the executive branch was designed or has actually functioned over time. Instead, as Loren Smith explains, "The government is a vast group of civil servants and a much smaller number of political appointees, organized into a mass of groups and confederations and subject to competing authority centers. They derive power, money, direction, and authority from different sources in different proportions that vary with time."[49] For better or worse, this is how our system of government functions. Central command authority is not one of the powers granted to the president by the Constitution or laws.

In his study of bureaus, Herbert Kaufman refutes the notion that the executive branch functions as a hierarchical model. In explaining that such a model is really "a vision" for organizing government, Kaufman notes that "some people apparently would like to shape the executive branch of the federal government, at least the regular executive departments, into the traditional pyramid with the president at the apex and with hierarchical directives unequivocally outweighing all other influences on everybody on it." Expanding on that concept, he explains that such advocates seek "to restrict the flow of authority to vertical channels and reduce or eliminate the lateral contacts that induce officials in the system to respond to other instructions, demands, and requests."[50] Kaufman's description here provides an excellent explanation of the unitary executive theory.

Kaufman states that such a model is impossible to realize. "The preeminence of Congress, the diffusion of power in Congress," he argues, "and the influence these conditions confer on groups outside the federal government thrust too hard in the other direction." In part, this has to do with the limited time that presidents and secretaries have available to devote to bureau chiefs and other parts of government. But, as Kaufman notes, other sources of influence (members of Congress, interest groups, etc.) "are in close, almost continuous contact—making demands, offering advice, and monitoring the responses."[51] Instead of working within a hierarchical model, bureau chiefs often have to reach out laterally, especially to Congress.

Another justification for the unitary executive theory goes as follows: even if the unitary executive has not been present historically, the needs of our modern society require the president to assume more direct command and control of the levers of government. But the reality is that recent efforts of presidents to gain control of the bureaucracy have just not been successful. Francis Rourke notes that these "attempts of the White House to establish unilateral control over executive agencies bear a strong resemblance to the congressional effort to achieve total legislative dominance over bureaucracy in the aftermath of the Civil War." Rourke explains that each side failed and then returned to "a point of equilibrium." The "idea of total control," Rourke concludes, "lies in a field of dreams."[52] An empirical study conducted by Thomas Hammond and Jack Knott came to a similar conclusion: "Control of the bureaucracy must be seen as a systemic matter: the president, House, and Senate *collectively* control the bureaucracy." Pointing to the principle of separation of powers, they argued that "no one institution may be able to do much about it."[53]

For the remainder of this chapter and into the next one, we analyze specific presidential powers often characterized as tools used by chief executives to provide direction and control over the executive branch. We provide a much-needed corrective to the idea that presidents occupy a hallowed position in the federal government that gives them the unilateral power to shape policy without involvement from others.

EXECUTIVE ORDERS

Adherents of the "strong" unitary executive theory believe that executive power is indivisible and therefore cannot be infringed upon by Congress or the courts. Viewed from their perspective, executive orders are a powerful tool that can be employed by presidents to control both the executive branch and public policymaking. As Chris Edelson states, the "strong" version of the theory is "designed to justify unilateral, unchecked presidential power unaccountable to the rule of law."[54]

Executive orders are presidential proclamations that have "general applicability and legal effect"; they are published in the *Federal Register*.[55] The exact number of executive orders that have been issued by presidents is not known, as the orders have not been adequately archived and recorded.[56] Presidents have used executive orders to provide policy direction and to manage the executive branch, especially in recent decades. For example, President George W. Bush issued Executive Order 13224 shortly after September 11, 2001, authorizing the blocking of property of individuals who commit, threaten, or support terrorism.[57] In 2009, President Barack Obama used an executive order to provide for the review and closing of the Guantanamo Bay detention center, which had been used to hold suspected terrorists.[58] More recently, President Donald J. Trump issued an executive order in 2017 calling for a review of national monument designations under the Antiquities Act of 1906.[59]

A president may believe that executive orders are powerful tools he may use to shape and direct administrative action in government, and they may indeed be useful in some cases, but the fundamental realities of governing remain in place. The fact is that executive orders provide a weak basis for lasting administrative action or control unless they are based on constitutional or statutory provisions. As Harold Krent explains: "Executive orders should not be considered 'law' in the conventional sense" as they often do not have adequate backing. "A violation of an executive order," he notes, "cannot lead to a legal sanction such as a fine or prison sentence."[60] At most, a president can—in the absence of "for cause" removal provisions—remove an executive branch official who refuses to adhere to an order. However, a president cannot use an executive order to override a statute that directs certain ministerial actions of officials, nor can the order contradict "congressional expressions."[61] In other words, the authority of executive orders stems from a system of checks and balances where the president must seek statutory guidance from Congress or look to the Constitution for an authoritative source.

In our constitutional system of government, the qualified nature of executive orders means that Congress and the courts may check them.[62] Perhaps the most famous example of a court striking down an executive order occurred in 1952. At that time, the Supreme Court held in the "Steel Seizure" case that President Harry Truman unconstitutionally attempted to seize the nation's steel mills.[63] In his study of executive orders, William Howell documented eighty-three court challenges to them between 1942 and 1998.[64] In concluding his analysis, Howell noted that in "the vast majority of challenges to executive orders, the courts ruled in favor of the president, not only endorsing presidents' past actions, but occasionally providing rationales for future presidents to further expand their base of power."[65]

Howell's conclusion here does not mean that challenges upheld in court will give presidents an unchecked executive power. In 1915, the Supreme Court in *United States v. Midwest Oil Company* upheld the president's use of an executive order to withdraw public lands from private party speculation while acknowledging that Congress could limit such a move.[66] The Court upheld this executive order even though it went against express statutory language that opened up public lands to private parties. The Court considered the question of whether the president had exercised a "dispensing power"—a right of English kings to ignore laws passed by Parliament—but decided the case on much narrower grounds. In the majority opinion, the Court reasoned that presidents had issued hundreds of executive orders withdrawing public lands over the course of eight decades, during which time "Congress did not repudiate the power claimed or the withdrawal orders made."[67] In noting that acquiescence by Congress "was equivalent to consent," the Court explained that presidents could "continue the practice until the power was revoked by some subsequent action by Congress."[68]

Congress had in fact passed the Pickett Act in 1910, which provided statutory support for the president to withdraw land while also restricting that power by keeping lands subject to federal mining laws open for "exploration, discovery, occupation, and purchase."[69] In 1958, Congress acted again, this time by passing the Engle Act, which mandated that land withdrawals of more than five thousand acres needed the legislature's acquiescence. Then, in 1976, it passed the Federal Land Policy and Management Act, which authorized the Department of the Interior to withdraw public lands totaling five thousand acres or less.[70] The pro–executive power court case and its subsequent history discussed here demonstrate the important ways that Congress can limit executive orders.

A more recent example of congressional pushback against a president's executive order occurred when President Barack Obama attempted at the start of his presidency to close the Guantanamo Bay detention camp. In his executive order, issued on January 22, 2009, President Obama stated he would close the detention camp "as soon as practicable, and no later than 1 year from the date of this order."[71] However, issuing an executive order is considerably easier than actually executing one. Obama needed to overcome two significant hurdles before closing the facility: first, the prisoners at the camp would need to be either prosecuted or moved elsewhere; and second, Congress would need to approve funding to help close down the camp.[72] In late 2010, Congress passed legislation banning the transfer of any individuals detained at Guantanamo to the United States and requiring the administration to notify Congress when it sent prisoners to another country. The Obama administration violated the latter provision when it sent five detainees to Qatar in 2014 without providing the necessary congressional notice.[73]

Despite the Obama administration's clear violation of the law, some legal scholars and civil rights proponents urged it to push past the boundaries of executive power.[74] For example, former State Department official and law professor Harold Koh argued that President Obama should unilaterally remove detainees from Guantanamo through a combination of various legal and constitutional claims that would give the president "legal space" to close the detention camp.[75] The situation led another legal scholar, Deborah Pearlstein, to write: "Which does the President think is more important? The strategic importance of closing Guantanamo on his watch? Or the structural, historical importance of holding the line on the expansion of presidential power in the United States?"[76] Other legal scholars supported Pearlstein's view that Obama should remain within the accepted limits of presidential power.[77] In the end, Obama continued to adhere to congressional restrictions and, despite the transferring of detainees to other countries, Guantanamo Bay remained open at the beginning of Donald J. Trump's presidency.

President Obama's executive order on Guantanamo Bay raises an important point about implementation: simply issuing an executive order is no guarantee that the president's administrative or policy direction will actually be followed. In his study of executive orders and bureaucratic responsiveness to them, Joshua Kennedy found that executive branch agencies do not necessarily respond to presidential orders.[78] Kennedy's finding runs counter to the dominant view of scholars, who see unilateral presidential tools as the ultimate trump card for presidents.[79] As Kennedy explains, "This is decidedly not the case."[80]

From the beginning of his presidency, Donald J. Trump has used a flurry of executive orders as a very public way to address his campaign promises and reverse Obama-era policies.[81] As William Howell noted in 2017, Trump is "just letting it rip on all manner of policy issues."[82] The president has chosen to emphasize executive orders despite enjoying Republican majorities in the House (at least, through 2018) and the Senate, which could have given his policy preferences a longer shelf life had he pursued them as bills that, with congressional approval, he could sign into law. So far, Trump has issued executive orders on repealing Obamacare,[83] building a wall between the United States and Mexico,[84] preventing people from certain Muslim countries from traveling to the United States,[85] and a host of other topics. Many of the initiatives undertaken through Trump's executive orders have ended up stalling in federal court.[86] These cases highlight a fairly clear and obvious fact: the use of executive orders does not automatically result in presidential success. To be certain, there is an allure of using executive orders to get things done, but often presidents run into institutional constraints and other impediments that prevent action. Such realities run counter to the very concept of the unitary executive theory.

SIGNING STATEMENTS

Presidential scholar Richard Waterman notes that the George W. Bush administration used signing statements to push for the "strong" unitary executive theory, a philosophy that for Waterman "raises serious legal questions about the boundaries of presidential power and Congress's ability to limit presidential discretion."[87] Unitary executive advocates see signing statements as a means for presidents to push back against legislative encroachments that interfere with their ability to manage the executive branch. Presidents not only can use signing statements to announce that they alone oversee the executive branch, but also can remove provisions from laws that unduly interfere with their ability to direct others. We argue here that giving signing statements the power to change or nullify the law turns the constitutional system of government on its head.

Broadly defined, a signing statement is an oral or written declaration by the president that accompanies a bill that he has signed into law. It may be released at the time of the bill's signing or later. According to Christopher Kelley, there are three generally recognized categories of signing statements: constitutional, political, and rhetorical. In a constitutional signing statement, a president not only points out flaws in a bill but also declares—often using vague language—his intent not to enforce certain provisions. Such statements may be different than ones that are political in nature. In political signing statements, a president gives executive branch agencies guidance on how to apply the law. Finally, the most common type of signing statements is rhetorical, whereby the intent of the president is to focus attention on one or more provisions for political gain.[88]

In their most pernicious form, constitutional signing statements presumably give presidents the ability to unilaterally prevent their power from being checked by the traditional legislative process. Unitary executive advocates contend that signing statements have a long-standing history in the legislative process. For example, Steven Calabresi and Christopher Yoo reference signing statements issued by Presidents James Monroe and Andrew Jackson to support their contention that the unitary executive theory has always been a well-established practice of government.[89] As law professor Neil Kinkopf observed, signing statements over time have served "a largely innocuous and ceremonial function"; they were not really used to change laws before President Reagan.[90] In fact, presidents did not aggressively use constitutional signing statements to provide unchecked presidential power until the Reagan administration. Therefore, history is not on the side of unitary executive advocates who would like to use signing statements as examples of long-standing presidential control over the executive branch.

Signing statements assumed greater prominence after Attorney General Edwin Meese announced a deal with West Publishing to include signing statements in the *US Code Congressional and Administrative News* "Legislative History" area. Up to that point, signing statements had been published in the *Weekly Compilation of Presidential Documents* and *Public Papers of the Presidents of the United States,* but this move essentially added them as "presidential history" to counterweigh against legislative histories that might be consulted by a judge.[91] Until this time, signing statements were widely considered, in Kelley's words, "nothing more than a press release."[92]

Despite the lack of precedent for the substantive use of signing statements, recent presidents such as George W. Bush have aggressively employed this tool to advance their view of an unchecked executive branch. President Bush, as Philip Cooper notes, was particularly apt at "quietly, systematically, and effectively develop[ing] the presidential signing statement to regularly revise legislation and pursue [his] goal of building the unified executive."[93] The public's focus on Bush's use of signing statements became so intense that the American Bar Association (ABA) created a taskforce in 2006 to study the controversy. The ABA eventually declared that the practice under Bush occurred on an unprecedented scale. Moreover, the group stated its strong opposition to the presidential usc of signing statements as a violation of principles of separated powers.[94]

Regardless of how many signing statements President George W. Bush employed,[95] all presidents since Reagan have used signing statements to undermine traditional governing checks and balances and the rule of law. In the modern era, an increasingly powerful and virtually unchecked executive has been aided by various factors, including what Gene Healy calls a "cult of the presidency,"[96] in which power-seeking presidents appear to be the norm, perhaps even the ideal. As a result, contemporary presidents' use of signing statements is the natural outcome of this phenomenon.

A recently published scholarly article questioned whether signing statements were really all that threatening.[97] We believe that they can be, under certain circumstances. Signing statements do not offend the

Constitution if they merely clarify the meaning of a law for the public. They are also properly used to simply provide guidance to subordinate officers within the executive branch on how the president believes certain provisions should be interpreted. A president could use other methods of delivery to convey such information, including press releases, news conferences, and intra–executive branch memorandums. Seen in this light, signing statements can be viewed as an effective tool for presidents to use to communicate with executive branch officials and employees in certain circumstances.

Signing statements become objectionable when a president attempts to transform statutory authority and circumvent the rule of law. To be sure, a president may find that certain provisions of legislative enactments violate executive authority or principles of separation of powers. Such weighty issues are appropriately resolved by a process of deliberation and accommodation between the political branches or, if not settled in that fashion, in court. We do not believe that such signing statements start a productive dialogue.[98] Instead, they invite interbranch conflict and encourage additional acts of presidential unilateralism. The more recent, aggressive use of signing statements has resulted in unnecessary battles between the branches of the federal government.

Members of Congress often object to signing statements because the presence of one sometimes means that the administration is attempting to settle a policy debate without legislative input. The proper time to exchange competing viewpoints is during the legislative process, which takes place before a bill is submitted to the president to sign. Presidents often make deals with members of Congress to provide legislative controls in a law to secure its passage. In 2009, President Obama did just that. In the process of convincing Congress to pass a funding measure for the International Monetary Fund and the World Bank, "Obama agreed to allow the Congress to set conditions on how the money would be spent" and to attach a reporting requirement provision. However, the president then turned around and issued a signing statement in which he argued that those restrictions would "interfere with my constitutional authority to conduct foreign relations." Congress was not happy with this turn of events. Representative Barney Frank (D-MA) wrote to the president and accused him of abandoning his promise. The House even passed a bill that barred funding of the president's challenges.[99]

Instead of encouraging dialogue and political accommodations, such actions by presidents can actually short-circuit the free exchange of ideas and may even poison relations with Congress, including lawmakers from the president's own party. If a proposed statute so clearly violates what the president views as vital constitutional principles, then he has an obligation to veto it. He should not agree to provisions during the legislative process and then turn around and effectively challenge them.

This approach not only increases distrust and promotes greater polarization on Capitol Hill but also goes against the text of the Constitution. Nowhere in Article I or Article II does the Constitution provide line-item veto authority to the chief executive. As George Washington explained, "From the nature of the constitution I must approve all the parts of a bill, or reject it *in toto*."[100] Even if a president makes constitutional objections during the lawmaking process, such protests do not make credible his actions of signing a bill and later challenging certain provisions through a signing statement. As Representative Frank remarked, presidents "have a legitimate right to tell us their constitutional concerns—that's different from having a signing statement." However, he explained, "Anyone who makes the argument that 'once we have told you we have constitutional concerns and then you pass it anyway, that justifies us in ignoring it'—that is a constitutional violation. Those play very different roles and you can't bootstrap one into the other."[101]

Louis Fisher cuts to the core of the problem with constitutional signing statements that purport to nullify statutory provisions. He argues that such statements "encourage the belief that the law is not what Congress puts in public law but what the administration decides to do later on." Fisher notes that "if the volume of signing statements gradually replaces Congress-made law with executive-made law and treats a statute as a mere starting point on what executive officials want to do, the threat to the rule of law is grave."[102] We agree. It is unilateral presidential decision-making itself that in this context strikes a serious blow against the core principles of separation of powers.

Another problem with constitutional signing statements is that they generally lack clarity and precision, which greatly hinders the idea that they could be used to help facilitate a dialogue between a president and Congress in the first place.[103] As noted earlier, signing statements are often crafted in a world of doublespeak where words are distorted to create confusion, and ambiguity is preferred in order to muddle the president's true intent. President George W. Bush received frequent criticism for his vague signing statements. Likewise, as Christopher Kelley explained, "There are numerous instances where Obama's signing statements resort to the vagaries seen in the Bush signing statements, where it becomes difficult to discern precisely what is being challenged or why."[104]

The benefits of the obfuscating language are clear. Even when a president intends to ignore a statutory provision, imprecise wording can sow enough confusion among reporters, scholars, members of Congress, and certainly the public to prevent any kind of universal response. Consider, for example, President Obama's April 15, 2011, signing statement dealing with the provision of a budget bill to cut off funding for certain czar positions within the White House. In his analysis of that statement, presidential scholar Robert Spitzer argued that Obama "offers a vague statement that leaves unclear what action, if any, the president would take, although political reporting suggested that this statement would not result in any challenge to the law."[105] Two of us took the opposing view and declared that the president's statement "effectively nullified" the anticzars provision.[106] If scholars can disagree about the intended meaning of presidential signing statements, it is doubtful that a casual observer could easily and clearly discern the president's intentions.

Obama's czar-related signing statement illustrates why it is so troubling that such claims of unilateral executive controls can both occur in a system of separated powers and then frequently go unchallenged. Here, the president and Congress negotiated for a long time over a budget bill. Each side was ultimately unhappy about certain provisions—no one got everything that they wanted. But the end result, a bill that passed through both houses of Congress and received the president's signature, was the outcome of a series of compromises between parties who ultimately (seemingly) agreed on the final product. After all of this, the president issued a signing statement effectively excising a provision of the legislation he had just signed. If the president may act in such a fashion without consequence, then checks and balances have little impact on claims of executive authority. In this case, the president's action stood because Congress did not resist, but the fact that Congress did not push back should not lend legitimacy to Obama's action.

Since becoming president and through the end of March 2020, President Trump has made 689 objections overall through fifty-five signing statements.[107] For example, he issued a signing statement objecting to provisions of a law he had signed that imposed sanctions on certain threatening foreign regimes. The president identified several specific provisions of the law that he considered in some way offensive to his authority as president, and he added that he would direct the executive branch to implement the law's provisions in a way that would not trample on "the President's constitutional authority to conduct foreign relations."[108] With so much to object to, of course, the president could have just vetoed the bill. The White House and Congress had devoted considerable effort to negotiating the legislation, but noteworthy in this case was the near certainty of a veto override after Congress passed the bill by overwhelming margins in both chambers. Wishing to avoid a veto override, the president approved the legislation despite his objections and then issued a signing statement over the parts of the legislation that he found objectionable.[109] Given its utility, the signing statement will likely continue to be a popular executive tool under President Trump and his successors.

FEDERAL EXECUTIVE CLEMENCY: THE PRESIDENT'S POWER TO PARDON

The unitary executive theory is generally aimed at providing a rationale for broad, even unchecked presidential power. However, there is at least one area of executive power where the president does not need a construct like the unitary executive theory to justify virtually unchecked power: clemency.

The president enjoys a nearly unlimited power to pardon federal crimes thanks to a single constitutional provision: Article II, Section 2, Clause 1 entrusts to the president the power to "grant reprieves and pardons for offenses against the United States, except in cases of impeachment." Practically speaking, presidential clemency is limited to federal (as opposed to state) offenses and may not be used to stop an impeachment proceeding. Several Supreme Court cases interpreting the constitutional Pardon Clause have generally granted the president a wide berth in how clemency may be used. For example, in the Civil War and Reconstruction era, the courts protected the president from congressional interference with his clemency power.[110]

Practically speaking, clemency is a check on the federal judiciary. The power is in turn limited by Congress. The legislature does not hold a direct check on clemency, but Congress may use the usual means at its disposal to direct public attention to possible wrongdoing: holding hearings, calling witnesses, subpoenaing documents, and so on. In more extreme cases, Congress may consider impeaching the president or even amending the Constitution.[111]

In an address to Congress, George Washington explained his decision to pardon two Whiskey Rebels by calling on the two appropriate rationales for justifying clemency decisions: as an act of mercy shown to a particular person, or as a decision made because the president determined it to be in the best interest of the public to grant mercy. Alexander Hamilton originally discussed these rationales in *Federalist* No. 74. They have since been picked up by two important Supreme Court cases, *United States v. Wilson* (1833) and *Biddle v. Perovich* (1927). Throughout American history, these two criteria have at least implicitly undergirded most clemency decisions made by presidents, with some notable exceptions.[112]

In recent years, controversial pardons made for a president's personal reasons have drawn attention to how presidents use clemency. For example, Bill Clinton pardoned a wealthy fugitive named Marc Rich and offered sentence commutations to members of the Fuerzas Armadas de Liberación Nacional (FALN), a Puerto Rican independence terrorist organization. These clemency decisions caused a media ruckus and led to criticism of the president, who apparently used clemency to secure votes (FALN) or to assist a generous donor to Democratic causes (Rich).[113]

Presidents also have used clemency inappropriately to help out political allies or friends caught up in federal justice proceedings. President George H. W. Bush pardoned the Iran-Contra defendants on Christmas Eve 1992 after Caspar Weinberger was reindicted by special counsel Lawrence Walsh and may have wanted Bush to testify at his trial. President George W. Bush commuted the prison sentence of I. Lewis "Scooter" Libby, who was Vice President Richard Cheney's chief of staff and ended up being a target of a special counsel investigation related to the scandal surrounding who may have leaked former agent Valerie Plame's secret CIA identity to the media. In these cases, the media pointed out (correctly) that none of these clemency recipients was likely granted a pardon or commutation because they deserved mercy or because the president was using clemency to serve some higher societal goal; rather, the president acted because granting clemency to these particular individuals satisfied some other end that he had.[114]

Most recently, clemency has been abused by President Donald J.

Trump, who, among his clemency decisions so far, has targeted prominent political supporters (Sheriff Joe Arpaio, the aforementioned "Scooter" Libby, and conservative commentator Dinesh D'Souza) and celebrities or celebrity-backed figures (the late boxer Jack Johnson, supported by Sylvester Stallone, and drug offender Alice Marie Johnson, who was endorsed by Kim Kardashian) for clemency even while ignoring thousands of petitions.[115]

In addition to his unusual choices for presidential mercy, Trump has ignored the usual process for evaluating the appropriateness of clemency for an applicant. The Office of the Pardon Attorney is an arm of the Department of Justice charged with assisting the president with clemency requests. Those seeking presidential mercy can go online to locate the proper form for the type of clemency they desire (usually a full pardon or a sentence commutation) and to complete and then submit the petition. At this point, a process begins that may include an investigation that winds its way through the federal justice system before ending with a clemency denial that often comes years later. Trump has apparently formed a "committee" to handle evaluations of clemency requests outside the normal process. It is the president's right to decide how (or whether) to investigate clemency requests before granting them, but Trump's approach so far has been extremely unusual among recent presidents.[116]

Perhaps most disturbing, Trump has on two occasions tweeted about the possibility that he may pardon himself, presumably to short-circuit an independent counsel investigation by Robert Mueller into any improper connections between Trump and Russian agents.[117] A self-pardon would seem to be the ultimate realization of a "unitary executive." Fortunately, the question is likely to remain theoretical, as the impeachment process looms large over any president who might be bold (or desperate) enough to attempt a self-pardon.

CONCLUSION

Under the Constitution and the law, presidents do not have complete discretionary control over the executive branch of government. Many governmental duties exist outside the direct supervision of the president. Court decisions have made clear that the president does not possess exclusive authority or control over every department or agency official. In fact, Congress has the authority to impose duties on government officers who ultimately are responsible to the Constitution and the law, not the sole discretion of the president. Where the law is clear as to the responsibilities of government officers, the president's discretion is limited accordingly.

Additionally, the federal government's administrative growth has made entirely impractical the idea that a president could ever exercise direct control over all executive branch officers. But even if a president claimed the right to do so, regardless of practical impediments, there is no convincing evidence that we can locate that would adequately support his right to do so.

Ultimately it is Congress that creates governmental structures, sets into law the policy discretion of departments and agencies, and provides appropriations. Furthermore, Congress possesses the responsibility to oversee and, if necessary, investigate the executive branch. It is difficult to shoehorn a theory of unitary executive power into a system so dominated by Congress.

Some advocates of a stronger presidency and executive branch might reasonably argue that the lack of true unitary control is a systemic flaw in our constitutional system. In such a scenario, there are remedies worth considering. However, we find little support for the view that the lack of unitary control was a mistake. Rather, it was an intentional design choice by the framers to limit the discretion of the president and to make him subject to the Constitution and the law, not the other way around. The argument for unitary control over the executive branch simply runs counter to principles of separated powers. Taken to its logical conclusion, the theory of a unitary executive eliminates the controls built into a system of separated powers and leaves the government under the direction of a single person—exactly what the framers of our Constitution sought to avoid.

CHAPTER 3

Domestic Powers

Part II

Advocates for a unitary executive argue that the president enjoys almost absolute command and control over the executive branch and its officials. Yet there are numerous constitutional, statutory, and even political constraints on what presidents can do regarding the appointment of officials and the removal of at least some of them. In the previous chapter, we reviewed discretionary and ministerial duties, the limits of the president's discretion, presidential power in the departments and bureaus, executive orders, signing statements, and federal executive clemency. Now we turn to the president's power to make appointments and to remove certain officials from office, which highlights well the fundamental flaws in the underlying rationale of the unitary executive theory.

APPOINTMENTS

The president's ability to make appointments, particularly those to the federal judiciary, has ebbed and flowed more than most other areas of presidential power. Some advocates for executive power declare that the Constitution leaves no room for legislative involvement or impediment in the nomination process.[1] If true, then the appointment and removal power could significantly aid in the notion that the president does have the tools to provide the command and control over the executive branch that unitary executive supporters contend. Those who advocate for presidential unilateralism with appointments reason that this is the only way to interpret the language of Article II, which reads, "[The president] shall nominate, and by and with the Advice and Consent of the Senate, shall appoint ambassadors, other public ministers and consuls, judges of the Supreme Court, and all other officers of the United States."[2] Alexander Hamilton is the best-known advocate for this point of view. In *Federalist* No. 66, he wrote: "It will be the office of the President to *nominate*, and, with the advice and consent of the Senate, to *appoint*. There will, of course, be no exertion of *choice* on the part of the Senate. They may defeat one choice of the Executive, and oblige him to make another; but they cannot themselves *choose*—they can only ratify or reject the choice he may have made."[3]

Hamilton could not have foreseen an important development in this process: as the constitutional system evolved, lawmakers assumed a significant role in choosing a nominee. This evolution happened *because of* the nature and text of the Constitution, not despite it. Appointments are a joint responsibility shared by the president and the Senate, and the power to reject is a vital factor in the appointment process. This joint responsibility requires the active participation of lawmakers well before a president formally nominates someone to federal office. Presidents recognize the pragmatic considerations involved in making appointments, and they understand that they need to comply with legislative preferences.

A textual reading of the Appointments Clause eventually gave way to a more nuanced interpretation based on actual practice. Early on, presidents searching for qualified candidates in the "pre nomination process" chose to consult with, and solicit recommendations from, lawmakers, particularly a senator or the highest-level elected office-holder (representative or governor) of the president's political party.[4] This practice is referred to as "senatorial courtesy" and is maintained with both judicial appointments (federal judges, US attorneys, and marshals) and others to this day. Senatorial courtesy dates back to George Washington's administration, during which the Senate rejected the nomination of Benjamin Fishbourn to be the naval officer for the Port of Savannah, Georgia. Senators deferred to the wishes of at least one of Georgia's home-state senators.[5]

Consultation also occurs with executive branch offices, including department-level, cadet/midshipmen, and postmaster appointments (until 1970, when President Richard M. Nixon and Congress transformed the Post Office Department into a government corporation). Lawmakers tend to recommend few specific candidates for appointments to cabinet-level positions. However, as G. Calvin Mackenzie has noted, "The President rarely announces a [cabinet] nomination without first assessing the sentiments of those individuals and interests most likely to be affected by the nomination," namely, members of Congress.[6] We agree that the practice of presidents keeping the lines of communication open with Senate leadership so that their candidate can earn support from senators is ideal.

Another important aspect of appointments is the ability of presidents to make recess appointments. The relevant constitutional clause is: "The president shall have power to fill up all vacancies that may happen during the recess of the senate, by granting commissions which shall expire at the end of their next session." With this language, the framers provided a way for presidents to staff the federal government at times when the Senate would not be in session. However, as with the Appointments Clause, the framers did not supply much by way of their own interpretation. Their missing guidance here could lead to a broad interpretation, perhaps wide-ranging enough to allow the president to have a nearly unlimited ability to act without Senate involvement. Advocates for a unitary executive power often rely on constitutional gray areas or imprecise language in the Constitution to justify their view that the chief executive can interpret any vague or blank spaces in the document however he pleases.

Most recess appointments have hinged on the interpretation of two words: "recess," that is, how long the Senate has to be on break to be considered in recess; and "happen," that is, does the vacancy need to have occurred during the recess of the Senate for the president to make a recess appointment? Most recent interbranch disputes regarding appointments have occurred over how to properly understand a "recess." In these cases, presidents have used their recess appointment power to bypass the confirmation process.

For example, President George W. Bush used his recess appointment power to place Fifth Circuit nominee Charles W. Pickering and Eleventh Circuit nominee William H. Pryor on the federal bench after Democratic senators successfully prevented confirmation votes from being taken. President Bush made Pickering's recess appointment on January 16, 2004, during an intersession recess of Congress.[7] Pickering's service on the federal bench expired on December 8, 2004, at which time he told Bush he did not want to be renominated. Pryor's case was more controversial than Pickering's, in that Bush made the Pryor appointment on February 20, 2004, during a ten-day

intrasession adjournment of Congress. It is important to note the difference here between "intersession" and "intrasession" and how that
can impact someone's term. As Louis Fisher explains, "Someone who
receives an intersession appointment serves until the end of the next
session, or about a year. An individual with an intrasession appointment made early during the session serves close to two years."[8] Pryor's
appointment was unsuccessfully challenged in the Eleventh Circuit.

During Bush's tenure, the Senate held pro forma sessions every
third day to prevent the president from abusing his recess appointment power. The Senate's refusal to go into a prolonged adjournment
seemingly meant that the president could not use the recess power to
place individuals into executive and judicial positions without senatorial consent. The Senate began holding pro forma sessions during
the 2007 recess after President Bush had made two recess appointments.[9] For nearly one and a half years, the Senate held more than
two dozen pro forma sessions to prevent Bush from making recess
appointments. Senate Historian Donald A. Ritchie said he believed
this was the first time the Senate had used pro forma sessions to block
recess appointments.[10]

In fall 2011, Senate Republicans began holding pro forma sessions
to prevent President Barack Obama from making recess appointments. As had been the case under Bush, the Senate convened for
only a few minutes (or less) and then closed without conducting any
business. Obama received advice from the Office of Legal Counsel
(OLC) that pro forma sessions did not bar the president from making
recess appointments, so he made four of them in early January 2012.[11]

The president's recess appointments triggered a lawsuit that challenged his authority to make those decisions. In January 2013, the
D.C. Circuit Court ruled that Obama could not make intrasession recess appointments based on the reasoning that the term "the recess"
does not contemplate the appointment power being used within a
session of the Senate. The appellate court also held that any recess
appointment made by the president could only apply to vacancies that
occurred during the actual recess. The case next went to the Supreme
Court. Although the Court rejected both points made by the D.C.
Circuit, it concluded that the Obama administration could not unilaterally decide when a recess occurs. The Court reasoned that it is
willing "to interpret the Clause as granting the President the power to
make appointments during a recess," but it would not offer a construction that would give "the President the authority routinely to avoid the
need for Senate confirmation."[12]

The Court therefore permitted the general use of intrasession recess appointments but disallowed it in cases where the recess lasts for less than ten days.[13] The Court's rationale behind the ten-day threshold focused on the lack of any available precedent. The Court also dismissed the Obama administration's view that the Senate's pro forma sessions were makeweight attempts to prevent the president from exercising his constitutional powers. Instead, the Court deferred to the Senate's authority to conduct its business as it saw fit and placed special emphasis on the chamber's capacity to act on legislation and nominations at any time during a pro forma session.[14]

Congress has used other mechanisms to limit the president's recess appointment power, such as passing funding restrictions. The original law regarding compensation for recess appointees was passed in 1863 and prohibited the use of funds to "be paid from the Treasury of the United States . . . to any person appointed during the recess of the Senate, to fill a vacancy in any existing office . . . until such appointee shall have been confirmed by the Senate."[15] In 1940, Congress revised its overly strict prohibition on salary payments for recess appointees. The law still retained the prohibition on payments to "an individual appointed during a recess of the Senate to fill a vacancy in an existing office, if the vacancy existed while the Senate was in session and was by law required to be filled by and with the advice and consent of the Senate, until the appointee has been confirmed by the Senate."[16]

However, Congress created three exceptions to make it easier for recess appointees to receive a salary. These three exceptions still exist today. First, payments can be made "if the vacancy arose within 30 days before the end of the session of the Senate." This exception recognized that the president and Senate have little time to consider a judicial replacement, let alone confirm that person. Second, payments are permitted if, by the end of a session, a nomination has been pending before the Senate (unless that nomination had already received a recess appointment). Given the time constraints confronted by the Senate at the end of a session, this provision is a reasonable accommodation to the circumstances. Third, payments can be made if a nomination "was rejected by the Senate within 30 days before the end of the session" (this option does not apply if the president then nominates the person who was rejected by the Senate).[17] This final exception is the Senate's attempt to ensure that presidents will not make recess appointments of rejected nominations. All three exceptions are subject to the qualification that a nomination must be sent to the Senate no later than forty days after the next session begins.[18]

Moving to the confirmation stage, the Senate holds a strong textual position, since appointments can only be made upon the advice and consent of that body. However, presidents from Franklin D. Roosevelt to Donald J. Trump have pressed their institutional role in the appointment process to varying degrees to seize the upper hand in shaping the federal judiciary. Even so, lawmakers have been able to counter presidential power through the years and remain firmly in control of the appointment process today. In the case of Obama, the Supreme Court rejected the president's use of recess appointments to sidestep the Senate's use of pro forma sessions, as discussed previously. Decades earlier, in 1937, President Franklin D. Roosevelt's infamous court-packing plan went down to defeat after pushback from his own political party.

The Senate usually conducts a rigorous review of nominees during the confirmation process. For judicial appointments, the Judiciary Committee sends each nominee a questionnaire designed to elicit information on the nominee's background. These questions focus on their education, employment record, draft status, bar association memberships, published writings, public statements, court cases (if the nominee has been a judge), public offices held, political affiliations, legal career, financial holdings, and various other concerns. The nominees also undergo a Federal Bureau of Investigation (FBI) background check and are vetted by committee staff. Another important aspect of the review process is the "blue slip" stage, named after the color of the paper used in the process. The committee counsel or nomination clerk will send out a blue slip to the senators of the state where the president has nominated an individual to serve in order to seek their assessment concerning appellate court, district court, US marshal, and US attorney nominations. Blue slips do not apply to nominees to be on the Supreme Court, or to be the attorney general, the solicitor general, or another position with a national scope. At times blue slips have been used to gain information about a nominee or have been used by home-state senators to block action on a nomination.[19]

Senators may resort to "holds" to delay or prevent a confirmation vote. Holds are informal devices that block action on measures scheduled for floor consideration. Unlike blue slips, holds are not normally publicly disclosed, have not been made available on a government or private website, and are not mentioned in the rules of the Senate. The majority leader, through his ability to set the Senate's agenda, decides if and for how long he will observe a hold. Generally, holds are honored because they are linked to the power of a senator to filibuster or to object when the majority leader asks for unanimous consent. Without the consent of its entire membership, no measure can easily pass in the Senate.

When obstruction by Senate Republicans under President Obama became too much for Democrats to tolerate in 2013, Senate majority leader Harry Reid (D-NV) decided to eliminate the filibuster for all executive branch nominations and most judicial nominations, excluding Supreme Court candidates.[20] This change came about after the failed cloture vote on Mel Watt's nomination to be the director of the Federal Housing Finance Agency in late October 2013, which, according to Democratic senator Jeff Merkley, "reopened" talks of using the nuclear option—a procedural tactic designed to eliminate the filibuster.[21] Upon making the decision to eliminate the filibuster, majority leader Reid said, "It's time to get the Senate working again."[22]

Democrats may have believed Reid's plan to be a good maneuver at the time, but it became problematic for them once the American public elected a Senate majority and a president of the opposing political party. When it appeared likely that Democrats would filibuster the Supreme Court nomination of Neil Gorsuch, President Donald J. Trump urged the Republican Senate to engage the nuclear option to ensure Gorsuch's confirmation. Senate majority leader Mitch McConnell did just that in April 2017: all fifty-two Republicans in the Senate voted in favor of the nuclear option, and all forty-eight Democrats voted against. The president did not stop there, however. The next month, he tweeted: "The U.S. Senate should switch to 51 votes, immediately, and get Healthcare and TAX CUTS approved, fast and easy. Dems would do it, no doubt!"[23] This has not yet happened, but it is worth noting that the issue is now being seriously discussed.

Gorsuch was confirmed by a 54 to 45 vote, with three Democrats voting in favor of his confirmation. The next year the nuclear option allowed Trump and Senate Republicans to push to a final floor vote the embattled Supreme Court nomination of Brett Kavanaugh. The Senate confirmed Kavanaugh by a 50 to 48 vote, with Senator Joe Manchin (D-WV) voting in favor and Senator Lisa Murkowski (R-AK) voting present to accommodate a colleague.[24]

The elimination of the filibuster first at the lower court level, and now with Supreme Court nominations, has resulted in a greater number of a president's selections being confirmed when the same political party controls both the White House and the Senate.[25] This was certainly the case immediately following the filibuster rule change in 2013. Speaking a year after the rule change took place, majority leader Reid boasted: "Senate Democrats were able to overcome political gridlock and confirm the highest number of district and circuit court judges in a single Congress in over thirty years."[26] This achievement is even more remarkable when one considers that Senate Democrats accomplished it in only a single year.

The new status quo requiring only a simple Senate majority for confirmation may tempt the president to nominate more ideologically extreme judges when his party controls the Senate. During debate over deploying the nuclear option to pave the way for Gorsuch's confirmation, Senator John McCain (R-AZ) forcefully argued: "Now that we are entering into an era where a simple majority decides all judicial nominations, we will see more and more nominees from the extremes of both the left and the right. I do not see how that will ensure a fair and impartial judiciary. In fact, I think the opposite will be true and Americans will no longer be confident of equal protection under the law."[27] McCain's statement is especially noteworthy, since he voted with his Republican colleagues in favor of the nuclear option. His comments lend credibility to the concern that partisanship will rise above all other factors in Senate deliberations over Supreme Court nominations.

A more fundamental question concerns the potential long-term implications that eliminating the filibuster will have for the relationship between presidents and the Senate. Does the absence of the filibuster make the upper chamber of the legislature weaker? Will future presidents press their advantage, especially when their own political party controls the Senate? Of course, the absence of the filibuster does not change the fact that every nomination must still be confirmed by a majority vote of the Senate.[28]

It is possible that the new reality of a filibuster-less appointment process might lessen the natural tension of governing. If it proves to be a benefit to getting things done, shouldn't the nuclear option be used routinely to ensure that Supreme Court nominations and legislation require only a simple majority vote to pass? Even before the election of Donald J. Trump as president, conservative pundit Charles Krauthammer publicly declared that Republicans should use the nuclear option to push legislation through the Senate.[29] Republican senator Mike Lee also came out in support of such a move.[30]

We disagree. Our government is built on principles of checks and balances and may indeed proceed at a pace that seems slow and sometimes even torturous. Even lawmakers intending to pursue the "collective good" by delaying and blocking judicial nominations may be painted as mere partisan ideologues by the opposing party. The day-to-day process can be frustrating or even jarring to observe. However, these are all predictable frustrations in a governing system where separate branches share the responsibility for judicial appointments. Without the filibuster, Senate leaders would have little incentive to run the institution in a way that promotes deliberation and dialogue. In cautioning against attempts to eliminate the filibuster, the late Robert C. Byrd (D-WV), a parliamentary expert and the Senate's longest-serving member, stated: "We must never, ever, tear down the only wall—the necessary fence—this nation has against the excesses of the Executive Branch and the resultant haste and tyranny of the majority."[31]

MYERS V. UNITED STATES: REMOVALS AND STATUTORY QUALIFICATIONS

Unitary executive advocates contend that the president has not only an absolute appointment power but also an unlimited ability to remove officials from office. In fact, this position has been advanced by Steven Calabresi and Christopher Yoo in their study on the unitary executive theory: "We show here that all forty-three presidents have consistently adhered to a practice of construing the Constitution as creating a unitary executive and giving them the removal power over the past 218 years."[32] In making this argument, the authors routinely praise Chief Justice William Howard Taft's majority opinion in *Myers v. United States*, noting that it "represents one of the cornerstones of unitary executive scholarship, and there can be no question but that the author of *Myers* was a vigorous defender of the unitary executive."[33]

Myers centered on the president's removal of a postmaster who had previously refused to resign his position. The law in question provided that postmasters "shall be appointed and may be removed by the President by and with the advice and consent of the Senate."[34] In this case, President Woodrow Wilson removed Frank Myers from his position without the approval of the Senate. In what can only be described as a pro-executive opinion, Chief Justice Taft's holding found the law to be unconstitutional, and he wrote, "The natural meaning of the term 'executive power' granted the President included the appointment and removal of executive subordinates."[35] Taft argued that "the power of removal must remain where the Constitution places it, with the President, as part of the executive power."[36]

However, despite their extensive coverage of *Myers,* Calabresi and Yoo neglected to mention that Taft had also argued that the president's removal power is not quite absolute:

> There may be duties so peculiarly and specifically committed to the discretion of a particular officer as to raise a question whether the President may overrule or revise the officer's interpretation of his statutory duty in a particular instance. Then there may be duties of a quasi-judicial character imposed on executive officers and members of executive tribunals whose decisions after hearing affect interests of individuals, the discharge of which the President can not in a particular case properly influence or control. But even in such a case he may consider the decision after its rendition as a reason for removing the officer, on the ground that the discretion regularly entrusted to that officer by statute has not been on the whole intelligently or wisely exercised. Otherwise he does not discharge his own constitutional duty of seeing that the laws be faithfully executed.[37]

Far from vouching for an absolute and unchecked presidential removal power, Taft actually placed a significant restriction on it, at least as applied to officials with a "quasi-judicial character." In doing so, Taft acknowledged the reality that Congress had already invested in officials' administrative and adjudicatory functions largely free from presidential control.[38]

Less than ten years later, the Supreme Court added to its earlier comments on the president's removal authority. *Humphrey's Executor v. United States* came about after President Franklin D. Roosevelt removed William Humphrey as a commissioner on the Federal Trade Commission (FTC) for policy differences, not—as the law stipulated—because of any "inefficiency, neglect of duty, or malfeasance in office" by Humphrey. Speaking for a unanimous Court, Justice George Sutherland noted that Congress had wanted "to limit the executive power of removal to the causes enumerated" as it concerned the FTC.[39] Sutherland explained that the Court's rationale in *Myers*, which acknowledged an unlimited presidential removal power, did not apply to the FTC: "The office of a postmaster is so essentially unlike the office now involved that the decision in the *Myers* case cannot be accepted as controlling our decision here. A postmaster is an executive officer restricted to the performance of executive functions. He is charged with no duty at all related to either the legislative or judicial power."[40] Sutherland concluded that it is

> plain under the Constitution that illimitable power of removal is not possessed by the President in respect of officers of [a quasi-legislative and quasi-judicial character]. The authority of Congress, in creating quasi-legislative or quasi-judicial agencies, to require them to act in discharge of their duties independently of executive control cannot well be doubted, and that authority includes, as an appropriate incident, power to fix the period during which they shall continue in office, and to forbid their removal except for cause in the meantime.[41]

Another aspect of *Myers* with significant implications for the unitary executive theory and presidential power has to do with the ability of Congress to place statutory qualifications on appointments. This important congressional ability is not mentioned by Calabresi and Yoo, and perhaps for good reason: if proponents of a unitary executive model claim that all executive powers belong to the president and are subject to his plenary control, then it is reasonable to infer that the appointment power should prevent Congress from adding more qualifications for those nominated by the president to serve in public office. This argument has been advanced by Saikrishna Prakash, a supporter of the unitary executive theory who believes that all statutory qualifications are unconstitutional restraints on a president's ability to appoint.[42]

However, Chief Justice Taft's opinion in *Myers* offers a different interpretation of the Constitution and the Appointments Clause than unitary executive supporters might expect: "To Congress under its legislative power is given the establishment of offices, the determination of their functions and jurisdiction, the prescribing of reasonable and relevant qualifications and rules of eligibility of appointees, and the fixing of the term for which they are to be appointed, and their compensation—all except as otherwise provided by the Constitution."[43] In this passage, Taft does not come across as quite the strong unitary executive supporter that Calabresi and Yoo claim he is. Driving home the point, presidential scholar Edward Corwin called these types of measures "by far the most important limitation on presidential autonomy" in the field of appointments and argued that Congress has the authority to "stipulate the qualifications" on offices that it creates.[44]

Congress's capacity to impose its own statutory qualifications undercuts Calabresi and Yoo's contention that "the executive branch's consistent opposition to congressional incursions on the unitary executive has been sufficiently consistent and sustained to refute any suggestion of presidential acquiescence in derogations from the unitary executive."[45] In fact, presidents have not only approved of statutory qualifications by signing them into law but also "consistently observed them" as well.[46] Reams of federal laws exist to prescribe qualifications for office. Typically, they stipulate political party, citizenship, residency, gender, professional qualifications, or civilian status. Many governmental boards or commissions require political balance of some sort. For example, the Equal Employment Opportunity Commission (EEOC) mandates that only three of its five members can be from the same political party.[47] This is also true for members of the Federal Communications Commission (FCC), the Federal Election Commission (FEC), and the Securities and Exchange Commission (SEC).[48] There are even laws requiring officeholders to be appointed without considering their political party affiliation. Similar restrictions apply for establishing and appointing inspectors general in federal departments and agencies.[49]

Other statutory restrictions abound. All "permanent officers and employees" of the Census Bureau are required to be "citizens of the United States," as are the directors of the US Patent and Trademark Office and the Office of Thrift Supervision.[50] Some offices require an appointee to live within the district for which he or she was chosen. Except for positions in the District of Columbia and in the Southern and Eastern Districts of New York, all US attorneys, assistant attorneys, and marshals must observe a residency requirement in order to hold office.[51] The position of director of the Women's Bureau at the Department of Labor must be held by a woman.[52]

Presidents of both political parties have accepted congressional restrictions on their appointment power by closely following the statutory qualification stipulations. In fact, presidents only started objecting to these limits on their ability to nominate during the Reagan administration.[53] Speaking in 2007, Deputy Assistant Attorney General John P. Elwood articulated the most commonly used rationale:

> As a mandatory directive to the President, [statutory qualifications] violate the Appointments Clause, U.S. Const., art. II, § 2, as each of the past four Presidents has noted in signing statements. If construed as a recommendation from Congress, however, these appointments provisions are constitutional and are often routinely followed. A constitutional signing statement on this issue, therefore, is not a declaration that the President will not follow the appointments provisions, but that he remains free to abide by them as a matter of policy.[54]

Contrary to what Elwood and others have argued, statutory qualifications are not merely "a recommendation from Congress." Rather, they are clear and direct legal requirements that define a position and promote the policy interests of Congress and in turn the president who signed the bill into law.

These statutory restrictions should not be seen as inflexible as Congress has granted exceptions to them on at least two occasions. The most famous case involved the 1950 appointment of General George C. Marshall as secretary of defense. Congress passed a law granting Marshall an exemption to the restriction that only civilians (or former military officers who have been out of active duty service for seven years) could serve as defense secretary, thereby allowing him to be eligible for the appointment.[55]

The second case occurred in the late 1990s, when President Bill Clinton sought a waiver from the legal restrictions placed on Charlene Barshefsky, his nominee to the position of US trade representative. Barshefsky once represented Canada in a trade controversy with the US and would have therefore been legally ineligible to serve without a waiver.[56] During the waiver-seeking process, the White House solicited an opinion from the OLC—an entity in the Justice Department that traditionally provides presidents with legal advice—regarding the constitutionality of the statute governing the appointment of the US trade representative. The OLC concluded that "a restriction ruling out a large portion of those persons best qualified by experience and knowledge to fill a particular office invades the constitutional power of the President and Senate to install the principal officers of the United States." The opinion went on to argue that the position dealt with foreign relations, which is "an area constitutionally committed to the President." Furthermore, the OLC contended that the position is closely linked to the president, and thus when an office "entails broad responsibility for advising the President and for making policy, the President must have expansive authority to choose his aides." The OLC concluded that the provision in question "is unconstitutional and cannot preclude the President's appointment of Ms. Barshefsky."[57] Of course, President Clinton did not follow the OLC's recommendation and sought a waiver for the appointment. After issuing the waiver, the Senate Finance Committee voted unanimously in favor of Barshefsky.[58] The Senate proceeded to confirm Barshefsky as well.[59]

The Marshall and Barshefsky appointments demonstrate that the Senate is willing to make accommodations for exceptional candidates. In the end, politics wins out over any doctrinaire position. Congressional waivers should be viewed as a useful tool that does not necessarily limit the discretion of the president or the appointing officer. Despite the OLC's opinion on Barshefsky's appointment restriction, President Clinton wisely sought to compromise with, rather than confront, Congress.

INDEPENDENT COUNSEL AND THE REMOVAL POWER

The Ethics in Government Act of 1978 is closely tied to debates over the removal power and is therefore highly criticized by unitary executive theorists. At the heart of their criticism of this law is their belief that the president has a responsibility to manage federal prosecutions and that any law which interferes with that power is unconstitutional.[60] The Ethics in Government Act of 1978 provided for the appointment of a special prosecutor by a panel of judges and the removal of the appointee by the attorney general only for "extraordinary impropriety, physical disability, mental incapacity, or any other condition that substantially impairs the performance of such special prosecutor's duties."[61]

To understand the reasons for these particular appointment and removal provisions, it is necessary to review a series of removals from office involving Justice Department officials that started on October 20, 1973, in what came to be known as the "Saturday Night Massacre."

This event came at a time when the press and the public suspected President Richard M. Nixon or his associates of having committed federal crimes in the Watergate scandal, but as yet had little knowledge of exactly what had occurred. In May 1973, President Nixon agreed to create a special prosecutor in the Department of Justice. That month, Nixon's attorney general, Elliot Richardson, established the Office of Watergate Special Counsel and named Archibald Cox, former John F. Kennedy administration solicitor general, as the special prosecutor.[62]

Richardson vested Cox with a significant level of independence and promised that he would not "countermand or interfere with the Special Prosecutor's decisions or actions." Richardson also vowed that Cox "will not be removed from his duties except for extraordinary improprieties on his part."[63] Richardson himself resigned after Nixon ordered him to remove Cox, who had requested that the president turn over tape-recorded conversations related to the Watergate break-in. Richardson's successor, Deputy Attorney General William Ruckelshaus, also refused to fire Cox and was himself terminated before he could resign. Solicitor General Robert Bork—third in line at the Department of Justice—took responsibility for the Justice Department and fired Cox.[64]

These incidents caused a firestorm of political protest. Public dissatisfaction over the "Massacre" was intense: Western Union deemed the flood of telegrams sent to Washington, DC, after Cox's termination to be "the heaviest volume on record."[65] Well-respected institutions and individuals, such as the director of the American Bar Association, *Time* magazine, and the AFL-CIO, urged Nixon's impeachment.[66] Criticism continued until a new special prosecutor—Leon Jaworksi—was named to continue the investigation.[67] Eventually, Nixon turned over the requested materials. One recording, of a June 23, 1972, conversation, became the "smoking gun" that revealed Nixon's culpability in covering up illegal activities and prompted his resignation. In the end, Watergate shattered public confidence in the chief executive and the Justice Department, and Congress believed that legislation was needed to protect a future independent counsel from being removed from her or his role by the president for political reasons.

Following Cox's dismissal, Congress considered legislation that would create a special prosecutor named by a court.[68] In the fall of 1973, two key bills—H.R. 11401 and S. 2611—were proposed to address the matter. They represented a change of perspective for Congress regarding responsibility for appointing special prosecutors. Instead of relying on the president or the attorney general to appoint a special prosecutor, or even trusting the president to act with the approval of the Senate, these bills called for the transfer of the appointment and removal powers for special prosecutors from the executive to the judicial branch.[69] The congressional hearings on these bills revealed that Congress could not trust the executive branch to investigate itself.[70]

By 1977, Congress worked out an agreement with newly elected president Jimmy Carter on a special prosecutor bill, and on October 26, 1978, the Ethics in Government Act became law.[71] The law broke from past procedure by permitting a special division of the US Court of Appeals for the D.C. Circuit, upon the attorney general's request, to appoint a temporary special prosecutor.[72] By dividing the responsibility for implementing a special prosecutor in this manner, members of Congress attempted to balance the president's ability to ensure the execution of the laws with Congress's desire for an independent investigation of the executive branch.[73]

Calabresi and Yoo noted in their book that President Carter "had little choice but to overlook the constitutional problems and sign the independent counsel bill into law."[74] The "little choice" they are referencing is, of course, the result of the "Saturday Night Massacre" and the public's significant loss of confidence in its belief that the executive branch could be trusted to properly investigate itself. However, if there were indeed "constitutional problems," then the president had a duty to veto the bill. Instead, Carter signed the bill into law with positive endorsements for the special prosecutor provision. In speaking about the removal provision, Carter noted it "gives the Special Prosecutor in the future, if needed, a great protection in carrying out his responsibilities without interference." Carter ended by declaring that he hoped "this act will help to restore public confidence in the integrity of our Government" and that the law could be used as "a guide" for state and local lawmakers "who might wish to imitate what has been done so well by the Congress this year."[75]

Despite Carter's positive endorsement, the Ethics in Government Act of 1978 came under fire during Ronald Reagan's administration, first by Attorney General William French Smith in 1981, and then later in the decade by other Justice Department officials. However, during that period, Congress reauthorized the law—and changed the name of the position from "special prosecutor" to "independent counsel"— and Reagan signed it without releasing any statement of concerns.[76] Reagan did not challenge the law until a 1987 signing statement issued after his administration had been investigated several times, including for the infamous Iran-Contra arms-for-hostages scandal. In that signing statement, Reagan argued that an "officer of the United States exercising executive authority in the core area of law enforcement necessarily, under our constitutional scheme, must be subject to executive branch appointment, review, and removal." He stated that there "is no other constitutionally permissible alternative." But in signing the law, Reagan noted that he was "gratified that the constitutional issues presented by the statute are now squarely before" the courts.[77]

The court dispute that Reagan referenced in his signing statement was *Morrison v. Olson*, which would be decided by the Supreme Court in 1988. Theodore Olson, a Justice Department official who had been investigated by an independent counsel, challenged the constitutionality of the law, arguing that it violated the Constitution's Article II Appointments Clause and intruded on the Article III responsibilities of judges.

In a 7–1 decision (Justice Anthony Kennedy did not participate; Antonin Scalia alone dissented), the Supreme Court ruled that the independent counsel statute was constitutional. Writing for the Court, Chief Justice William Rehnquist focused on the Appointments Clause in Article II, particularly the differences between "inferior" and "principal" officers. He acknowledged difficulty in finding the exact line between the two classes of officers, but argued that the independent counsel was clearly an "inferior" officer for these reasons: (1) the position is removable by the attorney general; (2) duties are limited to investigation and prosecution and do not include policymaking responsibilities; (3) "the office is limited in jurisdiction"; and (4) the position has a limited tenure in that it is set "to accomplish a single task."[78] Rehnquist next focused on the constitutionality of a judicial panel making the interbranch appointment of the independent counsel. He stated that the appointment method was constitutional and that Congress could "vest the power to appoint independent counsel in a specially created federal court."[79]

Turning to the Article III question, Rehnquist first touched on the ability of the judicial panel to define the jurisdiction of the independent counsel and stated, "Once it is accepted that the Appointments Clause gives Congress the power to vest the appointment of officials such as the independent counsel in the 'courts of Law,' there can be no Article III objection to the Special Division's exercise of that power, as the power itself derives from the Appointments Clause, a source of authority for judicial action that is independent of Article III."[80] He went on to state that Article III also does not prevent Congress from vesting in the judicial panel the ability to grant extensions, receive reports, award attorney's fees, and other miscellaneous powers.[81] The key rationale for the Court seemed to be that the stated powers "do not impermissibly trespass upon the authority of the Executive Branch," and, in fact, some of the powers were "passive" in nature.[82] Rehnquist did note that he was "more doubtful" about the ability of the judicial panel to terminate the office of independent counsel, but he read the statutory language narrowly to allow "termination" to occur only when the counsel's duties were completed.[83]

Finally, Rehnquist found that the limit placed on the attorney general in removing an independent counsel only for "good cause" did not violate the constitutional principle of separation of powers. At the heart of Rehnquist's analysis was the application of *Myers, Humphrey's Executor,* and other removal power cases. The appellees challenging the independent counsel law contended that the distinction between officials possessing "purely executive" as opposed to "quasi-legislative" and "quasi-judicial" responsibilities made the removal limitation unconstitutional. However, Rehnquist stated that the Court's conclusion "cannot be made to turn on whether or not that official is classified as 'purely executive.'"[84] This distinction is meant to "ensure Congress does not interfere with the President's exercise of the 'executive power' and his constitutionally appointed duty to 'take care that the laws be faithfully executed' under Article II."[85]

The "real question," Rehnquist explained, "is whether the removal restrictions are of such a nature that they impede the President's ability to perform his constitutional duty, and the functions of the officials in question must be analyzed in that light."[86] Rehnquist did not see a fundamental separation of powers issue, and he argued that, given the circumstances of the appointment and duties performed, the president's inability to remove the counsel "at will" is not a significant constitutional concern. The reason for this was obvious to the Court: the attorney general still retained through the "good cause" provision "ample authority to assure that the counsel is competently performing his or her statutory responsibilities in a manner that comports with the provisions of the Act."[87] In sum, Rehnquist found that Congress may place removal restrictions on purely executive officials and, likely, agencies as long as they do not "impede" the president in carrying out his executive functions.

In a blistering dissent, Justice Scalia scolded the majority. Taking issue with the portion of the act's language that required an attorney general to request an independent counsel unless there were "no reasonable grounds to believe that further investigation or prosecution [was] warranted," Scalia argued that political reality essentially required the attorney general to request an independent counsel even when one might not be appropriate under the circumstances.[88] One legal analyst referred to the provision as using "howitzers to combat mice," in that many investigations were begun, but few indictments resulted.[89] In essence, Scalia argued, Congress had used the independent counsel statute to ensnare executive branch officials in order to hurt the president and help itself. Also, under Scalia's strict interpretation of the Constitution, the independent counsel statute unconstitutionally vested executive power in someone other than the president.[90] The majority's suggestion that the president—via the attorney general—maintained "at least *some* control" over the independent counsel, Scalia suggested, was "somewhat like referring to shackles as an effective means of locomotion."[91]

According to Calabresi and Yoo, "The fact that the administration advanced [arguments against the independent counsel law] is sufficient to overcome any claims that the executive branch acquiesced in the institution of the independent counsel as a deviation from the unitary executive."[92] This statement misses the point—it does not matter if the president acquiesced or not. The Supreme Court upheld the independent counsel law as constitutional, and therefore limits could be, and were, placed on the removal power.

As mentioned earlier, President Reagan in his 1987 signing statement commended the fact that the "constitutional issues" were before the courts, and strongly implied that he believed they should be resolved there. Interestingly, Reagan's own solicitor general, Charles Fried, believed that the administration would lose the case, as the independent counsel law "had too strong an appeal to the public's common sense" and "the spectacle of the administration launching this rather arcane argument of principle in order to ward off investigations of the President's close friends was just too unattractive." As a result, Fried concluded, "The whole enterprise ran aground and was smashed to pieces."[93]

The independent counsel statute was a success and restored the public's confidence in the government's ability to investigate itself following the "Saturday Night Massacre." It lapsed in 1992, but Congress reauthorized it two years later. In a 1994 signing statement, President Bill Clinton said the law "is a foundation stone for the trust between the Government and our citizens. It ensures that no matter what party controls the Congress or the executive branch, an independent, non-partisan process will be in place to guarantee the integrity of public officials and ensure that no one is above the law."[94] At no point in this statement did Clinton object to the law or its constitutionality. Subsequent experiences—particularly the Kenneth Starr investigations of Clinton—under the independent counsel law, however, convinced the president to turn around and oppose its reauthorization in 1999.

Like many divisions in politics, the line between those who opposed and those who supported the law had less to do with any deep commitment to the unitary executive theory and more about who was in the White House at the time of a particular investigation. From the late 1970s through the Iran-Contra scandal, Republicans generally sympathized with the executive branch. Thus, critics of the independent counsel were, at first, primarily Republicans. Because Presidents Richard M. Nixon, Gerald Ford, Ronald Reagan, and George H. W. Bush were Republicans, this perspective is no surprise. Executive branch supporters viewed the independent counsel law as a weapon created by Congress "to render the President blind and lame by restricting his authority to appoint, direct, and remove the officers who wield executive power." They suggested that the statute was "an instrument for undermining the independence of executive officers themselves."[95] According to this point of view, the independent counsel statute was a way for the legislature to "undermin[e] public confidence in the ability of the President and his subordinates to faithfully execute the law, thereby paving the way for the Congress to assume the direction of the administration of the law through its oversight and investigatory powers."[96]

These criticisms over the independent counsel law seem misplaced. From 1978 to 1999, there were twenty independent counsel investigations. Indictments were sought in just eight of those twenty investigations. According to Louis Fisher, when "indictments and convictions were obtained, as with probes into corruption in executive departments (Housing and Urban Development, Agriculture) or the Iran-Contra affair, the abuses were substantial and needed attention."[97]

There is currently no statutory law in place to establish an independent counsel to investigate the executive branch. The Justice Department promulgated controlling regulations after the independent counsel law expired to give the attorney general the power to appoint a "special counsel" to investigate criminal wrongdoing.[98] The special counsel is not independent from the Justice Department, as the attorney general "may request that the Special Counsel provide an explanation for any investigative or prosecutorial step, and may after review conclude that the action is so inappropriate or unwarranted under established Departmental practices that it should not be pursued."[99]

Under President Donald J. Trump, the special counsel provision was invoked by Deputy Attorney General Rod Rosenstein[100] to appoint former FBI director Robert Mueller to investigate possible Russian interference in the 2016 presidential election.[101] During the course of an investigation lasting almost two years, Mueller obtained "seven guilty pleas and charges against 34 individuals and three separate companies,"[102] including Trump's 2016 campaign manager Paul Manafort, former national security adviser Michael Flynn, his personal attorney Michael Cohen, and others.

On March 22, 2019, Mueller gave a report on his findings to Attorney General William Barr.[103] Two days later, Barr issued a summary of Mueller's report in which the attorney general explained that Mueller found that Trump was not completely innocent of trying to obstruct justice, but that Trump's actions did not merit obstruction charges and, additionally, that Trump's administration had not worked with Russia to impact the 2016 presidential election. Mueller immediately disputed Barr's characterization of the report.[104]

On July 24, 2019, Mueller testified in front of Congress about the contents of the report. Notably, he remarked, "If we had had confidence that the President clearly did not commit a crime, we would have said so" (they did not say so) and that "charging the president with a crime was . . . not an option we could consider," because of an OLC memo from 1973 opining that a president currently serving in office could not be charged with crimes until he returned to private life.[105]

Now that the investigation is over and Mueller has testified to Congress, the big picture question going forward is whether the public and, more important, Congress have lost confidence in the executive branch's ability to investigate itself. If it has, Congress may need to enact another independent counsel law like it did after Watergate. Early indications suggest that, despite ongoing partisan divisions, the public still has confidence in the ability of the executive branch to police itself. According to the Pew Research Center, "Nearly two-thirds of Americans—including, for the first time, a majority of Republicans—say they are confident [Mueller] conducted a fair investigation into Russian interference in the 2016 election."[106] President Trump has called the Mueller probe "the Greatest Witch Hunt in U.S. history,"[107] but most Americans do not agree with that assessment.

CONCLUSION

Through this chapter's consideration of the various constraints on the presidential appointment and removal powers, we have argued that presidents do not exercise unitary control over the executive branch. Given the Senate's confirmation power, the president cannot unilaterally determine who gets a seat on a federal court, a cabinet secretary position, or even an ambassadorship. Moreover, the president may not simply impose his preferences on the Senate: in addition to the confirmation power, it also features the custom of "senatorial courtesy" and other practices that together give the Senate a formidable check on the presidential appointment power. Indeed, the Senate has not been reluctant to fully exercise this authority over time, and presidents have seen many of their nominees either turned away or forced to withdraw in the face of strong Senate opposition. The Senate has also resorted to using "holds" on nominations to try to force the president's hand on matters of policy. Congress generally has many mechanisms at its disposal to limit the president's recess appointment power and has used them effectively.

Presidents are often exasperated by the Senate's behavior on confirmations. They commonly complain about unreasonable delays, outright blocking of qualified nominees, and curbing the recess appointment power. In sum, they believe the Senate is putting up barriers that prevent the president from selecting his team to do the work of government. These complaints are often fair but are not at all relevant to the question of whether presidents possess some inherent right to place any appointees they might wish into Senate-confirmed positions.

The president's right to nominate someone for an appointed position also implies a right of removal, but even here the president's hands are often tied. Constitutionally, judicial appointments are for life and not subject to removal other than through Congress's ability to impeach and remove someone from public office. The public may not be aware that Congress has also created quasi-legislative and quasi-judicial agencies whose members serve fixed terms and may not be removed by the president. Congress alone has the authority to stipulate qualifications for offices that it creates. Thus, Congress establishes offices and determines their functions, jurisdictions, qualifications, and terms of appointment. Presidents generally have accepted these statutory stipulations without question.

Over time, special prosecutors, independent counsel, and now a special counsel have been created to help keep the executive branch in line. These first two offices were positions that were considered necessary to conduct truly independent investigations of the executive branch in response to allegations of Watergate-era wrongdoing. Until the Independent Counsel Act expired in 1999, these roles were a powerful additional check on the executive branch and a further reminder of that branch's subservience to the Constitution and to the law. Yet because of perceived overreach by independent counsel in past investigations, especially the then-ongoing inquiry focused on President Bill Clinton, the public did not support renewing the law.

The current Office of Special Counsel is part of the Department of Justice and thus belongs to the executive branch. Because the president possesses the full prosecution power granted by Article II of the Constitution, he may fire a special counsel even if that person and his or her staff are investigating the president. President Trump repeatedly criticized the Mueller investigation as a "witch hunt" but allowed special counsel Robert Mueller to complete his investigation into possible Russian meddling in the 2016 presidential election, even after Mueller took the extraordinary steps of having the FBI investigate the private residence of Trump's former campaign manager and the office of Trump's personal lawyer.

In sum, constitutional, statutory and political constraints on the presidential appointment and removal powers along with the special counsel mechanism all weigh against the theory that presidents have complete control over the executive branch and its officials.

CHAPTER 4

Domestic Powers

Part III

One of the key characteristics of the unitary executive theory is that the president enjoys sole authority over the entire executive branch. A recurring theme in our analysis and critique of the unitary executive theory so far has been to show that the president is not actually solely in command.

To this point we have explored congressional checks on presidential authority in key areas of domestic policy. In chapter 2, we considered discretionary and ministerial duties; the limits of the president's discretion; the ways that presidential power manifests in the departments and bureaus; and how presidents have used executive orders, signing statements, and federal executive clemency as tools to expand their influence. Chapter 3 contains an analysis of the president's ability to appoint and, in some cases, remove certain officials. We now continue that line of discussion here, where we review another set of tools that a president may call on to exert his influence over the direction of either domestic or foreign policy. Among the most important of these capabilities are using the legislative veto, exercising rulemaking authority, appointing White House czars, and asserting executive privilege.

THE LEGISLATIVE VETO

From the 1930s until a major Supreme Court decision in 1983,[1] Congress exercised a control over executive power known as the "legislative veto." In brief, Congress would delegate authority to the executive branch by enacting veto mechanisms in enabling laws. In doing so, Congress relied on an understanding it shared with the executive: we will grant more discretionary power to the executive branch only if we have the ability to control the outcome without having to pass an entirely new law. As a result, Congress often exerted its power over the executive through a one-house veto, although some legislative vetoes also occurred by joint resolution of Congress. Numerous important laws during this period contained provisions for a legislative veto, including, for example, the War Powers Resolution (1974).[2] The legislative veto option offered Congress a great degree of flexibility in the rulemaking process; if the legislature decided that agency or departmental actions violated legislative intent, it could easily pull back without needing to take any extra steps such as amending the law or challenging an executive action in court.[3] The legislative veto power was first formally recognized in the 1930s but has existed in various incarnations since the early years of the Republic.

Some proponents of unilateral executive powers see the legislative veto as a violation of the principles of separated powers. In their view, only the president may veto, since the Constitution does not grant veto authority to the legislative branch. Their belief is that when Congress passes a law, the president may veto the entire law, but Congress cannot undo what the two branches had mutually agreed on after going through the normal lawmaking process.

Supporters of the legislative veto, in contrast, maintain that the mechanism was mutually beneficial for the president and Congress, allowed a flexible approach to making and revising federal enactments, and generally worked well. They argue that the legislative veto was both consistent with long-standing practice and made the law- and rulemaking processes much more streamlined than a process that did not allow the mechanism. To supporters of the legislative veto, barring it would require Congress to concede to the executive an enormous amount of discretionary authority over implementing laws. In this scenario, Congress would have little incentive to challenge entire laws over differences of interpretation and would therefore be unlikely to contest many executive actions that appear to stretch legislative intent beyond what the legislature intended.

To proponents of unilateral presidential powers, the Supreme Court reached a definitive decision on the constitutionality of legislative vetoes in the 1983 case *INS v. Chadha*, where the majority struck down the mechanism as an unconstitutional violation of the principle of separation of powers.[4] First, the Court reasoned, a one-house veto violates the concept of bicameralism: one chamber of the legislature may not unilaterally decide the fate of a law. Second, the Court determined that the legislative veto violates the Presentment Clause, or the section of the Constitution that explains the path a bill must follow through Congress in order to become a law. The *Chadha* decision immediately raised questions about the constitutionality of nearly two hundred existing laws containing legislative veto provisions.

Unitary executive theory advocates point to the Court's decision in *Chadha* to strike down the legislative veto as a clear validation of their position. Steven Calabresi and Christopher Yoo maintain in their study of the unitary executive theory that the legislative veto had irritated presidents dating back to Woodrow Wilson, and that "the Supreme Court specifically relied on these presidents' consistent objections to this interference with their power over the execution of the law when declaring the legislative veto unconstitutional in *INS v. Chadha*."[5] Calabresi and Yoo argue, as they have done concerning other presidential powers, that presidents have over time refused to accept a legislative control on executive power. At one point, they declare that presidents "opposed the legislative veto with enough consistency to foreclose any suggestion that they acquiesced to this particular derogation of the unitary executive."[6] In another reference to the legislative veto, they contend that presidents "had consistently questioned" use of the mechanism.[7] Louis Fisher notes here Calabresi and Yoo's "softening of language" from "consistent objections" to "consistent questioning," but aside from this apt observation, ample evidence shows that presidents and many other executive branch officials have acquiesced to the legislative veto.[8] Indeed, the mechanism was established as a legitimate practice well before it became commonly known in the 1930s as the "legislative veto."

Over time the president and Congress have had their own practical reasons for including legislative veto provisions in laws. Each side benefited from the arrangement: the president received either the authority to make decisions or more flexibility to do so, while the legislature was able to supervise executive branch behavior more informally and without requiring additional legislative follow-up.[9] Indeed, one of the earliest rationales for the use of simple or concurrent resolutions as a legislative veto on executive action appears in an 1854 legal opinion by President Franklin Pierce's attorney general, Caleb Cushing. After describing the Presentment Clause and the veto override power of Congress, Cushing noted: "If, then, the President approves a law, which imperatively commands a thing to be done, ministerially, by a Head of Department, his approbation of the law, or its repassage after a veto, gives constitutionality to what would otherwise be the usurpation of executive power on the part of Congress."[10] As a result, "no separate resolution of either House can coerce a Head of Department, unless in some particular in which a law, duly enacted, has subjected him to the direct action of each; and in such case it is to be intended, that, by approving the law, the President has consented to the exercise of such coerciveness on the part of either House."[11]

One of the earliest examples of what later became known as the legislative veto occurred in the First Congress, which required the Treasury secretary to provide reports "to either branch of the legislature" as requested.[12] Congress did not begin to use the legislative veto as Cushing described it until the 1890s.[13] Legislative vetoes probably proliferated because Congress needed a way to protect itself as it began to delegate substantially more authority and discretion to departments and agencies.[14] Indeed, considerable evidence shows the growth and expansion of legislative vetoes dating from the late 1800s to the early twentieth century.[15] Calabresi and Yoo may contend that presidents "consistently questioned" legislative vetoes, but it seems this simply did not happen, nor would it have been a strong basis for claiming expansive presidential power even if it had occurred.[16]

Herbert Hoover is one example of a president who did not consistently oppose or question the use of the legislative veto, although some evidence exists of his occasional opposition to the mechanism. One such incident occurred in 1933, when he vetoed a bill that gave a joint congressional committee the power to make decisions on tax refunds over $20,000.[17] However, Hoover did not steadfastly oppose the use of the legislative veto. In fact, he called on Congress in his 1929 State of the Union address to *adopt* the legislative veto in a bill that would give him the power to reorganize the executive branch. "I can see no hope for the development of a sound reorganization of the Government unless Congress be willing to delegate its authority over the problem (subject to defined principles) to the Executive," Hoover stated, "who should act upon approval of a joint committee of Congress or with the reservation of power of revision by Congress within some limited period adequate for its consideration."[18] Congress acted on Hoover's request and granted him reorganization authority, subject to a legislative veto.[19]

Congress continued to reauthorize the president's reorganization authority (subject to a legislative veto) throughout much of the twentieth century. Even President Franklin D. Roosevelt capitulated to congressional demands to include a legislative veto when he realized that Congress would not authorize another reorganization measure without it. "Whatever constitutional misgivings Presidents had about the legislative veto of reorganization acts," Louis Fisher explains, "they acquiesced because they realized that Congress would not delegate such authority without attaching strings to it."[20] Calabresi and Yoo make a similar observation, as they note that presidents Ronald Reagan and George H. W. Bush "reportedly signed more than two hundred new legislative vetoes into law after *Chadha* and often complied with them."[21]

To be clear, several presidents questioned the legislative veto and then, as shown in the reorganization act examples described earlier, signed into law numerous bills containing legislative veto provisions. The president can posture in a statement, but his actual priorities become clear when he accepts legislative vetoes through explicit actions. A president's ultimate job is to govern, and this requires him to work with Congress. These demands of everyday governance come before any ideological notion of the proper scope of executive power or concern for furthering a "unitary" model of the presidency.

Despite the legislative veto's long history and its acceptance by presidents, Calabresi and Yoo strongly emphasize the Supreme Court's decision in *Chadha* holding the legislative veto unconstitutional.[22] But it is not certain that the Court completely forbade Congress from using the legislative veto via a single chamber resolution, or by way of both houses jointly issuing a concurrent resolution; in fact, forms of the legislative veto continue to exist even in the post-*Chadha* years.[23]

In its reasoning, the *Chadha* court emphasized the bicameral requirement and the Presentment Clause as justifications for striking down the legislative veto. It observed that the framers provided "that no law could take effect without the concurrence of the prescribed majority of the Members of both Houses."[24] In addition, the Court argued that the constitutional requirement "that all legislation be presented to the President before becoming law" was an essential feature to prevent the adoption of "oppressive, improvident, or ill-considered measures."[25]

The Court's *Chadha* opinion was badly reasoned and betrayed a poor understanding of both history and the procedures necessary for making laws. Louis Fisher eviscerates the Court's opinion, pointing out its various weaknesses and its "ignorance of history and congressional procedures."[26] Most notably, striking down the legislative veto cut off what the Court considered to be "legislative shortcuts" for Congress while leaving undisturbed similar "shortcuts" for the president and other executive officials, who can rely on executive orders and other unilateral devices to in effect make laws.[27]

Despite the Court's ruling in *Chadha*, legislative vetoes have not disappeared. In fact, the *Chadha* opinion has likely *strengthened* Congress's position vis-à-vis the executive branch.[28] Evidence of post-*Chadha* legislative vetoes abounds.[29] In one case, President Reagan objected to provisions in an appropriations bill that required the Appropriations Committee's approval for various actions by federal agencies. The House Appropriations Committee responded that it would repeal the authority of one of the agencies to exceed the spending caps placed in law. Soon after, the agency head wrote to the committee and said that he would not exceed the spending limit without first seeking legislators' approval.[30] Michael Berry found that since the *Chadha* decision, Congress has adapted and now employs other measures that in effect continue the legislative veto, particularly through the Appropriations Committee. Moreover, Berry argues that presidents have adapted, too, by issuing more signing statements appended to legislation to achieve similar flexibility.[31]

Not all presidents have agreed with the new reality, of course. Presidents George W. Bush and Barack Obama both objected to some committee-level vetoes. President Obama, citing *Chadha*, called them "impermissible forms of congressional aggrandizement in the execution of the laws."[32] But his argument, which mirrors that of his predecessors, fails to appreciate how the federal government actually works. The White House and the Department of Justice (DOJ) can certainly make pronouncements about how they think government should operate, but it is the other executive branch departments and agencies that must work with Congress to execute public policy. "Agency budget manuals, before and after *Chadha*," Fisher explains "are very specific in identifying which actions require committee approval."[33]

Despite what the Supreme Court or presidents might say, Congress will continue to direct, and often check, executive branch officials as they carry out public policy. In fact, by the end of 2013, Congress had placed into law nearly a thousand legislative vetoes since the *Chadha* decision in 1983.[34] Legislative vetoes still exist, the executive branch

continues to cooperate with them, and pro–unitary executive arguments are undercut by both of these facts.[35]

PRESIDENTS AND AGENCY-LEVEL RULEMAKING

Presidents have spent nearly the past fifty years trying to exert greater
influence and control over the agency-level rulemaking process.[36] In
1971, President Richard M. Nixon created the Quality of Life review
process, which authorized the Office of Management and Budget
(OMB) to review proposed rules of the Environmental Protection
Agency (EPA) and then share them with other agencies to solicit
their comments.[37] Presidents Gerald R. Ford and Jimmy Carter implemented their own limited changes to the process, but Ronald Reagan
was the first president to exert close control over the agency rule review process.[38]

In 1981, President Reagan issued an executive order requiring
agencies to send a copy of proposed rules to the Office of Information
and Regulatory Affairs (OIRA) within OMB. Agencies were charged
with preparing a cost-benefit analysis of major rules that would have
a financial impact on the economy of $100 million or more.[39] This
executive order joins a list of actions by various presidents who, over
the course of several decades, have attempted to solidify control over
the rulemaking process in ways similar to Reagan.[40] One of those efforts occurred in 1993 when President Bill Clinton issued an executive order, which generally maintained the overall regulatory review
framework, albeit with some minor naming details, such as using the
word "significant" instead of "major" to describe rules with a financial
impact on the economy of $100 million or more.[41] However, Clinton
made at least one noticeable revision: he emphasized that the benefits
of the rule need only justify the costs, whereas Reagan required the
benefits to outweigh the costs.[42]

Calabresi and Yoo argue that presidential efforts to provide White
House review of proposed agency regulations represent "one of the
most sweeping invocations of the unitary executive yet seen."[43] They
contend that the "sprawl of the federal bureaucracy and the con-
comitant increase in the difficulty of coordinating regulatory policy
across agencies made the evolution of some new means for coordinating regulatory policy inevitable."[44] They extol the benefits of these
changes, as agency heads now have a way to learn which regulations
are being promulgated by other agencies. The new procedures also

provide "both the means and the incentive for all levels of the agency to become actively involved in setting agency priorities and in shaping major regulatory initiatives." In the end, Calabresi and Yoo believe the review is "a reflection of the fundamental importance of the unitary control of the executive branch combined with the dramatic growth in the size and importance of the administrative state."[45]

Calabresi and Yoo's claim to unitary powers in this arena is much too broad. Even after the White House created a review process for agency-level regulations, there is little evidence to suggest that presidents enjoy anywhere near the degree of direction and command over agencies that unitary executive proponents describe. In fact, as William West has shown, the OIRA review process may provide the president with a *reactive* management tool for agency decisions and actions, but it is not a real "top-down planning and coordination" ability as is often associated with the unitary executive model.[46] West also notes that presidential power advocates "have made little attempt to support their claims with systematic evidence" but instead rely on the intuitively appealing argument that "a unitary actor" brings accountability "for the performance of government." He concludes that "advocates of a unified executive have been content with arguments that are superficially appealing but poorly specified."[47]

In looking at the effects of White House rulemaking, West maintains that "centralized administrative clearance has never entailed comprehensive oversight." He notes that OIRA does not have adequate staff to review the "two to three thousand rules developed by federal agencies each year."[48] In addition, he points to the "constraints on the president's legal authority." As he explains, congressional statutes create federal agencies so agencies "need to stay within their legal mandates," which "obviously limits presidents' ability to bring the diverse activities of the federal government into alignment."[49] Moreover, presidents lack a vision or drive to provide the kind of administrative management advanced by the unitary executive model.[50] As West states, "Presidents, themselves, do not have preexisting preferences with regard to many issues that arise in the administrative process."[51]

West believes that presidents are reluctant to take on broad policy supervision of the regulatory review process, a view he shares with former Clinton White House Domestic Policy Council staffer (and current Supreme Court justice) Elena Kagan. For example, Kagan noted that "Clinton's brand of presidential administration" was "driven more by discrete policy goals than by an overall theory of regulation."[52]

Indeed, regarding hazardous substances in the environment and workplace regulations, President Clinton "rarely took a public role in formulating agency rules." Kagan posits that this outlook "reflected his substantive interests as well as the structure and organization of the White House; but it also may have derived from a general, if unarticulated, sense that these actions involved significant levels of scientific expertise and thus offered less space for presidential involvement."[53] The limitations of presidential involvement also likely resulted from the political nature and interest of presidents, which requires the White House to "operate with an attitude of respect toward agency experts and with a set of processes that encourage consultation."[54]

Even if the efforts to successfully adapt the unitary executive model for use in the White House regulatory coordination efforts are overblown, presidents dating back to Richard M. Nixon have attempted to shape agency-level rulemaking to an extent unimaginable one hundred years ago. Still, acknowledging the rise of presidential involvement in rulemaking is a far cry from saying that the White House has succeeded in providing unilateral direction and control. "History, precedent, and policy," as Morton Rosenberg has noted, "all favor viewing rulemaking as an exclusive legislative function properly controlled by Congress."[55] Rosenberg may overstate the case a bit, but his contention that Congress is the actual source of rulemaking authority is still a much more accurate explanation than the pro-president one offered by unitary executive advocates.

A president's ability to exercise substantial review powers over agency regulations often comes from a statutory or even more ambiguous authority—it usually is not drawn from the Constitution. There is a significant constitutional dimension to the struggles of rulemaking, and one may certainly claim that issues are "grounded in separation of powers."[56] However, checks and balances are probably a better constitutional mechanism for understanding and managing the rulemaking process. In the rulemaking arena, Congress possesses significant powers to create agencies, enact enabling laws, and otherwise determine the nature and scope of its delegated authority.

Presidents have tried to centralize rulemaking management and review, but one should not underestimate the ingenuity of an agency seeking to insulate itself from the unitary executive model. Agencies have several options available for avoiding or bypassing White House review and carrying out their own views on policy (assuming they differ from the president's).

One of the most obvious ways that an agency can try to insulate itself from presidential interference is to simply take no action at all. Doing nothing clearly prevents an agency's rules from being reviewed by the OIRA.[57] In a study of the OIRA and federal rulemaking, Curtis Copeland explains that "some agencies have indicated that they do not even propose certain regulatory provisions because they believe that OIRA would find them objectionable."[58] While agency inaction might allow it to avoid OIRA review, anticipation of OIRA's impact may also cause an agency to change its behavior.

Another way to bypass White House review and control is agency-level adjudication, which involves an agency ruling on disputes between individuals and the government.[59] The outcomes of rulemaking and adjudication are often not that different, and both processes shape an agency's policy results. Although the shaping of policy is much clearer in the rulemaking process, adjudication often requires the parameters of existing rules to be molded in ways that give real effect to agency policies.[60] An additional advantage of adjudication is that the Administrative Procedure Act forbids ex parte communication once the process has begun.[61]

An agency can also use its litigation authority to advance its policy goals. Although the Justice Department has the general statutory authority to manage how to execute the law, Congress provides independent litigation authority to several agencies.[62] Agency litigation authority also reveals significant exceptions to the unitary executive model that exist within the executive branch. As Neal Devins has noted: "Statutory exceptions to Department of Justice litigation authority have likewise impeded Attorney General efforts to advocate a unitary executive voice."[63] This certainly was the case during the George H. W. Bush administration, when the US Postal Service successfully blocked Justice Department attempts to take over its independent litigation power.[64] As a result, agencies that have independent litigation power can now bypass White House review and work to enforce their own authority as set forth in existing laws and regulations.

Agencies enjoy still another avoidance tactic: issuing guidance documents.[65] Guidance documents were originally intended to provide agencies with an easy, legally nonbinding way to clarify existing rules. In practice, guidance documents can function like agency-level rules. As one administrative law scholar noted, they are treated as a means of "arm-twisting."[66] Since 2007, "significant" guidance documents have been subject to the OIRA review process. However, OIRA review of these documents "is much more limited [compared with proposed rules] and unsystematic in practice."[67] Guidance documents are not subject to the same level of scrutiny or statutory controls (i.e., the notice-and-comment procedures of the Administrative Procedure Act) at the agency level as are proposed rules, and therefore OIRA is not provided the equivalent amount of information to review.[68] An agency issuing guidance documents is therefore likely to have much greater freedom from White House scrutiny in shaping policy.

Notwithstanding the methods already described, presidents have left open an important and major method of avoiding White House review: issuing nonsignificant rules. Under President Clinton's 1993 executive order, which remains in effect today, only "significant" rules are reviewed by OIRA. Therefore, agencies can bypass OIRA review altogether by ensuring that the rules it creates are not deemed "significant."[69] Who (or what) decides whether a rule is "significant"? Each agency does so, and they have several options available for making that determination.[70] For example, an agency can avoid the economic impact feature (i.e., rules with a $100 million or more impact on the economy) by simply breaking up the rule so that its separate parts fall short of the $100 million threshold. OIRA can still identify significant rules itself, but rules considered nonsignificant are "more likely to go unnoticed."[71]

Congress can have an even more important impact on the White House's review of agency rules by creating independent regulatory agencies.[72] These agencies are considered "independent" from the president because they are multimember bodies with staggered terms whose members are only removable by the president for cause or for some specific reason stipulated by law. Congress often provides for certain appointment restrictions, which prevent a president from selecting a specific number of members from one political party.[73] As a result, presidents have no direct control over the regulations passed by the Securities and Exchange Commission, the Federal Trade Commission, or other independent regulatory agencies.[74]

As explained in an earlier chapter, Congress may choose to limit a president's removal power. For example, Congress could insulate other agencies from White House regulatory influences by subjecting the president's removal power to a "for cause" provision (i.e., an officeholder cannot be removed by the president except for inefficiency, neglect of duty, or malfeasance in office). Christopher Ahlers has advocated for establishing a "for cause" provision, and he sees

Congress's decision to apply removability restrictions to the adminis-trator of the EPA as insulating that agency from presidential influence in the rulemaking process.[75]

Recently, the "for cause" provision that applies to the director of the Consumer Financial Protection Bureau (CFPB) has been chal-lenged as unconstitutional. In 2016, a three-judge panel of the US Court of Appeals for the District of Columbia held the CFPB structure to be unconstitutional and said that the "for cause" provision must fall.[76] However, the entire D.C. Court of Appeals reheard the case and decided in January 2018 that the CFPB structure is constitutionally permissible by noting that "a degree of independence is fully conso-nant with the Constitution."[77] As of this writing, the Supreme Court is set to hear arguments about the CFPB's constitutional status.[78]

During the journey of the case through the courts, the Justice Department has taken both sides of the legal arguments. Under President Barack Obama the DOJ supported the CFPB, but un-der President Donald J. Trump the Justice Department has argued against the independence of the agency. In its amicus curiae brief before the D.C. Court of Appeals, Trump's Justice Department de-clared that the "removal restriction for the Director of the CFPB is an unwarranted limitation on the President's executive power."[79] The Justice Department seems concerned here with issues of direction and control, noting "there is a greater risk that an 'independent' agency headed by a single person will engage in extreme departures from the President's executive policy."[80] The brief did not define "the President's executive policy" or clarify what would be considered "ex-treme departures" from it.

Leaving aside the long-standing reality that departments and agen-cies have promulgated rules and regulations with little or no White House involvement, an adverse ruling for the CFPB would not end the discussion. Congress has the authority to create multimember inde-pendent regulatory agencies subject to "for cause" removal provisions. Changing the CFPB's structure in such a way would likely overcome the objections raised by the Justice Department and a potential nega-tive ruling by the Supreme Court.

REINING IN THE PRESIDENT'S CZARS

During the presidencies of George W. Bush and Barack Obama, sub-stantial controversy erupted over their appointments of numerous

White House "czars." Czars are officials unilaterally appointed by the president to oversee the administration of policies; to coordinate policies under the jurisdictions of multiple departments and agencies; and to oversee federal efforts to, for example, regulate the automotive industry or to distribute victims' funds, among other duties. Bush and Obama were not the first presidents to appoint so-called czars, but the vast number of czar appointments and the breadth of their duties generated a great deal of debate about whether czars should even be serving in government. These officials were controversial because they were not confirmed by the Senate and yet often had power and broad portfolios of duties that sometimes exceeded those of Senate-confirmed agency and department heads. A president who appoints czars in this way can enjoy broad authority to act without countervailing checks and balances. Thus, this approach to, and use of, White House czars fits within the framework of the unitary executive theory.

The George W. Bush presidency especially received significant scholarly attention for its explicit reliance on the unitary executive theory, through which it claimed the inherent power of the president to act unilaterally in several policy areas. Indeed, President Bush made broad-reaching and sometimes unprecedented efforts to increase the powers of his office.[81] One of the many ways that he did so was to expand the use of White House czars. Bush unilaterally appointed several new czars whose duties overlapped with those of cabinet secretaries and other confirmed officials. He also garnered legislative approval in the post-9/11 environment for multiple new positions that media sources commonly referred to as "czars."

The czars controversy has largely disappeared from public discussion, but czars remain very much a part of the federal government's governing structure. The growing powers of the presidency, combined with Congress's failure to sufficiently protect its own institutional prerogatives, has led to the demand for czars. Modern presidents are commonly expected to both set the national agenda and try to solve complex policy problems. They are often unwilling to wait for legislative action and may act on public policy initiatives even if they do not have clear legal authority to do so.

The White House czar position offers several features that might please advocates of the unitary executive theory. For one, czars are not vetted by Congress and therefore do not appear to have any obligation to testify before Congress even if called to do so. From a traditional separation of powers standpoint, this is deeply concerning.

These officials are far from mere advisers, as they often possess policy, budgetary, and regulatory powers. From a purely managerial standpoint, appointing czars might be a useful way to bring about unity and impose order on a chaotic executive branch. From a constitutional standpoint, however, czars are a troublesome feature in a republic built on checks and balances and accountability.

The president enjoys many constitutional and statutory powers, but appointing czars is not one of them: czars are not mentioned or even implied anywhere in the Constitution or in government manuals. A 1964 dictionary on political terms notes that the "czar" title is "applied to public men of dictatorial tendencies."[82] Using such a term as a label for executive branch officials seems highly inappropriate in a constitutional republic, but the term has caught on in media and academic accounts as a descriptor for a certain kind of extra-constitutional position in modern presidential administrations.

In a lengthy study of czars, two coauthors of this book defined them as executive branch officials who are not confirmed by the Senate but still exercise authority to promulgate rules, regulations, and other orders that bind government officials and the private sector. An overwhelming number of czars occupy positions created by presidents acting unilaterally, although some czar positions have been created by statute as well.[83] Czars should not be classified based on executive branch structure, but typically they would include heads, assistant heads, deputies, and any other top-level personnel within departments and agencies appointed solely by the president.[84]

Creating a czar position can be a complex process, as demonstrated by President George W. Bush's establishment of the White House Office of Faith-Based and Community Initiatives. Initially, the president sought legislative approval for the new office. When, after considerable debate, Congress withheld its blessing, the president simply brought the office into being by issuing an executive order. He also named a czar to run the new faith-based office. The faith-based czar, an official who was not confirmed by the Senate, nevertheless enjoyed policy, spending, and regulatory authority. George W. Bush's actions here created a precedent that continued in rebranded and expanded forms in both the Barack Obama and the Donald J. Trump administrations.

President George W. Bush's actions to strengthen unilateral presidential powers received much scrutiny, but his successor, Barack Obama, continued many of Bush's practices and even expanded on them. Regarding czars, Obama vastly increased both their number and their spheres of influence. During his presidency, he appointed czars for clean energy, green jobs, nonproliferation, urban affairs, the Troubled Asset Relief Program (TARP), and the auto industry bailout and recovery. He named separate czars to oversee the Great Lakes, Chesapeake Bay, and California water concerns, among many others. One person, Kenneth Feinberg, held two czar positions, serving as both the "claims czar" and the "pay czar" (on executive compensation). In appointing White House czars, Obama directly contradicted a 2008 presidential campaign promise: "The biggest problems we're facing right now have to do with George Bush trying to bring more and more power into the executive branch and not go through Congress at all. And that's what I intend to reverse when I am president of the United States."[85]

Czars can create significant governing concerns, as illustrated by two Obama-era officials. In 2009, Obama named Steven Rattner as his car czar, a particularly important position thanks to the near collapse of the automotive industry and the bankruptcies of General Motors and Chrysler. Rattner, working as a non-Senate-confirmed official, held the title of chief adviser to the Treasury Department on the automobile industry and had the responsibility to decide whether to distribute billions of federal dollars to General Motors, Chrysler, and GMAC to allow those companies to avoid financial collapse. He headed the fourteen-member President's Task Force on the Automotive Industry and reported to the Treasury secretary, Timothy Geithner.

As the two auto companies emerged from bankruptcy in July 2009, Rattner resigned after becoming embroiled in a financing scandal. But he exercised enormous power over the auto industry during the six-month period that he served as car czar. According to *New York* magazine, Rattner had "rewrit[ten] the understanding between the car companies and the unions while bending the companies' financiers—his friends and peers—to his will. With what seemed a cool, almost arrogant confidence—his casual dismissal of GM CEO Rick Wagoner reflected this quality—he had played a large role in restructuring the American car industry."[86]

Rattner's role as car czar and the auto bailouts were both based on questionable legal authority. The Troubled Asset Relief Program, created by Congress when it passed the Emergency Economic Stabilization Act (EESA), ostensibly gave Rattner the authority to manage the auto bailout. However, Congress created TARP to bail out financial institutions, not automobile manufacturers. Even the Congressional Oversight Panel created specifically to provide oversight of TARP expressed skepticism on this point, noting in a report that the EESA "does not explicitly state that the TARP is available to provide assistance to the automotive industry."[87] It appears that the "crisis atmosphere" permitted agreement to a rather liberal interpretation of the law.[88] Legislative consent seemed lacking, and this permitted Rattner to act without much (if any) congressional oversight. Rattner proudly wrote in his own account of the auto bailout: "The auto rescue succeeded in no small part because we did not have to deal with Congress." He went on to say that "if the task force had not been able to operate under the aegis of TARP, we would have been subject to endless congressional posturing, deliberating, bickering, and micromanagement, in the midst of which one or more of the troubled companies under our care would have gone bankrupt."[89] It is no surprise that Rattner, a former czar, would disparage Congress and the system of checks and balances in order to promote the view that unlimited and quick actions by executive officials should win out. If such a view prevails, then executive action, above all other concerns or interests, becomes the ultimate purpose of government.

New York attorney general Andrew Cuomo prosecuted Rattner for receiving kickbacks in a scandal involving the New York pension fund. As part of a settlement deal, Rattner agreed to pay $10 million and not appear "in any capacity before a public pension fund" for a period of five years. In a separate settlement with the Securities and Exchange Commission, Rattner agreed to pay $6 million and accept a two-year ban from working in the securities field. [90] These penalties stemmed from Rattner's apparently illegal actions before he was selected by President Obama to be an executive branch czar.

Would Rattner, or anyone else with ongoing legal issues, have been appointed by the president knowing he would face a Senate confirmation vetting process that included an FBI review? Probably not. There is no guarantee that a normal vetting process would have revealed Rattner's past misdeeds, of course, but it most likely would have done so. And what were Rattner's qualifications for a job with such tremendous responsibilities? He began his professional career as a reporter and transitioned into mergers and acquisitions. Along the way, he donated millions of dollars to Hillary Clinton, Barack Obama, and other Democratic Party candidates for public office. President Obama may have been persuaded to overlook these obvious complications to

simply unilaterally name this wealthy contributor to a non-Senate-confirmed post.

Carol Browner was another Obama-era czar whose situation demonstrated the growing concerns with individuals holding czar positions.
Browner was named the Obama White House's energy and climate
czar and asked to be the administration's leader in pushing forward
climate change initiatives, a job that was actually far more important than the responsibilities held by the president's EPA head, Lisa
Jackson. For example, Browner played a key role in brokering a deal
with automakers and the states to reduce greenhouse gas emissions.
Her czar appointment thus elevated her above EPA administrator
Jackson, who held an actual Senate-confirmed, cabinet secretary–level
position. Indeed, during Browner's tenure in the czar role, her profile
and policy influence so vastly surpassed Jackson's that very few people outside of the Washington, DC, political world would likely even
recognize Jackson's name. Browner is probably the most conspicuous
example of a czar whose authority completely overshadowed that of
a cabinet head occupying the same policy space. As a czar, Browner
did not hold a Senate-confirmed appointment and refused to testify
on the Hill. During the first two years of the Obama administration,
congressional Republicans vehemently opposed Browner's expansive
policy role and promised to challenge her authority if they were to
achieve majority status in that chamber. Soon after the GOP took
control of the House in January 2011, Browner resigned from her
position.[91]

The czars phenomenon has not become a systemic problem. But
the fact that recent presidents use them more frequently is still a cause
for concern and requires reflection on the position's implications for
presidential power and governing.[92] Before the rise of the modern
presidency and the vast expansion of executive powers, presidents generally understood that they were not free to create positions allowing
officeholders to exercise policy, regulatory, and spending authority
without first obtaining congressional consent. Moreover, presidents
usually did not use unilateral action to assume authority to circumvent statutory officers or legislatively enacted programs. Regrettably,
these traditional rules and norms of the presidency have gradually
eroded and brought about detrimental consequences for our democratic republic.

Modern presidents enjoy enormous leeway to act from both expanded powers and congressional deference, and they increasingly

turn to czars to resolve the pressures they face to lead on many policy fronts. But czars represent a constitutional abnormality when they are empowered to oversee public policy over Senate-approved officeholders who are accountable to Congress and the law. Confirmed department or agency officials have a duty to the law; temporary czars do not. Indeed, Senator Robert Byrd (D-WV) raised similar issues early in the Obama presidency, writing:

> The rapid and easy accumulation of power by White House staff can threaten the Constitutional system of checks and balances. At the worst, White House staff members have taken direction and control of programmatic areas that are the statutory responsibility of Senate-confirmed officials. They have even limited access to the president by his own cabinet members. As presidential assistants and advisers, these White House staffers are not accountable for their actions to the Congress, to cabinet officials, and to virtually anyone but the president.[93]

In fact, a czar's commitment is often to the president and his campaign promises rather than to statutory government programs. Even more important, czars owe little accountability to Congress, and presidents can therefore use them as unilateral tools for achieving their policy goals.

Presidents most likely have the best intentions when creating czar positions, but simply having czars around encourages isolated thinking among top executive branch staff. Modern presidents are increasingly looking inward for advice and analysis even though they would be better served by obtaining different perspectives from outside the White House and the executive branch. Czars only exacerbate this trend toward increased presidential isolation by acting in ways that are easier for presidents to keep secret from Congress and the public. Such practices create insular thinking that is not subject to a rigorous outside review process that might reveal deficiencies in a plan or policy. The risks of failure can increase in the absence of an outside review process.

Richard Pious makes this key point in his book *Why Presidents Fail.* Pious argues that the modern institutionalized presidency, featuring a centralized command and control operation within the White House aimed at helping the president to make better decisions, "has increased rather than reduced the risks of failure."[94] He finds that executive branch officials and presidents are often ill-equipped to manage public policy issues alone. The fact is, he contends, presidents need Congress's help. In questioning the role of modern White House staff (including some czars), Pious explains, "Too many aides meddle in too much departmental business, antagonize too many legislators, and provide fodder for too many reporters looking to add to their collection of White House scalps."[95] Pious believes that a better alternative to presidents centralizing power and acting unilaterally is for them to concur with "framework legislation mandating collaborative governance with Congress."[96] We agree. Since most czars have no place in the Constitution or the laws, they operate in a system of governance created by the president. Pious's presidential failure thesis holds regarding czars.

Finally, czars have compiled an unimpressive track record over time at advancing coordination, government efficiency, and presidential policy goals. Consider, for example, President Woodrow Wilson's creation of the War Industries Board (WIB) during World War I. Wilson charged Bernard Baruch with ramping up wartime production of defense materials. However, industrial production peaked in May 1917, that is, a full year before Wilson set up the WIB. More recently, President Richard M. Nixon's czars on inflation and the economy both failed at their primary tasks. The same is true of the nation's first drug czar. Nearly ten years later, the federal government revived the "War on Drugs," and First Lady Nancy Reagan led the way with her "Just Say No" campaign. Various presidents have appointed multiple czars who together have not made a noticeable dent in illicit drug use. Finally, George W. Bush charged Tom Ridge, the homeland security czar, with the responsibility to coordinate federal policies in the so-called war on terror. The resulting enormously complex bureaucracy largely failed to carry out a patchwork of policies and regulations.

The czar phenomenon has yielded a combination of "worst-case scenario" outcomes for governing: czars have further fueled the concentration of executive power, limited access to presidents, and insulated the executive branch from congressional oversight, all while adding more layers of decision-making in government. Despite their efforts, czars have generally not made the executive branch bureaucracy more effective and efficient. A basic assumption of the unitary executive theory is that increased presidential discretion and control over the White House would improve administration and further the national interest. Real-life experience with White House czars has strongly refuted this theoretical belief.

EXECUTIVE PRIVILEGE: CONSTITUTIONAL, YET LIMITED

Executive privilege is one of the president's defensive tools and is therefore different from other presidential powers. In brief, executive privilege is a constitutional principle that permits the chief executive and high-level executive branch officers to withhold information from Congress, the courts, and the public. This presidential capability is not enumerated anywhere in the Constitution, but it is accepted today as a legitimate implied power. It has existed in some form since the time of President George Washington, although the phrase "executive privilege" was not officially used by a presidential administration until the 1950s.

Presidential use of executive privilege has ebbed and flowed. Like all constitutional powers, executive privilege is subject to a balancing test. The test begins with the assumption that presidents and their staff need confidentiality and the ability to keep some deliberations private. Over time, presidents have made their strongest cases for executive privilege in circumstances that implicate national security issues. A competing, and equally legitimate, assumption is that Congress must be able to access executive branch information to carry out its legislative and oversight functions. The need for confidentiality between presidents and their advisers will sometimes conflict with Congress's own need for access to that same secret information in order to do its job.

In these circumstances, presidential power advocates will contend that the burden is on Congress to prove it has a legislative interest before it may access executive branch information. Congress's burden, they argue, becomes heavier as that information nears the president's orbit. However, this understanding is flawed. In fact, the exact opposite is true, as the burden of proof is really on the executive branch to show it has a significant justification to withhold information. This is a consequence of our constitutional system, where separate institutions share power and government is based on accountability. Presidents have often abused executive privilege for political reasons. Perhaps most (in)famously, Richard M. Nixon tried to use executive privilege to cover up embarrassing and politically inconvenient information regarding the Watergate scandal.

Three recent presidents, George W. Bush, Barack Obama, and Donald J. Trump, have made executive privilege claims, albeit more sparingly than Bill Clinton, who made more executive privilege claims than all other post-Watergate presidents combined. Bush's executive privilege claims should be viewed in the context of his administration's attempt to restore what it believed to be executive influence that was unconstitutionally stolen by legislative encroachment.[97] Bush tried to protect presidential papers by giving former presidents the right to make executive privilege claims on their own papers, a decision that President Obama overturned on his first day in office. In other cases, Bush refused to disclose decades-old DOJ material to a congressional committee and made executive privilege claims on documents and testimony in a US attorneys firing scandal.

The "Fast and Furious" case under President Obama highlights the presidential misuse of executive privilege, a dynamic that occurs all too often. Beginning in March 2011, the House Oversight Committee launched an investigation into Operation Fast and Furious, a program within the Bureau of Alcohol, Tobacco, Firearms, and Explosives that was designed to trace thousands of firearms from the United States to Mexico and then catch Mexican drug cartel members. Controversy over Fast and Furious arose after two of these weapons were found at the murder scene of a US Border Patrol agent named Brian Terry.[98]

Over the course of a year, the Department of Justice withheld documents and misled Congress about the nature of the Fast and Furious program. The DOJ eventually had to retract a February 4, 2011 letter to Congress denying the allegation that guns had been allowed to "walk." In October 2011, the Oversight Committee again subpoenaed the Justice Department for more information about the case. The Obama administration again refused to disclose the information. By May 2012, after repeated requests for the Obama administration to comply with the subpoena, House Speaker John Boehner (R-OH) wrote to Attorney General Eric Holder and informed him that he risked being charged with contempt of Congress if his department continued to refuse to satisfy the information request. In a June meeting between Holder and House Oversight chair Representative Darrell Issa (R-CA), the attorney general offered a "fair compilation" of the subpoenaed documents that the administration had so far refused to disclose, but only on the condition that the contempt vote be canceled and that Issa accept the validity of the documents even before he had a chance to review them. Issa turned down the proffered deal.[99]

Soon after the meeting between Holder and Issa, President Obama invoked executive privilege without providing a rationale for making the claim. In a letter to Issa, Deputy Attorney General James Cole tried to offer some justification for the executive privilege claim, noting that disclosure of information would "inhibit . . . candor" and therefore "significantly impair" the executive branch.[100] Such an argument, as Louis Fisher notes, "is vastly overplayed," and the rationale, which was "always of questionable merit, has lost even more credibility in recent years" as presidents of both parties frequently talk about and disclose sensitive information to the media about national security and domestic policy issues.[101] Neither the Oversight Committee nor the House accepted the administration's rationale, and both bodies held Holder in contempt, marking the first time in the history of the United States that a cabinet officer had been held in contempt of Congress.

Under federal law, the Justice Department, acting through the US attorney in the District of Columbia, must enforce a contempt resolution. However, the Obama Justice Department, acting much like it did under President Bush during the US attorneys firing scandal, refused to enforce the citation. The House followed with a lawsuit that asked the D.C. District Court to dismiss Obama's executive privilege claim and compel Holder to produce the documents. The Obama administration argued before D.C. District Court judge Amy Berman Jackson that it had "an unreviewable right to withhold materials from the legislature."[102] After nearly three years of court battles, Judge Jackson finally ruled in January 2016 that the Justice Department's Inspector General Report released to the public in 2012 made the administration's stonewalling moot. "There is no need to balance the need against the impact that the revelation of any record could have on candor in future executive decision making," Jackson noted in the opinion, "since any harm that might flow from the public revelation of the deliberations at issue here has already been self-inflicted."[103]

In April 2016, Obama's Justice Department finally complied with the October 2011 House subpoena and released the documents that it had refused to disclose for years.[104] In a letter to House Oversight chair Jason Chaffetz (R-UT), Assistant Attorney General Peter Kadzik stated, "In light of the passage of time and other considerations, such as the Department's interests in moving past this litigation and building upon our cooperative working relationship with the Committee and other congressional committees, the Department has decided that it is not in the Executive Branch's interest to continue litigating this issue at this time."[105] Why would the passage of time and other considerations be the deciding factors in releasing long-withheld documents? Considering the result, the entire episode appears to be pointless stonewalling by the Obama administration.

Fast and Furious is far too often becoming the rule, rather than the exception, in executive privilege cases. More and more, the executive branch resists being subject to the traditional system of checks and balances and resists Congress for as long as it can, often without justification. Obama's actions, described here, and similar behavior by other presidents hinder a fundamental principle of our government: the need for proper checks and balances. A closed-off executive branch prevents Congress from carrying out many of its essential functions. Far from its stated goal of protecting vital national security information, the Obama administration's stonewalling in Fast and Furious prevented Congress from viewing documents and material that related to key aspects of the inner workings of government. Determining whether a program of government is working and investigating the death of a border patrol agent are more than reasonable justifications for receiving information from the executive branch.

At this writing, in mid-2020 just past the halfway point of the Trump presidency, there have been three significant executive privilege controversies: (1) the Russia investigation and Mueller Report; (2) the citizenship question regarding the 2020 Census; and (3) the White House security clearances investigation.[106] Whereas most past executive privilege controversies occurred within the framework of recognized constitutional separation of powers issues, the Trump administration has asserted an unusual concept: a "protective executive privilege" that recognizes no countervailing or balancing powers against those of the executive branch. This concept amounts to an argument for a wholly unconstrained executive power with broad implications beyond issues of executive privilege. Or, in the case of the White House security clearances investigation, the Trump administration has slow-walked the accommodation process and used other declarations of privilege claims, apart from executive privilege, to defend its claimed institutional interests. Here we describe and analyze the first of the three executive privilege controversies—concerning Russian interference in the 2016 US elections and the Robert Mueller investigation.

On June 13, 2017, early on in the congressional investigation of Russian meddling in the 2016 US elections, Attorney General Jeff Sessions appeared before the Senate Intelligence Committee and refused to answer certain questions on the basis that they might be covered by executive privilege. A revealing back-and-forth developed between the attorney general and the senators over the application of executive privilege in the Trump White House. Asked whether he was refusing to answer some questions due to a claim of executive privilege, the attorney general said and repeated several times that he had no such authority, that only the president may claim that power. But, when pushed, Sessions said that he could not answer some questions because doing so might reveal information that at some point could be subject to a presidential claim of executive privilege.[107]

Senators then asked Sessions to identify which legal standard, other than executive privilege, prevented him from answering their questions at that hearing. Again, Sessions maintained that since the president might assert executive privilege over something, to answer questions prior to a formal claim of privilege would be tantamount to taking that authority away from the president. At one point, he stated, "I'm protecting the president's constitutional right by not giving it away before he has a chance to review it." Senators objected that Sessions was "having it both ways"—assuming all the benefits of a claim of executive privilege without making a formal claim, and with no other legal foundation established for refusing to answer questions. Sessions kept returning to the same point: "I'm protecting the right of the president to assert it if he chooses and there may be other privileges that could apply in this circumstance."[108]

In the end, there was no winning this back-and-forth for the senators—they made no headway in getting Sessions to open up. For the senators, the frustration was that a formal claim of executive privilege at least would provide a basis for negotiating some compromise with the administration over access to information germane to their investigation. The position that Sessions took was basically that the White House could refuse to provide any information because someday something might be subject to a claim of executive privilege, and thus there was no room for a negotiated settlement with Congress. This enabled the president at times to make the incredible claim that he and his administration were being transparent because he had not used executive privilege to prevent officials from talking to investigators.

Upon the limited release of Robert Mueller's report on the Russian investigation, House Judiciary Committee chair Jerry Nadler (D-NY) sought to gain access to the entire report and underlying documents. Attorney General William Barr, who is the legal custodian of the report, refused, so the House Judiciary Committee on April 18, 2019, issued a subpoena for Barr to compel him to produce the entire report. Less than a month later, the House Judiciary Committee voted to hold Barr in contempt of Congress for failing to comply with the subpoena.[109] This was the second time that an attorney general had been held in contempt by a congressional committee. The first time it had happened was under President Barack Obama, when the House Judiciary Committee voted to hold his attorney general, Eric Holder, in contempt in the Fast and Furious investigation.

Anticipating the contempt vote, President Trump made an executive privilege claim over the subpoenaed materials. In a letter from Assistant Attorney General Stephen Boyd to Nadler, the administration explained that the president was making a "protective assertion of executive privilege," which uses legal-sounding language to justify the practice of refusing to provide testimony or documents on the basis that they might be subject to a claim of executive privilege.[110] Surprisingly, this concept is not entirely new, as the Trump administration referenced an Office of Legal Counsel opinion issued by President Bill Clinton's attorney general Janet Reno, who defined the contours of the privilege claim. It was a misguided precedent at that time, but like many such actions, once established it found new life in a future administration under a different name.[111] "The Clinton administration went so far as to categorize certain documents as 'subject to executive privilege' as a way to wall off those documents without having to make an actual claim of executive privilege."[112]

Eventually the DOJ agreed to a compromise in which it would provide to the House Judiciary Committee certain key evidence and findings from the Mueller Report that had been withheld. The compromise deal allowed committee members to review key evidence privately, although there was no announcement of whether and perhaps when the materials would be made public. The committee had initially demanded full access to all of the Mueller Report evidence, unredacted, but committee chair Nadler eventually agreed that he was "prepared to prioritize production of materials that would provide the Committee with the most insight into certain incidents when the Special Counsel found 'substantial evidence' of obstruction of justice."[113]

In May 2019, the House Judiciary Committee subpoenaed former White House counsel Don McGahn to turn over official documents and to testify about Russian interference in the US elections and possible coordination of that effort by Trump. Although McGahn at that point was a private citizen and not easily protected by any form of privilege, the president objected and eventually claimed executive privilege to block McGahn from cooperating with Congress. The president's logic was that he already had allowed McGahn to speak with the Office of Special Counsel: "I let him interview the lawyer, the

White House lawyer, for 30 hours. Think of that—30 hours. I let him interview other people. I didn't have to let him interview anybody. I didn't have to give any documents. I was totally transparent because I knew I did nothing wrong."[114]

Because executive privilege exists to protect certain information from disclosure, the fact that the president had allowed McGahn and others to speak at length with the Mueller investigation team substantially weakened the basis of any later claim the Trump administration might make for executive privilege over that same information. The Mueller Report had been published at that point. It was a national best seller and being constantly dissected by media and political analysts. To many, the president appeared to have already waived the privilege by allowing his White House counsel and others to cooperate with the special counsel investigation, so it was odd for Trump to later claim executive privilege over information that had largely already been made public. To members of Congress seeking documents and testimony, the Trump administration's refusal to cooperate with their investigation stung, especially since the president had already cooperated with a special counsel but now would not allow the legislative branch access to information needed for its own investigation. The Trump administration retort was that since the special counsel is situated in the DOJ, and therefore is a part of the executive branch, it was therefore legitimate to share information within the executive branch while claiming executive privilege over that same information when requested by Congress.

The Trump administration's claim of what it called the protective executive privilege overstepped all past legal and customary boundaries for executive privilege claims. To be sure, past administrations have made overbroad claims of executive privilege, but Trump's claim put a somewhat new twist on the exercise of this power, in that it was clearly intended to erect an unbreachable barrier in front of congressional efforts to obtain documents, testimony, and other sources of evidence of potential White House and administration wrongdoing.

Creating a closed-door policy where the executive branch alone decides these important issues removes Congress from the governing picture and does much to hinder our constitutional form of government. Executive privilege does not provide presidents with the power to do whatever they want, whenever they want, or to conceal information that might be politically embarrassing or disadvantageous in some other way. Instead, our government is based on the premise of accountability. When the public does not know what the executive branch is doing, no one can be held accountable for its actions and any potential resulting wrongdoing.

CONCLUSION

Unitary executive advocates identify numerous domestic sources of the president's authority to act unilaterally, but there is little evidence that such broad-reaching executive powers exist. Presidents remain constrained by constitutional checks and balances, even when they claim to have authority to act directly in the national interest. The legislative veto has a long history as a vehicle for balancing the powers of the legislature and the chief executive and forging greater cooperation between the two. Although it has come under constitutional challenge, it continues to operate in different forms even today. Rulemaking has long served as a mechanism to give Congress the ability to review and direct policy implementation according to the legislative will without having to fundamentally alter policies. This flexibility has served the needs of both political branches well. The modern practice of presidents appointing so-called czars without legislative authorization and consent is a clear violation of separated powers and remains highly controversial. Finally, presidents have long claimed the right to withhold information under the power of executive privilege. Although it is a recognized and legitimate power, it is still subject to the limitations of legislative and judicial challenges.

CHAPTER 5

Foreign Affairs Powers

Part I

The unitary executive theory focused exclusively on the president's domestic powers for roughly two decades. At that point, its advocates began to argue for the theory's applicability in the realm of foreign affairs, too, taking advantage of its obvious utility for eliminating restrictions on executive power. The 9/11 terror attacks on the World Trade Center and the Pentagon provided the perfect opportunity for unitary executive proponents inside the George W. Bush administration to advance the most aggressive form of the unitary executive theory to date. In David Bodenhamer's words: "The unitary executive theory, combined with the president's role as commander-in-chief, became the centerpiece of the response to terrorist threats during the presidency of George W. Bush."[1] Indeed, President Bush surrounded himself with experienced veterans of previous administrations who had worked for post-Watergate presidents and believed they had witnessed decades of decline in all areas of presidential power.

One of the most vocal critics of this post-Watergate decline was Bush's vice president, Richard Cheney. Cheney had served as White House chief of staff under President Gerald Ford and as secretary of defense under George H. W. Bush. His extensive experience working in the executive branch in the years following President Richard M. Nixon's resignation only heightened his resolve to strengthen the presidency. In 2005, Cheney provided a detailed summary of his perspective:

> I do have the view that over the years there had been an erosion of presidential power and authority, that it's reflected in a

number of developments—the War Powers Act . . . the Budget
and Impoundment Control Act . . . a lot of the things around
Watergate and Vietnam, both, in the '70s served to erode the
authority, I think, the President needs to be effective especially in
a national security area.

Continuing, Cheney noted that the Iran-Contra Minority Report provides a good summary of his position, in that it "lay[s] out a robust
view of the President's prerogatives with respect to the conduct of
especially foreign policy and national security matters." Cheney de-
emphasized the importance of the legislature when the country is facing a foreign threat, noting that he "served in the Congress for 10
years" and has an "enormous regard" for the institution, but that "the
nature of the threats we face, it was true during the Cold War, as well
as I think what is true now, the President of the United States needs to
have his constitutional powers unimpaired, if you will, in terms of the
conduct of national security policy."[2]

In 1987, then representative Cheney wrote most of the Iran-Contra
Minority Report, although Republican representatives William Broomfield, Henry Hyde, Jim Courter, Bill McCollum, and Michael DeWine
and Senators James McClure and Orrin Hatch also signed it. The report offers valuable insights into Cheney's thoughts on presidential
power. Moreover, it provides a glimpse at what would become some of
the core arguments advanced not only by unitary executive advocates
in the George W. Bush administration but also by Presidents Barack
Obama and Donald J. Trump, who likewise believed they could unilaterally act outside the Constitution and laws. The Minority Report takes
a remarkably defensive tone in framing its support for presidential
power: "To acknowledge the existence of a struggle is a far cry from
seeing the Constitution as if it permits any branch to go after another's
powers, without bounds." The report attacked the notion of a "boundless view of Congressional power," which allegedly became popular in
the 1970s and argued that the Necessary and Proper Clause was only
meant to guarantee "legislative supremacy" in the rarest of cases.[3]

The report focused largely on selective quotes from both the
delegates to the Constitutional Convention and the authors of *The
Federalist Papers*. It relied heavily on Alexander Hamilton's statement
in *Federalist* No. 70 about "energy" in the executive: "They have, with
great propriety, considered energy as the most necessary qualification

in the former, and have regarded this as most applicable to power in a single hand; while they have, with equal propriety, considered the latter as best adapted to deliberation."[4] In citing Hamilton, the report's writers argued: "No government, democratic or otherwise, could long survive unless its Executive could respond to the uncertainties of international relations."[5] This passage implied an interpretation of executive energy free from legislative control, a sentiment that was expressly indicated in other parts of the report.

In its review of American history, the report tried to justify an expansive presidential power by citing as precedent Thomas Jefferson's purchase of the Louisiana territory, a transaction conducted without express constitutional or statutory authority. The report noted how "the President decided to go through with the Purchase, without abandoning his view that the Constitution severely limited the President, by asserting an inherent, *extra*constitutional prerogative power for the Executive that was more sweeping than anything Hamilton had ever put forward."[6] After reviewing other examples, the report declared that "Presidents exercised a broad range of foreign policy powers for which they neither sought nor received Congressional sanction through statute." In its conclusion the report declared that history "leaves little, if any doubt that the President was expected to have the primary role of conducting the foreign policy of the United States."[7]

Cheney and the other Minority Report drafters had two primary objectives. Their first goal was to defend President Ronald Reagan, a fellow Republican caught up in the Iran-Contra affair, a significant scandal that could have led to his impeachment. Their second goal was to lay the foundation for a robust defense of an aggressive use of presidential power in foreign affairs. After George W. Bush became president, unitary executive theory advocates could combine the general framework of the unitary executive theory with the Minority Report's specific assertations of unilateral presidential powers in foreign affairs. Now, their mission broadened from merely providing the president with control over domestic affairs to also dominating foreign affairs, thus ensuring near-complete control over most aspects of governing. In their own critical assessment of the Iran-Contra Minority Report, Frederick Schwarz Jr. and Aziz Huq argued that the Reagan administration and the Minority Report authors, in particular, "crystallized the most aggressive version of unitary executive theory in national security and foreign affairs."[8]

THE UNITARY EXECUTIVE AND
THE COMMANDER-IN-CHIEF CLAUSE

John Yoo served as deputy assistant attorney general in the Department of Justice during the early days of the George W. Bush administration. He is one of the chief architects of a robust justification for plenary presidential powers in matters of war. Yoo helped introduce the unitary executive theory into the realm of foreign policy and war by assisting the Bush administration with constructing an aggressive model of presidential power based primarily on the Constitution's "Commander-in-Chief" Clause. For example, in a 2002 memorandum, Yoo asserted: "The President enjoys complete discretion in the exercise of his Commander-in-Chief authority and in conducting operations against hostile forces."[9] In another memorandum, Yoo again asserts, "We conclude that the Constitution vests the President with the plenary authority, as Commander in Chief and the sole organ of the Nation in its foreign relations, to use military force abroad—especially in response to grave national emergencies created by sudden, unforeseen attacks on the people and territory of the United States."[10] Yoo generally advocated for extremely broad unilateral authority based on the unitary executive theory: "The *centralization of authority in the President alone* is particularly crucial in matters of national defense, war, and foreign policy, where a *unitary executive* can evaluate threats, consider policy choices, and mobilize national resources with a speed and energy that is far superior to any other branch."[11] He also downplayed the role of Congress, declaring that there is no statutory authority that "can place any limits on the President's determinations as to any terrorist threat, the amount of military force to be used in response, or the method, timing, and nature of the response. These decisions, under our Constitution, are for the President alone to make."[12]

Yoo's 1996 law review article "The Continuation of Politics by Other Means: The Original Understanding of War Powers" contains some of the thinking that is expressed later in his Bush administration memos.[13] In the article, Yoo acknowledges that his views run counter to the "uniformity of opinion" held by most scholars.[14] In truth, he made arguments and assertations there so grandiose that, as James Pfiffner noted, they "stretch the text of the Constitution and the deliberations of the framers beyond reasonable interpretation."[15] In Yoo's analysis, "the war power provisions of the Constitution are best understood as an adoption, rather than a rejection, of the traditional British approach to war powers."[16] In other words, Yoo argued that the framers were not trying to limit the president's war powers but instead were awarding him complete control. Yoo repeatedly cites the Commander-in-Chief Clause to justify what he calls the "President's leadership role in war."[17]

Accepting Yoo's assertion of presidential control over war power requires ignoring Article I, Section 8 of the Constitution, which grants to Congress the ability to define and punish piracies and felonies on the high seas and offenses against the law of nations; declare war; raise and support armies; provide and maintain a navy; make rules for regulating land and naval forces; call forth the militia; organize, arm, and discipline the militia; and make all laws necessary and proper for carrying out these powers. Yoo's argument seems to be outweighed here by the Constitution's evidence supporting a prominent role for the legislature in questions of war.

In addition, Yoo's interpretation of the Commander-in-Chief Clause as a key source of authority for a president with plenary power over matters of war also fails to withstand closer scrutiny. As explained by David Gray Adler, the "commander-in-chief" title dates back to seventeenth-century England, where it was assigned to "the ranking military authority in each theater of battle."[18] This military figure, or commander in chief, would be subject to civilian command (in this case, Parliament), which required him to obey all orders received from his commander.

Looking closely at how early Americans applied this British term, the Continental Congress placed similar restrictions on George Washington when it dubbed him commander in chief, a role that included the mandate "to observe and follow such orders and directions, from time to time, as you shall receive from this, or a future Congress of the United Colonies or Committee of Congress."[19] As David Barron and Martin Lederman explained, "All evidence indicates that, at least at that time, there was nothing inherent in the [commander-in-chief] title that precluded its bearer from being subject to detailed congressional control."[20] In fact, Adler noted how the "practice of subordinating the commander in chief to a political superior, whether a king, parliament, or congress, was firmly established for 150 years and thoroughly familiar to the Framers."[21]

An early American court case also provides evidence to refute Yoo's view that presidents enjoy plenary war powers. In 1804, the Supreme

Court in *Little v. Barreme* addressed whether a president could extend the meaning of a congressional statute to provide him with the authority to seize vessels traveling to French ports. In his opinion for the Court, Chief Justice John Marshall acknowledged the possibility that, in exercising his powers under the Take Care and Commander-in-Chief Clauses, the president might have empowered a broader meaning of the seizure power granted by the statute.[22] However, Marshall noted that the law in question "limits that authority to the seizure of vessels bound or sailing to a French port," which meant that Congress occupied the field and created a legal obligation that the president could not ignore. Having answered the question at hand, Marshall admitted that "the first bias of my mind" was to give some latitude to the president. Even though the president could not provide an expanded meaning to the statute, Marshall thought that the person who made the unlawful seizure could be excused from having to pay damages. However, Marshall acquiesced to the reasoning of his colleagues and declared that the president's "instructions cannot change the nature of the transaction" or, more plainly, since the president had no legal authority to order the seizure, doing so violated the rights of the vessel owners, and they could therefore seek damages.

Little shows that when Congress provides statutory direction for the use of the armed forces, in this case, naval power, its command is binding on a president. One could also look to *Bas v. Tingy* (1800) and *Talbot v. Seeman* (1801), two other Supreme Court cases where the Court focused on Congress, not the president, to answer questions about presidential use of the war power. Barron and Lederman reached a similar conclusion in their study of the Commander-in-Chief Clause: "There is surprisingly little Founding-era evidence supporting the notion that the conduct of military campaigns is beyond legislative control and a fair amount of evidence that affirmatively undermines it."[23]

Yoo and others in the George W. Bush administration disregarded much of the relevant history and instead relied on cherry-picked facts to support their claims to broad presidential power. They offered arguments that initially appeared strong but failed to withstand closer examination. For example, in his September 2001 memorandum, Yoo points to the *Prize Cases* as the justification for substantial presidential plenary powers in wartime: "The Court explained that, whether the President 'in fulfilling his duties as Commander in-Chief' has met with a situation justifying treating the southern States as belligerents and instituting a blockade, was a question 'to be decided *by him*' and which the Court could not question, but must leave to 'the political department of the Government to which this power was entrusted.' "[24] However, Yoo neglects to mention that the Lincoln administration, while defending the president's actions before the Supreme Court, actually argued that the president does *not* have plenary powers in matters of war. In fact, the position of the Lincoln administration was that in "case of civil war, the President may, in the absence of any Act of Congress on the subject, meet the war by the exercise of belligerent maritime capture."[25] This position is much more qualified and limited and acknowledges an important role for the legislative branch.

What role should Congress play, according to the Lincoln administration? The administration argued that "Congress should be a council of war in perpetual session to determine when and how long and how far this or that belligerent right shall be exerted."[26] Continuing, the administration noted that the "function to use the army and navy being in the President, the mode of using them, within the rules of civilized warfare, and subject to established laws of Congress, must be subject to his discretion as a necessary incident to the use, in the absence of any act of Congress controlling him."[27]

THE DECLARE WAR CLAUSE: A HOLLOW LEGISLATIVE POWER?

As explained earlier, Yoo did not acknowledge the Lincoln administration's qualifications on presidential power in the *Prize Cases*. Instead, he applied his own expansive reading of war powers to the case. His academic writings and Bush administration memorandums devote considerable space to making the Commander-in-Chief Clause seem more vital than it actually is to resolving the power question. Curiously, while puffing up the Commander-in-Chief Clause, he simultaneously tries to deflate the Declare War Clause. In his 2001 memorandum, Yoo declared that "the President's authority to commit the armed forces to combat is very broad."[28] This view can be traced directly back to his 1996 *California Law Review* article, where he writes, "The Constitution gives the President the initiative in war by virtue of his powers over foreign relations and the military." And, as Yoo notes, "Contrary to the arguments by today's scholars, the Declare War Clause does not add to Congress' store of war powers at the expense of the President." Instead, it merely "gives Congress a judicial role in declaring that a state of war exists between the United States and another nation, which bears significant legal ramifications concerning the rights and duties of American citizens."[29]

Yoo's view of the Declare War Clause runs counter to the constitutional text, the framers' words, and prevailing scholarship. First, the text of the Constitution reads: "The Congress shall have Power . . . to declare War." Yoo admits that Congress can declare a war but argues that this constitutional grant is more of a legal formality, and that presidents are still free to make war on their own. Second, this line of reasoning cannot be derived from the debates on drafting the Constitution at the Constitutional Convention. As Louis Fisher explains, "The framers were determined to withhold from the president the power to take the country to war against another nation."[30] An early version of the proposed constitutional language had granted Congress the power "to make war." Charles Pinckney said he supported "a vigorous Executive but was afraid the Executive powers of the existing Congress might extend to peace & war &c which would render the Executive a Monarchy, of the worst kind, to wit an elective one." Pierce Butler, the lone voice for giving the president the war initiative, said "he was for vesting the power in the president, who will have all the requisite qualities, and will not make war but when the nation will support it."[31] Elbridge Gerry declared that he "never expected to hear in a republic a motion to empower the Executive alone to declare war." George Mason agreed, noting he "was agst. giving the power of war to the Executive, because not safely to be trusted with it, ... He was for clogging rather than facilitating war." The delegates eventually settled on the word "declare" instead of "make," which, as James Madison and Gerry noted, left "to the Executive the power to repeal sudden attacks."[32]

It seems clear that the delegates entrusted the ability to initiate war to the legislature, not the president. They also designated the president to be commander in chief, but, as noted previously, this role was meant to be less dynamic than how Yoo would describe it. In many respects, the commander-in-chief role is a managerial position that must be activated by Congress rather than the president (unless he is repelling enemy attacks). The president is the commander of the army and navy, but only if Congress first establishes and funds them both and sets out any restrictions on how they may be used. Even then, the president needs Congress to either declare or authorize war before he can send American troops into battle.

Yoo's expansive reading of presidential power is also not supported

by the debates during the ratification process. Speaking at the
Pennsylvania ratifying convention, James Wilson noted that the war
power included in the Constitution "will not hurry us into war; it is
calculated to guard against it. It will not be in the power of a single
man, or a single body of men, to involve us in such distress, for the important power of declaring war is vested in the legislature at large."[33]
Likewise, Alexander Hamilton—the same founder cited today as
having favored a forceful and energetic chief executive—explained
in *Federalist* No. 69 the critical differences between the British king
and the newly created position of "president" regarding war powers:
"The President will have only the occasional command of such part
of the militia of the nation as by legislative provision may be called
into the actual service of the Union." Hamilton explained that the
president is certainly the "commander-in-chief of the army and navy
of the United States." And in that respect, he argued, the president's
"authority would be nominally the same with that of the king of Great
Britain, but in substance much inferior to it." Hamilton expressed his
belief that the commander-in-chief role amounts "to nothing more
than the supreme command and direction of the military and naval
forces" whereas, in stark contrast, the king's position "extends to the
declaring of war and to the raising and regulating of fleets and armies,
all which, by the Constitution under consideration, would appertain
to the legislature."[34]

Various constitutional and presidential scholars agree that Yoo's
analysis misses the mark. As Louis Fisher explains, the framers "de-
liberately transferred the power to initiate war from the executive to
the legislature."[35] Likewise, James Pfiffner writes: "There can be little
doubt that the framers intended to give Congress and not the president the authority to decide about whether to go to war."[36] These
scholars have sound reasons for reaching this conclusion. The framers
created a government under the Articles of Confederation without an
executive branch; consequently, its members had to make collective
decisions. To be sure, the delegates to the Constitutional Convention
supported the creation of a president under the new Constitution
as a response to the challenges of governing under the Articles of
Confederation. However, as David Gray Adler argued, "The Founders'
profound distrust of executive power was, indeed, a key factor that led
them to break from the executive model for warmaking, but equally
compelling in their configuration of the War Clause was their attach-
ment to the republican principle of collective decision making, the

premise that the conjoined wisdom of the many is superior to that of one."[37]

LEGAL OBFUSCATION TO TAKE UNITARY ACTION

Modern presidential administrations of both parties are masterly at finding ways around the Constitution and laws so they can unilaterally involve the country in armed conflicts worldwide. To be sure, some of these administrations predate the rise of the unitary executive model, but their actions and the rationales used to justify them still fit well with unitary executive theorists' mission to expand presidential power.

As a recent example, consider President Obama's decision to launch sustained military strikes in Libya, which eventually led to the end of Libyan dictator Muammar Gaddafi's government (and life). Here, Obama accepted the legal opinions of White House counsel Robert Bauer and State Department legal adviser Harold Koh instead of those offered by Acting Office of Legal Counsel (OLC) director Caroline Krass and Pentagon general counsel Jeh Johnson.[38] Obama's move to act against the advice of an OLC opinion was unprecedented and caused much debate in various legal circles. As Yale law professor Jack Balkin noted: "It is difficult to escape the conclusion that from the outset Obama was prospecting for opinions that would tell him that his actions were legal, and once he found them, he felt comfortable in rejecting the opinion of the OLC."[39]

Equally concerning is how Obama accepted Harold Koh's rationale that the term "hostilities" under the War Powers Resolution (WPR) can be read so narrowly that acts of war that do not place American armed forces in danger would not trigger the sixty-day withdrawal provision.[40] Obama's action meant that, for the first time since the passage of the WPR, a president would disregard the sixty-day time limit to end hostilities unless Congress provided authorization.[41]

Obama's decision freed him from following the Constitution and laws and allowed him to act unilaterally. This action was extraordinary not only for the way that he ignored the OLC's advice and the WPR but also for how it went against his stated belief that the "President does not have power under the Constitution to unilaterally authorize a military attack in a situation that does not involve stopping an actual or imminent threat to the nation."[42] It is important to mention here that Obama would have had a more difficult time claiming that the

WPR does not matter had he not used groundwork previously laid by Bush and other presidents.

Obama's actions were not without consequence. The House voted 295 to 123, with 70 Democrats in favor, to reject a bill that would have given Obama clear authority to carry out a military campaign in Libya.[43] This vote sent the first clear signal from a chamber of Congress that the president was going farther than he should. In addition, the intervention was widely seen as a failure, with one account noting that, if judging the intervention by Obama's own standards, "Libya has not only failed to evolve into a democracy; it has devolved into a failed state."[44] This assessment aligns with Obama's own: although he has not admitted to any overreach regarding the Constitution or the law, Obama has conceded that his Libya war effort was poorly planned and stands as his "worst mistake" as president.[45]

More recently, President Trump ordered a missile strike against Syria in response to a chemical weapons attack.[46] In an OLC opinion, Trump's administration rationalized the president's decision by claiming the use of force was "in the national interest" of the country and noted that the "hostilities would not rise to the level of a war in the constitutional sense."[47] This rationale, which bypasses the Constitution and the law, matches well with former president Obama's own views from 2013 when he articulated a unilateral approach to war on humanitarian grounds to punish or deter the use of chemical weapons.[48]

Regarding Iran, President Trump has also adopted the view that he can act without Congress. In an exchange with the press, Trump noted that while he liked keeping Congress informed, "I don't have to do it legally."[49] Instead of ignoring the Constitution and controlling legal authority, the Trump administration appears to believe that the 2001 Authorization for Use of Military Force (AUMF) gives the president the ability to attack Iran.[50] This is not a new argument, as President Obama claimed that the AUMF gave him the authority to act on at least nineteen occasions, including many missions undertaken against terrorist groups that did not even exist in 2001 or, if they did exist, had nothing to do with 9/11.[51] As a result, the nearly twenty-year-old military authorization has often been treated as a blank check by presidents to cover military operations unrelated to the 9/11 terrorist attacks.[52]

One legal scholar called Trump's AUMF justification to attack Iran "quite a stretch" and not in keeping with "what members of Congress intended when they authorized the president to go after those who attacked the U.S. on 9/11 and those who harbored them."[53] Another scholar noted that Trump has no way around the Constitution, as the president must gain Congress's "approval before he orders military action against Iran, unless an emergency makes it impossible to do so."[54] The House expressed similar views as it voted to block funding of any military action in Iran that does not have congressional authorization.[55]

In January 2020, a US drone strike killed Iran major general Qasem Soleimani, an order given to the US military by President Trump—the third time within weeks the administration used airstrikes to attack Iran.[56] At the time of the killing, Congress had not been informed about the president's order or the military strike. An immediate statement by the Department of Defense after the killing noted that Soleimani "was actively developing plans to attack American diplomats and service members in Iraq and throughout the region."[57] However, critics have questioned the evidence used to justify the attack while the administration began to change its reasons for killing Soleimani.[58]

Regardless of the underlying reasons for killing Soleimani, the constitutionality of the action stands on weak ground. The attack occurred without Congress providing authorization or even being consulted.[59] As we have explained, the 2001 AUMF is not a reasonable congressional authorization for the president to launch offensive attacks against Iran. The House of Representatives agreed. On January 9, 2020, the House voted 224 to 194 to restrict Trump's ability to authorize a military attack against Iran without the approval of Congress.[60]

The approved bill—which invokes provisions of the 1973 War Powers Resolution—does itself run into questions of its constitutionality as it comes in the form of a concurrent resolution that only needs to be passed by both chambers of Congress and is not presented to the president for a signature. The reason the concurrent resolution's constitutionality comes into question is the result of the 1983 Supreme Court decision in *INS v. Chadha* where a similar piece of legislation was held to be unconstitutional.[61] In that case, the Supreme Court reasoned that congressional action that has the force of law must follow constitutional procedures for creating laws, which includes the presentation of bills to the president for his signature.

A little over a month after the House voted to limit President Trump's ability to attack Iran, in a 55–45 vote (with eight Republicans approving) the Senate moved through separate legislation to also curtail the president's war powers.[62] Specifically, the Senate approved a joint resolution—authored by Senator Tim Kaine (D-VA)—which read: "Congress has not yet declared war upon, nor enacted a specific statutory authorization for use of military force against, the Islamic Republic of Iran" and therefore ordered the termination of hostilities with Iran.[63] The passage of the resolution came despite President Trump's attacks against it. In two tweets, Trump declared, "It is very important for our Country's SECURITY that the United States Senate not vote for the Iran War Powers Resolution" and added, "If my hands were tied, Iran would have a field day."[64] A month later, the House also approved the Senate's resolution by a 227–186 vote (with six Republicans in favor).[65] On Wednesday, May 6, President Trump vetoed the "very insulting" war powers resolution.[66] The following day, senators who supported the measure failed to secure enough votes to override Trump's veto.[67]

AN EMERGENCY PRESIDENTIAL POWER?

The historical record shows that Congress did indeed control presidential use of the war power by deciding as a body whether the country should go to war or take military action.[68] One can trace Congress's fidelity to the Constitution from its decision to statutorily authorize the use of military force in the Quasi-War with France in 1798 to its declarations of war in World War I and World War II. However, presidential willingness to carry out the principles embodied in the Constitution's Declare War Clause changed significantly with the Korean War. President Harry Truman committed the country to war at that time without congressional authorization, relying instead on a United Nations resolution for the needed authority. Since then, presidents such as Obama and Trump have taken the lead in exercising the war power with minimal or even zero congressional involvement.

Some of the strongest arguments for plenary presidential power in matters of war stem from a president's claim of an emergency. However, these arguments are still premised on a weak foundation, which includes assertations of overly broad presidential power and what seems to be at times an almost willful disregard for the text, history, and scholarly understanding of the Constitution. In many respects, unitary executive theory advocates seem to be contending that a president can exercise emergency war powers, a position that would fit into the mainstream of scholarly thought. In fact, Yoo made this point in his famous memorandum of September 25, 2001: "The historical record demonstrates that the power to initiate military hostilities, particularly in response to the threat of an armed attack, rests exclusively with the President."[69] But a commonly accepted need for emergency presidential power can quickly lead to the more controversial view that the president needs access to broad, unilateral war power in case of a sudden attack or other immediate threat to the nation. This view is shared by others, such as President Bush's attorney general, Alberto Gonzales, who explained in a 2015 article that "today's threats require the President to have the authority to act quickly and decisively."[70]

Before turning to emergency presidential powers, we will explore some basic concepts that are fundamental to understanding the Constitution. First, presidents and Congress both carry out their duties based on the Constitution's enumerated and implied powers. Enumerated powers are provided expressly in the text of the Constitution, whereas implied powers, although not specifically mentioned, may be reasonably inferred from the text. In the Supreme Court case *McCulloch v. Maryland,* Chief Justice John Marshall held that Congress had the implied authority to establish a national bank.

Some scholars, including Steven Calabresi and Christopher Yoo, use the word "inherent" interchangeably with "implied," a practice that has created confusion and muddied the larger debate over presidential powers.[71] This practice is not limited to scholars, of course, as various presidential administrations have also made similar attempts to redefine constitutional language to expand presidential powers. As Justice Robert Jackson once noted, "Loose and irresponsible use of adjectives colors all nonlegal and much legal discussion of presidential powers. 'Inherent' powers, 'implied' powers, 'incidental' powers, 'plenary' powers, 'war' powers and 'emergency' powers are used, often interchangeably and without fixed or ascertainable meanings."[72] This is why Jackson cautioned against entertaining such rationales for expanding presidential power. He explained, "Nothing in my experience convinces me that such risks are warranted by any real necessity, although such powers would, of course, be an executive convenience."[73]

The words "inherent" and "implied" have significantly different meanings. Inherent powers are not derived from the text of the Constitution but are justified simply by the status or position of being the president. Inherent powers can give chief executives the ability to act without concern for the Constitution or controlling legal authority.

Louis Fisher explains that the "claim and exercise of inherent powers move a nation from one of limited powers to boundless and ill-
defined authority. The assertion of inherent power in the president
threatens the doctrine of separated powers and the system of checks
and balances. Sovereignty moves from the constitutional principles of
self-government, popular control, and republican government to the
White House."[74]

The debate over inherent powers is not new. In fact, it can be traced
back to the concept of prerogative powers, which are rooted in the
English governing system. The framers drew significantly from various
British constitutional customs in developing a new governing structure. They were aware that the British monarch had possessed the
prerogative power, or the right to act outside the law when he deemed
it to be in the public interest to do so. This power was "inherent in
the crown" and permitted the "king to do things which no one else
could do, and his power to do them in a way in which no one else
could do them."[75] The king not only could exercise authority established in law but could even act against any legal restrictions if carrying out the public good.[76] Among other advantages, the prerogative
power provided the English monarch with the authority to initiate
wars, raise armies, make treaties, create offices, appropriate money,
and set aside statutes.[77] The king's prerogative power remained strong
even at the dawn of the American Revolution. As William Blackstone
wrote: "By the word prerogative we usually understand that special
pre-eminence, which the king hath, over and above all other persons,
and out of the ordinary course of the common law, in right of his regal
dignity."[78]

Upon their declaration of freedom from England, the American
colonies rejected a model of the executive that would include a prerogative power. Instead, the new nation established a central government under the Articles of Confederation that did not even include
an independent executive. At the state level, the powers of governors
were greatly limited, and overwhelming authority was vested in the
legislative branch.[79] After the failings of the Continental Congress to
efficiently manage the war, the framers realized that they needed a different governing structure. But this situation did not herald a return
to monarchial domination. Rather, the framers chose to restrict and
check executive power. In fact, regarding war, spending, and administration, powers that once belonged to the English king alone were
either taken away from the executive altogether or became subject to

a check exercised by the legislative branch. Delegate James Wilson, a proponent of a strong presidency, noted that he "did not consider the Prerogatives of the British Monarch as a proper guide in defining the Executive powers. Some of these prerogatives were of a Legislative nature. Among others that of war & peace &c."[80] The framers corralled any vestiges of a king's prerogative power squarely within the four corners of the Constitution, and this included transferring the ability to declare war from the executive to the legislative branch.

The framers' rejection of such broad prerogative presidential powers does not mean that every argument made by unitary executive supporters can be uniformly dismissed. However, we contend that even a broadly defined war power cannot exist outside the Constitution, which means that its text is important to consider. Returning to the Commander-in-Chief Clause, we have noted how it is used to justify plenary presidential powers and action in war. Presidential advocates often cite as an example President Abraham Lincoln's actions against the South before Congress authorized war. However, as we have explained, even the Lincoln administration's defense of its actions did not advance a plenary presidential power in war. The Lincoln administration itself argued that the president was operating within the confines of the Constitution, particularly when the president needed to act resolutely during a civil war. These nuances are not helpful to their general line of argument so unitary executive advocates fall back on making sweeping generalizations and then cite Lincoln's actions stripped away from their necessary context.

One can trace some of the roots of emergency presidential power back to Theodore Roosevelt, who adopted a mild version of the prerogative power concept used by the British monarch. For Roosevelt, presidents could be reasonably expected to act for the public good, unless in doing so their actions directly violated the Constitution or laws.[81] This new, broadened understanding of presidential behavior set the stage for a more aggressive model of the presidency's powers in wartime. More recently, the George W. Bush administration adopted and expanded this model. Roosevelt alone should not bear the blame for the status of the model today, of course, as his definition was refined and expanded through the words and actions of his successors.

One of those successors, President Woodrow Wilson, held and applied an equally expansive view of the presidency. In his view, it was the only institution that could provide active political leadership by channeling public opinion "independent of any constitutional grant of authority, or of constitutional constraints."[82] Wilson placed the president's independence and power above all other considerations. Because, as he argued, the president represents the "whole people," he should be free to govern, since the "object of constitutional government is to bring the active, planning will of each part of the government into accord with the prevailing popular thought and need, and thus make it an impartial instrument of symmetrical national development."[83]

Since the presidencies of Roosevelt and Wilson, their more expansive view of the president's war power has largely been accepted and adopted by their successors. However, even as modern presidents have cited the actions of Roosevelt and Wilson as justification to use emergency powers during wartime, they are still obligated to tie their decisions to conventional and contemporary constitutional and legal arguments. The presidency in the twenty-first century is unquestionably more powerful than anything the framers could have imagined. Even so, the president is still constrained by a constitutional republic and may not act on his own for long before facing consequences.

Turning again to the rationale for exercising emergency powers as expressed by Yoo and Gonzales, they point to the requirement that there must be a "threat" in order for a president to "act quickly and decisively." This rationale fits well within the Lincoln precedent and focuses the debate over emergency presidential powers on the particular situations in which they are used. The 1890 Supreme Court case of *In re Neagle* is instructive here. In that case, the Supreme Court held that the US attorney general had the power even in the absence of statutory authority to assign a US marshal to protect Supreme Court justice Stephen Field from possible threats on his life.[84] We think it beyond question that the president likewise possesses similar powers that may be exercised in an emergency.

Once again, Lincoln's actions during the Civil War are relevant. In the *Prize Cases*, the Supreme Court acknowledged the legality of Lincoln's blockade order. While noting that the president "has no power to initiate or declare a war," the Court also pointed out that, if facing an invasion, "the President is not only authorized but bound to resist force by force . . . without waiting for any special legislative authority."[85] Recognizing a role for emergency powers does not mean they are unlimited, though. Only a few short years after the Civil War, the Supreme Court held in *Ex parte Milligan* that military courts could not function in territories where the civilian courts were still open and operating. In their decision, the Court rejected a presidential power doctrine in war that would give the chief executive the ability to suspend the law:

> No doctrine, involving more pernicious consequences, was ever invented by the wit of man than that any of its provisions can be suspended during any of the great exigencies of government. Such a doctrine leads directly to anarchy or despotism, but the theory of necessity on which it is based is false; for the government, within the Constitution, has all the powers granted to it, which are necessary to preserve its existence; as has been happily proved by the result of the great effort to throw off its just authority.[86]

Of course, it is considerably easier to rebuff presidential power after a war has ended; the courts have generally been reluctant to question contemporaneous wartime decisions.[87]

Youngstown Sheet & Tube Company v. Sawyer is another case in which the Court has defined and established limits on a president's emergency powers; there, it held that President Harry Truman did not have the constitutional or legal authority to order the seizure of privately owned steel mills.[88] The Truman administration argued that the president "acting within the aggregate of his constitutional powers as the Nation's Chief Executive and the Commander in Chief of the Armed Forces of the United States" could take action in a "grave emergency."[89] Justice Hugo Black, writing for the Court, rejected this contention: "We cannot with faithfulness to our constitutional system hold that the Commander in Chief of the Armed Forces has the ultimate power as such to take possession of private property in order to keep labor disputes from stopping production."[90]

In a concurring opinion, Justice Robert Jackson reinforced Black's view: "No doctrine that the Court could promulgate would seem to me more sinister and alarming than that a President whose conduct of foreign affairs is so largely uncontrolled, and often even is unknown, can vastly enlarge his mastery over the internal affairs of the country by his own commitment of the Nation's armed forces to some foreign venture."[91] Then, Jackson laid out one of the more articulate rationales against an expansive view of the Commander-in-Chief Clause:

There are indications that the Constitution did not contemplate that the title Commander in Chief *of the Army and Navy* will constitute him also Commander in Chief of the country, its industries and its inhabitants. He has no monopoly of "war powers," whatever they are. While Congress cannot deprive the President of the command of the army and navy, only Congress can provide him an army or navy to command. It is also empowered to make rules for the "Government and Regulation of land and naval Forces," by which it may, to some unknown extent, impinge upon even command functions.[92]

Jackson believed that Congress could subject the commander-in-chief role to various limitations that were perfectly "consistent with a constitutional Republic."[93] He believed that emergency powers should not be completely separated from either the law or the Constitution. Consistent with Jackson's understanding of emergency presidential powers, Congress has established a useful, albeit imperfect, system in the *United States Code* that relies on statutes to both define and activate emergency presidential powers.[94] Only in the context of a genuine national emergency may the president activate these powers.[95] Two of the more familiar emergency powers statutes are the Trading with the Enemy Act and the International Emergency Economic Powers Act.[96]

Our view is that Congress wisely gave the president significant emergency powers that provide him with ample discretionary authority to address emergency circumstances. We remain unconvinced, however, that living in a dangerous modern world that is constantly under the threat of terrorism necessarily requires the country to accept undefined and expansive presidential powers. Granting a president such latitude, unmoored from constitutional controls or other legal constraints, would cause a paradigm shift that could essentially end the system of separated powers and checks and balances as we have known it for more than two hundred years.

Even statutorily granted emergency powers are not perfect, of course. Unfortunately, the judiciary rarely enacts limits on presidential power, and presidents can sometimes expand their influence even beyond statutorily granted delegations of emergency powers. A prominent example occurs in *Dames & Moore v. Regan*, where Justice William Rehnquist argued that congressional acquiescence, along with "inferences . . . drawn from the character of the legislation Congress has enacted," justified an expansion of the president's power.[97] The Court rationalized this holding by noting that "Congress cannot anticipate and legislate with regard to every possible action the President may find it necessary to take or every possible situation in which he might act."[98]

"SOLE ORGAN" DOCTRINE

Rehnquist's opinion in *Dames & Moore v. Regan* is just one recent example of the Supreme Court both accepting and actively expanding presidential power. The 1936 case *United States v. Curtiss-Wright* is the genesis of several arguments that support plenary presidential powers in foreign affairs.[99] Various presidential administrations, including George W. Bush's, have cited this case as support for wide-ranging presidential power.[100] Writing for the majority, Justice George Sutherland supported "the very delicate, plenary and exclusive power of the President as the sole organ of the federal government in the field of international relations—a power which does not require as a basis for its exercise an act of Congress but which, of course, like every other governmental power, must be exercised in subordination to the applicable provisions of the Constitution."[101] The basis of Sutherland's statement is a citation to Chief Justice John Marshall, who, as a member of the House of Representatives, described the president as "the sole organ of the nation in its external relations, and its sole representative with foreign nations."[102]

Some presidential power advocates argue that this language suggests that presidents can unilaterally exercise power in foreign affairs. However, Marshall was not actually advancing this idea at all. Rather, he was merely arguing that presidents have the responsibility to faithfully carry out treaties as part of his defense of President John Adams, whom Marshall believed had the duty to fulfill an extradition treaty with Great Britain. Far from advancing plenary presidential powers, Marshall acknowledged a presidential obligation to honor controlling legal authority, in this case, a treaty that both the president and the Senate had agreed to. Along these lines, Edward Corwin explained, "Clearly, what Marshall had foremost in mind was simply the President's role as *instrument of communication* with other governments."[103] Louis Fisher likewise confirmed that "the context of [Marshall's] speech makes it clear that he was speaking of presidential power to execute *the policy of Congress*, whether expressed in statute or treaty."[104]

Unfortunately, the judiciary continues to misuse Marshall's "sole organ" speech even today in ways that advance the concentration of presidential power in the foreign affairs arena, perhaps most notably in the Supreme Court's *Zivotofsky v. Kerry* decision.[105] Here, the Court held that the president has the exclusive power to formally recognize foreign governments. In a poorly reasoned and weakly justified decision, Justice Anthony Kennedy claimed, "The text and structure of the Constitution grant the President the power to recognize foreign nations and governments."[106] However, he cited provisions of the Constitution (the Treaty and Nomination Clauses) that do not clearly do this and that are, in fact, powers the president actually shares with the Senate. In addition, he referenced Emer De Vattel, an international legal expert who died nearly twenty years before the Constitutional Convention was held, as authoritative on the meaning of the receiving power granted to presidents in Article II, Section 3 of the Constitution. A more instructive view for determining original meaning, which Kennedy also cites, is Alexander Hamilton's statement that the power is "more a matter of dignity than of authority."[107]

However, Kennedy concludes that Congress has no role here, and that the president alone must decide these questions. In doing so, he implicitly revives Sutherland's "sole organ" doctrine understanding of the presidency. "Recognition is a topic," Kennedy writes, "on which the Nation must 'speak . . . with one voice.'" He decides: "That voice must be the President's" as "only the Executive has the characteristic of unity at all times." As Kennedy notes, giving Congress any role in this enterprise "would not only prevent the Nation from speaking with one voice but also prevent the Executive itself from doing so in conducting foreign relations."[108]

We find the principles laid out here by Sutherland and Kennedy to be misguided. These two Supreme Court justices overemphasize the importance of presidential unity in the field of foreign affairs and, in doing so, damage collective decision-making, shared powers, and checks and balances—the very foundations of our form of government. We argue that these opinions should not be treated as controlling when addressing questions about presidential power in foreign affairs. Among other defects, the fundamental flaw of Kennedy's opinion is its focus on the "functional considerations" of government, namely, his insistence that the country "must speak with one voice."[109] Why is unity so crucial to Kennedy in this context, and why does he seem to be mistakenly placing efficiency and unilateralism above collaboration and compromise?

In his dissent, Justice Antonin Scalia took Kennedy to task. Scalia argued that the "vices of this mode of analysis go beyond mere lack of footing in the Constitution." He contended that Kennedy's view, which Scalia labeled "functionalism," "will *systematically* favor the unitary President over the plural Congress in disputes involving foreign affairs." Scalia surmised that a functionalist approach may "make for more effective foreign policy, perhaps as effective as that of a monarchy." But he argued that "in the long run," following such a principle "will erode the structure of separated powers that the People established for the protection of their liberty." Later, Scalia made an important point regarding how to maintain a system of checks and balances:

> That is not the chief magistrate under which the American People agreed to live when they adopted the national charter. They believed that "the accumulation of all powers, legislative, executive, and judiciary, in the same hands, . . . may justly be pronounced the very definition of tyranny." [citation omitted] For this reason, they did not entrust either the President or Congress with sole power to adopt uncontradictable policies about *any* subject— foreign-sovereignty disputes included. They instead gave each political department its own powers, and with that the freedom to contradict the other's policies.[110]

Scalia usually supported broad presidential power and the tenets of the unitary executive theory, which makes his observation here somewhat surprising. We agree with his position in this case that the general purpose of the Constitution is to establish departments that would check one another. As James Madison famously noted in *Federalist* No. 51, "Ambition must be made to counteract ambition."[111]

By bestowing a unilateral power on one branch of the federal government, Kennedy's opinion in *Zivotofsky* weakens important, long-standing dynamics between the three branches. For this reason, we contend his opinion should be treated more as an anomaly than as a controlling judicial command. We believe that the framers created a governing system not only to provide autonomy between the branches but, more important, to give each branch the means to counter the power, and particularly the abuses, of the other two. The federal judiciary disrupts that dynamic when, as in *Zivotofsky*, it introduces new, plenary powers with little historical, textual, or other evidence. As Madison explains in *Federalist* No. 51, the framers gave "to those who administer each department, the necessary constitutional means, and personal motives, to resist encroachments of the others."[112] The government established by the Constitution contained structures designed to curb the "personal motives" that might arise within each branch and lead to abuse of power. With this approach, the framers created a government that could control itself, especially at times when the general public had neither the inclination nor the ability to do so itself.

CONCLUSION

The George W. Bush administration used the unitary executive theory as a theoretical justification for its claims of expansive presidential powers in foreign affairs. Bush administration official John Yoo and other unitary executive supporters pressed for a more robust model of the presidency at a time when the country feared more terrorist attacks. Consequently, national security concerns trumped all others. Vice President Cheney became the link between the George W. Bush presidency and a robust vision of the presidency expressed decades earlier by then representative Cheney (and others) during the Iran-Contra scandal. Since then, presidents such as Obama and Trump have made justifications to ignore the Constitution and laws so they could unilaterally undertake military action.

However, such expansive claims to act unilaterally are often based on novel legal theories and selective history, and they run counter to the "uniformity of opinion" held by most scholars. Yoo leveraged his prominent position in a presidential administration to push for an extreme view of presidential power that distorted commonly accepted definitions of both the Commander-in-Chief Clause and the Declare War Clause. The same can be said of Harold Koh, with whom President Obama sided over an OLC opinion, indicating that military action in Libya was controlled by the WPR.

Our analysis and critique of the expansive view of presidential power advocated by Yoo, Koh, and others should not be understood as an endorsement of a weak model of the presidency. We believe that presidents should, and do, have ample power in foreign affairs to engage in diplomacy and manage wars, among other duties. However, we believe that constitutional powers must be subject to checks by the other branches of government in order to protect liberty. No one branch should have a monopoly on a power that the other two branches cannot reach. With this understanding of presidential power in mind, we continue our look at the unitary executive theory in foreign affairs. In the next chapter, we focus on military commissions and habeas corpus, foreign surveillance, torture, extraordinary rendition, and the state secrets privilege.

CHAPTER 6

Foreign Affairs Powers

Part II

The unitary executive theory played a larger role in foreign affairs matters after 9/11. Following the terrorist attacks in New York City and Washington, DC, Vice President Richard Cheney and others in the George W. Bush administration made a forceful case for unchecked presidential authority in various wartime contexts to prevent further destruction and loss of American life. Deputy Assistant Attorney General John Yoo's post-9/11 memorandum provided a potent constitutional argument for broader executive authority: "In light of the text, plan, and history of the Constitution, its interpretation by both past Administrations and the courts, the longstanding practice of the Executive Branch, and the express affirmation of the President's constitutional authorities by Congress, we think it beyond question that the President has the plenary constitutional power to take such military actions as he deems necessary and appropriate."[1]

The broad claims by Yoo and others to justify such expansive, indeed, nearly unconstrained, presidential powers have had a significant impact on ideas and practices related to the separation of powers. Here we further explore the impact of the unitary executive theory in the realm of foreign affairs. Our view is that the unitary executive theory falls short as a justification for specific exercises of power, including the creation of military commissions; foreign and domestic surveillance; torture; extraordinary rendition; and state secrets privilege. We do not intend to suggest that all these powers are illegitimate, but merely that the unitary executive theory and its sweeping justifications for such practices are not the most stable foundation for them.

MILITARY COMMISSIONS AND HABEAS CORPUS

President George W. Bush's first robust use of his war powers came
in October 2001 when he sent US military troops to Afghanistan.
Congress backed Bush's decision by passing the Authorization for
Use of Military Force (AUMF)—a public law enacted only days after
the 9/11 attacks.[2] However, actually carrying out a "war on terror" required the Bush administration to establish an infrastructure to allow
it to detain suspected terrorists and gather information to prevent future attacks. Accordingly, nearly a month after sending US forces into
Afghanistan, President Bush issued a military order authorizing the
detention of any "individuals subject to this order . . . at an appropriate location designated by the Secretary of Defense outside or within
the United States."[3] The president's order also established military
commissions to try noncitizens who were members of al Qaeda or
individuals who may have assisted terrorists.

An Office of Legal Counsel (OLC) memorandum provided the legal rationale Bush needed to unilaterally create a detention system
and establish military commissions. The memorandum backed the
president's authority to make unilateral decisions about detaining individuals and establishing trial procedures that applied to them. The
memorandum went so far as to dismiss the controlling legal authority for establishing military tribunals found in the Uniform Code of
Military Justice by declaring that "the President has inherent authority
as Commander in Chief to convene such tribunals even without authorization from Congress."[4]

Patrick Philbin, the author of the OLC memorandum, cited two
nineteenth-century cases to support this sweeping assertion of executive authority. However, in each of those cases, it was US generals—
not the president himself—who had established military tribunals and
did so without any statutory authority. Further limiting the preceden-
tial value of what these two generals did is the fact that one of them,
General Winfield Scott, who established a military tribunal in 1847,
never believed his authority was as sweeping as Philbin's memo suggested. Instead, the general argued that he acted in order to maintain
control over unruly volunteer soldiers who had "committed, with im-
punity, all sorts of atrocities on the persons and property of Mexicans."
General Scott only established the tribunals "until Congress could be
stimulated to legislate on the subject."[5] General Scott was not exercising some form of plenary authority that he derived from his role

as battlefield commander in chief. Rather, he believed his actions should be controlled by Congress. Taken in this light, the Uniform Code of Military Justice's explanation of the authority for, and restrictions imposed on, military tribunals assumes even greater importance. However, to Philbin (and to the Bush administration more generally), the Constitution granted the president "inherent" authority to act unilaterally in this context.

The legal community immediately criticized President Bush's military order. In December 2001, four hundred law professors wrote to Senate Judiciary Committee chair Patrick Leahy (D-VT), arguing that the military tribunals established by the order "are legally deficient, unnecessary, and unwise." They contended that the order "undermines the tradition of the Separation of Powers" and argued that they knew of "no Court [which] has upheld unilateral action by the Executive that provided for as dramatic a departure from constitutional norms as does this Order."[6] Their assessment also received support from an American Bar Association Task Force, which argued: "The scope of the President's power to act alone with respect to military commissions has not been developed in case law."[7]

President Bush had limited his military order to non-US citizens, but authorities in Afghanistan quickly captured a US citizen, Yaser Hamdi, and later arrested another American, Jose Padilla, in Chicago. Because Hamdi and Padilla were American citizens, a debate erupted over how the Bush administration should treat them. Some advocates argued that Hamdi and Padilla should receive at least minimal due process rights. The Bush administration and its supporters made the opposite case, noting that the two men were considered "enemy combatants," and pointed out that the US government had detained and tried other American citizens as enemy combatants under similar conditions.

The Bush administration defended its actions regarding Hamdi and Padilla by invoking President Franklin D. Roosevelt. They cited as precedent Roosevelt's decision in World War II to create a similar detention and military commission system to try a small group of Nazi saboteurs, including one individual who held dual US-German citizenship. Eventually the Supreme Court upheld Roosevelt's military commission in *Ex parte Quirin*.[8] The Bush administration and its supporters hoped that *Quirin* would be the key to obtaining judicial sanction for their own detention and military commission system. As two former Justice Department officials noted, *Quirin* was a "most apt precedent" in deciding the fate of Bush's military commissions.[9]

However, *Quirin* was actually a deeply flawed opinion. It had been authored by a Supreme Court operating under significant time constraints, and the defendants had already been executed by the US government before the opinion was issued. The Supreme Court in that case was particularly concerned about how to uphold the trial and conviction of dual US-German citizen Herbert Hans Haupt, who was located inside the United States and therefore outside a war zone. The controlling authority under the circumstances appeared to be the 1866 Supreme Court case *Ex parte Milligan*, in which the Court had held that a US citizen who is located outside a war zone could not be tried by a military commission while civilian courts were available.[10] However, the *Quirin* Court ended up distinguishing the case from *Milligan* by reasoning that Milligan, who lived in a Union state, was a civilian who attempted to commit sabotage; Haupt, by contrast, was a member of the German armed forces who entered the United States to wage war.[11]

In a more recent case, *Hamdi v. Rumsfeld*, the Court called *Quirin* "the most apposite precedent that we have on the question of whether citizens may be detained" but dismissed its relevance as a controlling opinion.[12] In *Hamdi*, Justice Sandra Day O'Connor—writing a plurality opinion for the Court—held that the US government can detain a citizen, but that there are some minimum protections that must be provided, including notice of the reasons for a detainee's classification as an enemy combatant; access to legal counsel; and an opportunity to have a neutral decision maker hear a challenge to the US government.[13] The Court in *Hamdi* did not simply accept the Bush administration's argument that *Quirin* allowed the president to establish military commissions however and wherever he wishes; rather, the Court narrowed this wide-ranging assertation of executive power.

Still, the Bush administration fought on many fronts to maintain unilateral presidential control over post-9/11 war on terror concerns. This broad approach meant that military commission issues often became entangled with questions of detainee access to the courts. In fact, as early as December 2001, Patrick Philbin and John Yoo argued that the federal courts "could not properly exercise habeas jurisdiction over an alien detained at GBC."[14] They used this line of argument to try to prevent the federal courts from exercising habeas corpus jurisdiction over the American detention facility located in Guantanamo Bay, Cuba.

In *Rasul v. Bush*, the Supreme Court held that the federal courts do, in fact, have jurisdiction to hear challenges from foreign nationals regarding the legality of their detention.[15] In this case, the Bush administration argued that a different Supreme Court precedent, *Johnson v. Eisentrager,* controlled the detainees' jurisdictional concerns. In *Eisentrager,* the Supreme Court ruled that German prisoners held in Germany could not access the US courts.[16] However, the *Rasul* Court distinguished *Eisentrager* by noting that the individuals held at Guantanamo "are not nationals of countries at war with the United States, and they deny that they have engaged in or plotted acts of aggression against the United States; they have never been afforded access to any tribunal, much less charged with and convicted of wrongdoing; and for more than two years they have been imprisoned in territory over which the United States exercises exclusive jurisdiction and control."[17] As a result, the Court reasoned that US courts do indeed have jurisdiction over the Guantanamo detainees.

After its failed effort to exercise total control over detainees and military commissions, the Bush administration next created the Combatant Status Review Tribunal comprising a panel of three military officers that would give detainees an opportunity to challenge their designation as enemy combatants.[18] The Bush administration knew that many detainees were captured using less than perfect information, an unfortunate consequence of following leads provided by unreliable sources, people hoping to score a quick reward by identifying someone as a terrorist who may not be.[19] It had hoped that the Combatant Status Review Tribunal process would create a review system that would address flaws raised by the Supreme Court in *Rasul,* particularly the Court's concern that the detainees were being held indefinitely without access to any legal proceedings to determine their status.[20]

Unfortunately for the Bush administration, news reports and photos surfaced that showed inhumane treatment and prisoner abuse at the Abu Ghraib prison in Iraq. Responding to the outcry generated by these stories and pictures, Congress passed the Detainee Treatment Act (DTA), which would prohibit "cruel, inhuman, or degrading treatment or punishment."[21] The new legislation also attempted to do the Bush administration a favor by limiting detainees' rights to access US courts in a provision of the law that seemed to be a direct response to *Rasul.*[22] Despite the legislature's help to limit the reach of the courts, President Bush fell back on the unitary executive theory and issued a signing statement noting that he would interpret the DTA "in a manner consistent with the constitutional authority of the President to supervise the unitary executive branch and as Commander in Chief and consistent with the constitutional limitations on the judicial power."[23]

Senator Dianne Feinstein (D-CA) noted at the time that Bush's willingness to issue such signing statements effectively meant "that if he doesn't like a law, he won't carry it out nor will any post of the Executive Branch."[24] As we have argued in earlier chapters, modern presidents of both political parties have used several tools to advance the unitary executive theory. In this case, President Bush released a signing statement indicating that he would carry out his duties "in a manner consistent with" his constitutional responsibilities instead of saying he would act *in compliance with* the new law.

Shortly after the passage of the DTA, the Bush administration experienced yet another defeat in its push to retain control over detainees and military commissions. The Supreme Court held in *Hamdan v. Rumsfeld* that the military commissions established by the president were not authorized by law.[25] Moreover, these commissions violated both the Geneva Conventions and the Uniform Code of Military Justice. As the Court noted, in attempting to try detainees, "the Executive is bound to comply with the rule of law."[26] In sum, instead of having its expansive views of presidential power vindicated by the Court, the Bush administration repeatedly experienced obstacles, ranging from setbacks to outright rejections, whenever it tried to use unilateral presidential powers to establish or control military commissions.

In the wake of *Hamdan*, Congress passed the Military Commissions Act, which statutorily created military commissions while providing certain procedural protections for detainees, including access to witnesses and evidence.[27] The law also tried to strip the federal courts of habeas corpus jurisdiction in cases where prisoners are determined to be "enemy combatants" according to the DTA. However, the Supreme Court held two years later in *Boumediene v. Bush* that the detainees in Guantanamo had a constitutional right of habeas corpus review and that Congress had failed to provide an adequate substitute for that review via the DTA.[28] The effects of *Boumediene* were substantial. Almost immediately, US district judge Richard Leon ordered the release of Boumediene and four other detainees, noting, "To rest [their continued detention] on so thin a reed would be inconsistent with this court's obligation."[29]

In 2009, President Barack Obama ordered the US government

to temporarily stop using military commissions and called for a review of their procedures, hoping to eventually recommend reforms to Congress.[30] Although opponents of military commissions hailed Obama's plan as a much-needed rebuke of Bush-era practices, the Obama administration decided after concluding its review that the commissions actually served a necessary purpose and should continue. This was a new position for Obama: as a presidential candidate in 2008, he was highly critical of military commissions and declared that other judicial avenues should be used instead. But, after his own official presidential review, he concluded that the commissions "allow for the protection of sensitive sources and methods of intelligence-gathering; they allow for the safety and security of participants; and for the presentation of evidence gathered from the battlefield that cannot always be effectively presented in federal courts."[31] Jack Goldsmith, who served in the Bush OLC, pointed out that Obama had now adopted his predecessor's view on military commissions: "This was precisely the Bush rationale."[32] Obama's ultimate decision to maintain continuity with many Bush-era practices in this area is another example of how powers once exercised by a president are rarely scaled back by his successors.

President Obama did recommend reforms to military commission practices, and Congress took up the issue for consideration. Eventually, Congress passed the Military Commissions Act of 2009, which provided greater procedural protections for detainees, including the prohibition against the admissibility of statements derived via torture or by cruel, inhuman, or degrading treatment; the ability to present evidence; and the ability to examine and respond to evidence.[33] The very act of a president going to Congress to request modifications to military commission procedures was a sea change from just a few years before.

Despite Obama's acquiescence with some controversial Bush-era practices, Bush's preferred line of argument in the aftermath of 9/11 that the president has "inherent authority" to create military commissions without congressional authorization had failed by the end of Obama's first year in office. The Bush administration's push for wide-ranging unilateral presidential power was rejected by the courts, and military commissions were brought under statutory control by Congress.

In 2016, GOP presidential nominee Donald J. Trump reignited the military commissions debate when he said that he opposed using the judicial system to try US citizens who are alleged terrorists or collaborators and preferred to try these persons by commission at Guantanamo Bay: "Well, I know that they want to try them in our regular court systems, and I don't like that at all. I don't like that at all. I would say that they could be tried there [Guantanamo Bay], that would be fine."[34] Because of legislation passed in 2006 and 2009, this practice would violate the law.

President Trump issued an executive order to reverse Obama's plan to close the Guantanamo Bay detention facility, which had remained open throughout Obama's presidency despite Obama having identified closing it as one of his earliest policy priorities. The executive order included the following relevant language: "The United States may transport additional detainees to U.S. Naval Station Guantanamo Bay when lawful and necessary to protect the Nation."[35] To date, the Trump administration's practices (if one ignores the president's rhetoric) have been consistent with those of both the Bush and Obama administrations.

FOREIGN AND DOMESTIC SURVEILLANCE

One of the most audacious claims of inherent presidential authority by the George W. Bush administration was its approval of the federal government electronically surveilling persons in the United States calling and e-mailing people overseas. The administration's Terrorist Surveillance Program (TSP) was an operation led by the National Security Agency (NSA) that conducted such monitoring without a warrant and was therefore blatantly illegal.

In the 1970s, Congress responded to revelations that Americans were being surveilled in their own country for political purposes by the Lyndon B. Johnson and (especially) Richard M. Nixon administrations by passing the Foreign Intelligence Surveillance Act (FISA). This act, signed into law by President Jimmy Carter in 1978, established procedures for the surveillance and collection of "foreign intelligence information" between "foreign powers" and "agents of foreign powers" suspected of treason or espionage. Under the law, the president may approve electronic surveillance of foreign powers without first obtaining a warrant, provided the operation will not reveal any information about an American citizen. If the president wishes to launch a surveillance operation to observe an American citizen who may be conspiring against the United States by cooperating with another country, he must seek a FISA warrant, and the time allowed for the operation will be limited unless reapproval is secured. FISA established a special court specifically to review administration requests to conduct surveillance of a US citizen.

The 1978 law closed off (at least in theory) the possibility that a US citizen could be surveilled without a FISA warrant. It established clear procedures that the Bush administration (or any other presidential administration) could follow in order to legally undertake surveillance of US citizens suspected of having terrorist ties abroad. Unfortunately, the Bush administration decided to act unilaterally rather than follow these legally established procedures. James Pfiffner makes the unarguable point: "President Bush could have followed the process set out by law; that is, he could have required NSA to get warrants from the special FISA court." Although the Bush administration argued that doing so on a case-by-case basis would have been unnecessarily time-consuming, Pfiffner points out that the FISA court was "about as close to a rubber stamp as one could wish," having approved, from 1978 to 2005, a staggering 18,748 warrants while refusing to sanction only five requests. The NSA also had the legal option to move right away and then ask a court within the next three days to approve its actions. In brief, the Bush administration's chosen actions were both illegal and unnecessary. Moreover, Pfiffner notes, if the president thought FISA was still too restrictive, he could have easily appealed to Congress to amend the law, as it had done on multiple occasions since 9/11. President Bush did not do so for several years, at which point political opposition to his actions, even within his own Department of Justice, was simply too much to overcome.[36]

The president and his administration thoroughly rejected the argument that the TSP was in any way illegal. In a 2005 press conference, the president directly addressed the issue of his authority to act: "As President, and Commander in Chief, I have the constitutional responsibility and the constitutional authority to protect our country. Article II of the Constitution gives me that responsibility and the authority necessary to fulfill it."[37]

President Bush's statement here is a classic defense of the view that Article II gives the president broad discretion to act outside the written law when he determines that it is necessary to do so to protect the nation. When the media revealed that Bush had ordered the NSA to undertake surveillance of foreign sources with possible ties to al Qaeda and US citizens, he argued that journalists were harming national security and even went so far as to threaten punitive action against those who had revealed the existence of NSA surveillance activities.

In response to legislative pushback, President Bush maintained that his administration had not committed any separation of powers violations, as it had consulted with congressional leadership (although not with Congress as a whole) about the program. As a general principle, the president's conversations with selected legislative leaders simply may not confer the equivalent of congressional consent to his actions. Accepting this argument would be tantamount to saying that the president may unilaterally override any legislative requirement, provided he consults with at least some members of Congress about doing so.

The Bush administration's first official answer to Congress about the legality of its actions was contained in a December 22, 2005, letter to legislative leaders from Assistant Attorney General William Moschella. In the letter, Moschella articulated the classic dilemma of balancing privacy and security interests and concluded that the nation's security must come first. He noted that the September 18, 2001 AUMF was the primary legal justification for Bush's action. Moschella elaborated that the AUMF "clearly contemplates action within the United States" and that it gave the president wide latitude to do whatever he believed to be necessary to prevent terrorism against the United States.[38] Here, Moschella provided a very broad interpretation of the legislative intent of the AUMF; Congress certainly did not create the AUMF to either override FISA or sweep away other legislative and judicial restraints on presidential powers.

The Bush administration claimed further legal validation of its actions in a January 19, 2006 OLC memorandum. In that memorandum, the OLC argued that the AUMF authorized the federal government to conduct surveillance actions in a manner that was both legal and consistent with the requirements of FISA and the civil liberties protected by the Fourth Amendment to the Constitution.[39] The memorandum went so far as to claim that "the AUMF places the President at the zenith of his powers in authorizing the NSA activities."[40]

Revelations of the NSA surveillance actions created substantial political and legal headwinds pushing against the Bush White House. Some members of the Department of Justice who were strongly opposed to these questionable activities even threatened to resign. In May 2007, a federal judge ruled that the TSP practice could not continue under FISA. By August 2007, Congress acted, and the president signed a law that effectively authorized much of what the administration had been doing under TSP. The new law approved a TSP-like program under the direction of the director of national intelligence (DNI) and the attorney general.[41] Of course, the new law only established the legality of certain administration surveillance actions that occurred *after* its enactment; it did not legally validate what had transpired before. As a result, the president's overextension of his executive authority was not mitigated by the new law. In July 2008, Congress amended the FISA law to allow for a somewhat more limited surveillance program that would target individuals located outside the United States.[42]

The release of NSA documents by Edward Snowden in 2013 greatly aided in the reevaluation by Congress of the limits on FISA.[43] The documents revealed that, among other things, the federal government had been collecting bulk phone data on US citizens; this revelation started a vigorous debate regarding national security and privacy. Two years later, Congress passed the USA Freedom Act, revising provisions of FISA by changing many of the operations of the NSA and requiring the federal government to undergo court review procedures to approve requests for gathering electronic surveillance data.[44] Finally, on January 19, 2018, President Donald J. Trump signed into law the FISA Amendments Reauthorization Act of 2017, which reauthorized certain FISA provisions that granted the NSA authority to conduct warrantless surveillance of foreigners' communications but also introduced new oversight and control mechanisms into law. The legislation barely passed in the Senate, where it was met with fierce opposition from Republican and Democratic senators. Senators Rand Paul (R-KY), Ron Wyden (D-OR), Mike Lee (R-UT), and Patrick Leahy (D-VT) joined together in attacking the bill, noting that it failed to provide adequate safeguards and, instead, "further expands the risks of unconstitutional spying on innocent Americans."[45]

The evolution of FISA's support in Congress since 9/11 signifies well the struggle the country is having over the power and reach of the federal government into the personal lives of its citizens. The bipartisan efforts of a number of senators did not succeed in providing for the most robust protections. But legislative successes in 2008, 2015, and even 2018 to provide additional controls on FISA counter President Bush's claim of constitutional authority to conduct warrantless spying. Instead, the debate over the NSA's authority is clearly grounded in law and has been governed by a long line of legislative measures that can be traced back for decades.

TORURE

The George W. Bush administration's most controversial antiter-
rorism measure was its approval of "enhanced interrogation" techniques against so-called enemy combatants held by US authorities.[46]
Although torture was technically banned by both US law and international laws and norms, various members of the Bush administration
justified highly controversial practices as both legitimate and vital to
gathering critical information that might identify possible terrorists
and short-circuit future attacks.

For example, White House counsel Alberto Gonzales wrote a memo
to President Bush dated January 25, 2002, in which he laid out several
reasons why, in the context of a war on terror, the Geneva Convention
should not protect al Qaeda and Taliban fighters in US custody, including Gonzales's observation that after 9/11 there is a "new paradigm [that] renders obsolete Geneva's strict limitations on questions
of enemy prisoners and renders quaint some of its provisions."[47]
Responding to correspondence from the Department of Justice and
the attorney general, President Bush wrote on February 7, 2002, how
he agreed that, regarding suspected terrorists, the United States was
not bound by the Geneva Convention Relative to the Treatment of
Prisoners of War of August 12, 1949.[48]

The "Bybee memo," authored by Assistant Attorney General Jay
Bybee on August 1, 2002, to Gonzales discussing 18 U.S.C. Section
2340, or the "torture statute," carved out a broad sphere for President
Bush's use of his war powers under the Commander-in-Chief Clause.
Bybee argued that Bush had "the constitutional authority to order
interrogations of enemy combatants to gain intelligence information
concerning the military plans of the enemy" and that "any effort to
apply Section 2340A in a manner that interferes with the President's
direction of such core matters as the detention and interrogation
of enemy combatants thus would be unconstitutional."[49] Bybee
noted elsewhere in the memo that the torture statute "must be con-
strued as not applying to interrogations undertaken pursuant to his
Commander-in-Chief authority."[50] In other words, Bybee argued that
even if a practice was forbidden in the torture statute (that is, banned
in a law passed by Congress), the president could exercise his own
constitutional authority and undertake that practice anyway. This dynamic is at the very heart of the unitary executive theory as presidents

are placed above laws and given powers that cannot be checked by the other branches.

So, to what extent did the Bush administration seek to utilize its unitary powers in the realm of torture? A good indicator is its discussion of the infliction of pain on a detainee by US interrogators. The "Bybee memo" advised that the "torture statute" required a detainee to experience "severe pain" for his treatment to constitute torture. In Bybee's words, "Such damage must rise to the level of death, organ failure, or the permanent impairment of significant bodily function."[51] The "Levin memo" issued in December 2004 "supersedes the [Bybee] August 2002 Memorandum in its entirety," including the sections analyzing "severe" pain and the "commander-in-chief" power.[52]

Secretary of State Donald Rumsfeld approved several interrogation techniques, such as "Fear Up Harsh," "Fear Up Mild," and "Reduced Fear" in a memo dated April 16, 2003.[53] He noted that even though "the Geneva Convention [was] not applicable to the interrogation of unlawful combatants," American military forces should keep in mind that "other nations" that believed the Geneva Convention *was* applicable would be watching.[54] In several memos from 2005, Steven Bradbury of the Department of Justice's OLC described several techniques used in "a prototypical interrogation," which may feature a detainee "stripped of his clothes, shackled and hooded" before the detainee endured "sleep deprivation," "dietary manipulation," and even nudity, aside from a diaper.[55] In one memo, Bradbury opined that neither preventing a detainee from sleeping for long periods of time nor waterboarding is considered to be torture.[56]

On July 20, 2007, George W. Bush issued Executive Order 13440. In it, he reiterated his earlier belief that Geneva Convention 3 did not protect "enemy combatants" or members of the Taliban or al Qaeda and noted his continuing support for the CIA's interrogation program.[57] When Barack Obama became president, he quickly issued Executive Order 13491—titled "Ensuring Lawful Interrogations"—which revoked Executive Order 13440 and replaced it, requiring compliance with standards established in Army Field Manual 2-22.3.[58]

During his presidential campaign in 2016, Republican Donald J. Trump criticized the Obama policy to end the use of torture as a tool in the fight against terrorism. During the presidential transition period, Trump had considered appointing General David Petraeus to a high-level cabinet post until he learned that the general had publicly opposed using torture. Shortly after assuming office, Trump said "torture works" in an ABC News interview and affirmed his plan to bring back waterboarding and other torture techniques.[59]

EXTRAORDINARY RENDITION

"Rendition" is a legal and internationally accepted practice. Many countries hand detainees over to stand trial for crimes committed elsewhere. Internationally, there are numerous long-standing laws and treaties governing the practice of rendition. However, "extraordinary rendition" is significantly different and rests on a considerably shakier legal foundation than rendition. The practice of extraordinary rendition can be defined as the "transfer of an individual, without the benefit of a legal proceeding in which the individual can challenge the transfer, to a country where he or she is at risk of torture."[60] The United States has transferred detainees to other countries primarily to coerce information out of them and bypass antitorture laws. After 9/11, this practice expanded substantially and often led to heated debates about the limits of executive authority and sometimes even constitutional challenges. Although President George W. Bush may not have directly claimed the right to extraordinary rendition as a manifestation of the unitary executive theory, the practice was part of a larger set of unusual and related post-9/11 measures that Bush unquestionably wanted the world to recognize as within his sphere of "unitary" influence.

For most of US history, renditions were acceptable under prevailing legal obligations often spelled out in treaties, and Congress played a significant role in the practice. During President George Washington's administration, Secretary of State Thomas Jefferson addressed the logistics of transferring a fugitive to a different country. In 1791, Jefferson looked at other countries' practices and noted that because renditions were based on treaties, it was Congress's duty to determine the seriousness of the crime in question and then decide whether to return a fugitive to his or her country.[61] In 1793, the French minister Edmond-Charles Genêt requested that the United States return certain individuals who had committed crimes against France. Jefferson said that American laws "take no notice of crimes committed out of their jurisdiction."[62] Jefferson's words and actions established the long-standing precedent that Congress has the authority to determine whether to transfer an accused criminal to another country.

If Congress determined a crime was serious enough to transfer an individual, it could do so via treaty. Attorney General William Wirt wrote about the president's authority to return criminal suspects to another country, noting that "the President has no power to make the delivery" unless, as Louis Fisher points out, the legislature has approved a law or treaty granting the president that ability.[63] Four years after Wirt wrote this line, Secretary of State John Quincy Adams responded as follows to a governor of Canada who had asked for the United States to deliver a fugitive: "I am instructed by the President to express his regret to your Excellency that the request . . . cannot be complied with under any authority now vested in the executive government of the United States."[64]

Attorney General Hugh Legare advised in 1841 that Congress was the proper body to handle renditions, noting "The president is not considered as authorized, in the absence of any express provision by treaty, to order the delivering up of fugitives from justice."[56] Although congressional authority had been widely recognized as a legitimate basis for transferring fugitives to their native lands, a president attempted to challenge Congress's authority in this arena for the first time during the Civil War period. President Abraham Lincoln had ordered the return of a Spanish subject, Jose Arguelles, without a treaty in place to describe exactly how that should happen.[66] The Senate and the House described Lincoln's actions as an abuse of power, while Lincoln's attorney general attempted to defend the president. Apart from this incident, all three branches of the federal government had until that time understood that Congress had the exclusive power to implement a rendition.

The Supreme Court has ruled on rendition questions on several occasions. For example, in an 1840 case, *Holmes v. Jennison*, George Holmes was being held in the United States because a governor of Canada was requesting that he be delivered to that country to face punishment for crimes that Holmes had allegedly committed. Holmes's attorney argued, "No President of the U.S., no Governor of Canada, and lastly, no King of England, has ventured to act in a case of this kind, except by legislative authority, or by treaty, which is tantamount to a law."[67] The Court's opinion noted that Congress's treaty-making power was the source of the government's ability to transfer a fugitive. Chief Justice Roger Taney wrote, "And as the rights and duties of nations towards one another in relation to fugitives from justice are a part of the law of nations and have always been treated as such by the writers upon public law, it follows that the treaty-making power must have authority to decide how far the right of a foreign nation in this respect will be recognized and enforced when it demands the surrender of anyone charged with offenses against it."[68] Chief Justice Taney stated that because the president shares the treaty-making power with Congress, the power to decide whether a fugitive should be transferred rests with both. Justice Smith Thompson further explains the constitutionality of rendition: "This power to surrender fugitives from justice to a foreign government has its foundation—its very life and being—in a treaty to be made between the United States and such foreign government and is not by the Constitution vested in any department of our government without a treaty."[69]

In 1936, the Supreme Court ruled on the case of *Valentine v. United States*, which stemmed from a request by the French government that native-born citizens of the United States be delivered to France for crimes they committed against France. The alleged criminals sued to avoid being handed over to the French government and claimed that the Franco-American Extradition Treaty of 1909 exempted US citizens from extradition.[70] The Supreme Court used its opinion in this case as the vehicle through which to give its own interpretation of the process of rendition. The Court ruled unanimously that the president does not have authority on this issue:

> It rests upon the fundamental consideration that the Constitution creates no executive prerogative to dispose of the liberty of the individual. Proceedings against him must be authorized by law. There is no executive discretion to surrender him to a foreign government unless that discretion is granted by law. It necessarily follows that as the legal authority does not exist save as it is given by act of Congress or by the terms of a treaty, it is not enough that statute or treaty does not deny the power to surrender. It must be found that statute or treaty confers the power.[71]

All three branches of the federal government understood that Congress and the president possessed the power to transfer a fugitive (rendition) through their shared power of treaty-making. In the absence of a treaty between the United States and the other relevant country, the president did not have the power to transfer someone to that other country. Over time, though, this understanding has evolved, starting with presidents Ronald Reagan, George H. W. Bush,

Bill Clinton, and finally culminating in the extraordinary rendition controversy in the post-9/11 George W. Bush administration.

President Reagan adopted the technique known as "rendition to justice," which was designed to capture suspected terrorists outside American borders and then bring them back to stand trial in the federal courts. In 1986, the president ordered the CIA to capture alleged terrorists. Reagan's successor, President George H. W. Bush, continued the practice and directed that Panamanian leader Manuel Noriega be "taken into custody" by American law enforcement; the Supreme Court upheld the president's action in *United States v. Alvarez-Machain*.[72] American authorities justified Noriega's arrest with a controversial 1989 OLC opinion titled "Authority of the FBI to Override Customary or Other International Law in the Course of Extraterritorial Law Enforcement Activities." The memorandum overruled a Carter administration Department of Justice opinion from 1980 and instead determined that the FBI could legally apprehend fugitives abroad without the permission of the host country.[73]

President Bill Clinton expanded the concept of "rendition to justice" to include practices that became known as "extraordinary rendition." Clinton signed Presidential Decision Directive 30, which authorized the secretary of state and the attorney general to use all legal means needed to remove terrorist threats from the United States. As a result, under President Clinton, rendition worked as a way to apprehend terrorist suspects by covert means in a foreign country without its knowledge or consent while giving no rights to those captured. This practice remained uncommon until after 9/11, when it became the standard policy of the Bush administration.

Under President George W. Bush, rendition fully gave way to "extraordinary" rendition. The old practice was expanded to allow the United States to send "individuals to countries not for the purpose of trial, but rather to gather intelligence about future wrongdoing through unlawful detentions and coercive interrogation."[74] The Bush administration defended this policy as a deterrent to terrorists and as a means for saving American lives. For example, Secretary of State Condoleezza Rice stated, "Renditions are permissible under international law and are consistent with the responsibilities of those governments to protect their citizens."[75]

Bush's successor, President Barack Obama, issued several executive orders concerning extraordinary renditions. The first of these,

Executive Order 13491, ensured lawful interrogations. It revoked President Bush's executive order and instead required interrogations to be done according to the Army Field Manual and also created a special task force to review the practice of rendition of detainees to third countries and ensure that torture does not ensue.[76] The second executive order, 13492, reviewed how to close Guantanamo Bay and discussed what could be done with the detainees already located there.[77] The third executive order, 13493, created another task force to review lawful options for the apprehension, detention, trial, and release of detainees.[78] Overall, President Obama did not make major changes to the practice of extraordinary rendition as it existed under George W. Bush; instead, he tweaked it to align more with the practice administered by President Clinton.[79] Obama's version of rendition was a more monitored exercise than was rendition under the Bush administration, but like Bush, Obama still ordered the transfer of suspected terrorists to other countries. The director of the Central Intelligence Agency, Leon Panetta, noted the Obama administration's concern for using rendition responsibly: "Our people have to make very sure that people won't be mistreated."[80]

It is still unclear if President Trump has adopted George W. Bush's policies regarding rendition. His CIA director, Gina Haspel, previously worked for the CIA's rendition, detention, and interrogation program. During her Senate confirmation hearing, she pledged not to restart the CIA detention or "enhanced interrogation" program. In a letter to Senator Mark Warner (D-VA), she identified the advantages and drawbacks of the program and noted, "With the benefit of hindsight and my experience as a senior Agency leader, the enhanced interrogation program is not one the CIA should have undertaken."[81] Whether the Trump administration may have reestablished the extraordinary rendition program anyway is not known, as it has not been transparent on this issue.

STATE SECRETS PRIVILEGE

Much like executive privilege in the domestic sphere, state secrets privilege is best seen as one of the president's "defensive tools" that helps the executive branch keep national security information in civil legal proceedings a secret from the courts, Congress, the press, and the public. Seen in this light, it is a pernicious power that skews our system of checks and balances and provides a significant advantage to presidents vis-à-vis the courts and Congress. Though its origin remains unclear and its effects are vague, the state secrets privilege has been established over time as a legitimate, though limited, executive power. President George W. Bush frequently called on the state secrets privilege to justify some of his more controversial actions in the war on terror.

The state secrets privilege is sometimes confused with executive privilege. William Weaver and Robert Pallitto distinguish the two as follows: the state secrets privilege "relies more on practicality than constitutional principle for its justification. Although judges occasionally ground the privilege in separation of powers, the ultimate reason for upholding its use is on the practical grounds that it is necessary to the survival of the state."[82] Another common distinction is that executive privilege applies broadly to different categories, such as protecting the privacy of internal White House deliberations and information related to ongoing investigations in the Department of Justice. In contrast, the state secrets privilege is significantly narrower and applies only to national security.

Advocates of the state secrets privilege maintain that its origins date back to the founding of the Republic and the Constitution. They consider this power to be an inherent characteristic of the executive branch and reference Alexander Hamilton, James Madison, and John Jay's mentions of secrecy and national security in *Federalist* No. 64 and *Federalist* No. 84.

In *United States v. Reynolds*, the Supreme Court established the legitimacy of the state secrets privilege in the modern era while also showcasing the potential for that power to be abused.[83] In that case, the widows of three civilians who died in the crash of a military plane in Georgia filed a wrongful death action against the US government. The secretary of the air force filed a formal claim of privilege, contending that the accident report contained information about secret military equipment and that the release of this information would cause undue harm to national security. When the report was declassified in 1995, it revealed no secret equipment, but instead provided evidence that the government had covered up its own negligence. However, the Court's decision in 1953 affirmed the government's position.

The Supreme Court in *Reynolds* applied the *Duncan* framework to reach its conclusion. In England in 1942, the case *Duncan v. Cammell* gave the power to withhold information, or the "crown privilege," only to the executive.[84] This case involved family members of seamen killed in submarine trials. The Crown asserted that to protect national security it would not release documents related to this accident. The *Reynolds* Court later adopted this idea of absolute authority of the executive to withhold such documents and set up a framework for how to rule in favor of the privilege, as described by Lee Tien:

> (1) it belongs to the government; (2) it must be properly invoked by means of a "formal claim of privilege, lodged by the head of the department which has control over the matter" after "actual personal consideration"; (3) the court must then "determine whether the circumstances are appropriate for the claim of privilege, and yet do so without forcing a disclosure of the very thing the privilege is designed to protect"; (4) the precise nature, extent, and manner of this inquiry depends in part on the extent of a party's need for the information sought tested against the strength of the government's claim of privilege; and (5) *in camera* review can be appropriate, but not in all cases.[85]

The Court in *Reynolds* concluded that the judiciary determines whether the privilege should be applied; here, however, the majority agreed that the state secrets privilege was appropriate without even making the effort to see the documents themselves. The *Reynolds* case is a highly problematic precedent because it did not establish any standard as to what kind of information is dangerous to release. Lower courts have implemented an impact test to deal with the confusion left behind by *Reynolds*: they ask if there is a "reasonable danger" to national security if certain information is released.[86] Of course, national security is not always clearly defined, which allows substantial space for the executive to claim the need to protect various sources of information that may not actually have anything to do with national security.

Louis Fisher's work highlights contemporary abuses of the state secrets privilege. For example, he references *Barlow v. United States,* where Defense Department employee Richard Barlow's job was in jeopardy because Pakistan's nuclear potential spurred disagreements between the executive and legislative branches.[87] Barlow wanted access to documents that he claimed would help prove his innocence. However, the CIA director blocked Barlow's request by making a formal claim of state secrets privilege. The CIA director stated, "I recognize it is the Court's decision rather than mine to determine whether requested material is relevant to matters being addressed in litigation."[88] The Court concluded that the documents were, in fact, privileged. Courts have expanded the use of the state secrets privilege in civil cases to protect against subpoenas, discovery motions, and other judicial requests for information.

In the context of the war on terror, the Bush administration successfully invoked the state secrets privilege in a lawsuit by Khaled al-Masri, who had sued the CIA and others for being held against his will and tortured.[89] As a candidate for president in 2008, Barack Obama strongly criticized the Bush administration's use of the state secrets doctrine. When he was president, though, Obama's administration continued Bush-era practices by, for example, claiming state secrets privilege in a lawsuit brought by Nasser al-Awlaki, Anwar al-Awlaki's father, against the United States roughly a year after Obama ordered a drone attack to kill Anwar, an American citizen, without first offering him a hearing.[90] The Trump administration invoked the state secrets privilege in 2017, claiming national security concerns in its attempt to prevent CIA officials from testifying in a lawsuit brought by alleged victims of CIA interrogators who tortured them at a "black site."[91]

Like executive privilege, state secrets privilege is not directly an area of presidential power where the battle of the unitary executive theory is fought. However, as we have highlighted, it is a power that presidents employ to limit the ability of the other branches to check presidential power. In that way, state secrets privilege is a vital mechanism of presidents in that it permits them to conduct foreign policy largely unfettered from Congress, the courts, and public and to do so in ways that conform to the unitary executive theory. By being able to shield information and executive branch actions via a state secrets privilege, presidents have, in effect, eroded the ability of the other branches to hold the presidency to account.

CONCLUSION

The unitary executive theory is an insufficient basis for unilateral presidential action in the areas of military commissions, foreign and domestic surveillance, torture, extraordinary rendition, and states secrets privilege. As President George W. Bush formulated responses to volatile circumstances brought about by the terrorist attacks on 9/11, these exercises of executive powers became sources of national and even international controversy.

The Bush administration tried to unilaterally control the terms of military commissions and was repeatedly defeated in the courts. Congress eventually passed the Military Commissions Act of 2009 and assumed control of them itself. President Trump's general approach to military commissions has been similar to the approaches of Bush and Obama. However, Trump has issued an executive order to keep Guantanamo Bay open and available as an option for trying US citizens accused of terrorism even though doing so would violate current law.

In the realm of foreign and domestic surveillance, the Bush administration violated the Constitution and broke the law by surveilling American citizens without first obtaining a FISA warrant. In 2015, President Obama signed the USA Freedom Act, in what he called "sensible reform legislation," as a means for, in House Speaker John Boehner's words, both "keeping Americans safe from terrorism and protecting their civil liberties."[92] President Donald J. Trump signed into law the FISA Amendments Reauthorization Act of 2017, which, among other measures, required the federal government to submit to court review when attempting to gather electronic surveillance data.

President George W. Bush wrote in a memo dated February 7, 2002, that the United States was not bound by the Geneva Convention regarding treatment of suspected terrorists.[93] Several Bush administration figures offered support for extraordinary executive power. Perhaps most notable was Assistant Attorney General Jay Bybee's advice in the August 1, 2002 "Bybee memo" that the president's commander-in-chief power allowed Bush to ignore a law banning torture if the president believed it would interfere with his own constitutional responsibilities.[94] The "Bybee memo" was superseded by the "Levin memo" in December 2004. Bush's justifications for enhanced interrogation were rejected by his successor, Barack Obama, but on the presidential campaign trail in 2016, Republican nominee Donald J. Trump commented on waterboarding, "You bet your ass I'd approve it . . . in a heartbeat."[95]

On rendition, the framers believed Congress and the president should share responsibility. This understanding stood largely unchallenged until the Civil War. Rendition did not become continuously "extraordinary" until the George W. Bush administration. The addition of one word made a big difference: as Louis Fisher noted, "Putting 'extraordinary' in front of rendition changes the meaning fundamentally. . . . Presidents claimed the right not only to act in the absence of statutory or treaty authority but even in violation of it."[96]

Finally, the state secrets privilege is a legitimate power intended to protect the government from having to disclose information that may threaten national security. Unfortunately, as illustrated by the *Reynolds* case, the privilege can often be abused by a government more concerned about avoiding embarrassment than protecting information that meets classification standards. In recent years, presidents Bush, Obama, and Trump have all successfully claimed state secrets privilege in lawsuits stemming from the war on terror to prevent sensitive national security documents from being disclosed in court.

Conclusion

The unitary executive theory is largely about power. Whether Democrat or Republican, any president wants to have as much flexibility as possible to address the many concerns that find their way to the Oval Office. At the same time, the president is just one actor in a system of separated powers and checks and balances that the framers designed to frustrate the ability of any single branch of the federal government to unilaterally impose its will on the other two. Unitary executive supporters have developed their theory of expansive presidential power to work around constraints that may be imposed by Congress and the courts. The president and Congress have fought many a political battle over the years, and the unitary executive theory has become a relevant consideration weighing in on the side of the president mostly in the past four decades, beginning when attorneys within President Ronald Reagan's Department of Justice began to make arguments for the theory.

Contrary to core arguments of the unitary executive theory, however, the Constitution establishes Congress, not the president, as the lead player in the federal government. In Article I, Section 8, the framers ascribed a laundry list of seventeen key government powers to Congress, including responsibility over the federal purse and the ability to "declare war." They vested "the executive power" in a president of the United States in Article II at a time when the chief executive was not widely recognized as having nearly the reach that he does today. History has tilted the scales to increasingly favor the president, but even now, as ever, he may be reined in by a Congress with the public support or the political will to do so. Lack of political will, not some alleged secondary constitutional status, has rendered Congress much weaker than the role expected of it by the framers.

At times, presidents need to be able to act quickly and decisively, and the framers recognized that. As the post-9/11 presidency of George W. Bush best demonstrates, presidents can most easily make the case for extraordinary powers when the country is under attack. Following Bush's lead, Presidents Barack Obama and Donald J. Trump have also tried to expand the boundaries of their constitutional authority, although without the circumstance of an attack on the US homeland during their times in office. For example, as we describe in the introduction, President Trump tried (and failed) to require state and local law enforcement to accept orders from the federal government regarding suspected illegal immigrants as a requirement for continuing to receive federal grants. Had this move been successful in court, it would have substituted the president's judgment for that of Congress. Trump has also made wide-ranging claims of exclusive executive authority with his "travel ban" and his trade policies with China, among other areas. Unitary executive proponents have laid the intellectual groundwork for a theory of presidential power that, in its most extreme form, accommodates such broad claims of executive authority.

The unitary executive theory gives intellectual substance and legitimacy to a potentially dangerous accumulation of presidential power and is even more threatening because it is not likely to dissipate on its own. Unless the next US president consciously returns to Congress powers assumed for wartime demands (as Lincoln did), or at least seeks congressional support for them, the prerogatives claimed by presidents under extraordinary circumstances may establish a baseline for future presidents in ordinary times. Those later presidents will then be reluctant to give back powers once acquired, no matter what they may have promised during their campaigns for the presidency, as happened recently regarding President Obama. As a candidate for the presidency, Obama had pledged to respect legislative authority and limits on presidential powers, but by 2014, even he had come around: "I've got a pen and I've got a phone. And I can use that pen to sign executive orders and take executive actions and administrative actions that move the ball forward."[1] This dynamic would have continued to be in place no matter who followed President Obama into office, although President Trump has made broad-ranging claims of his own in several areas that push against boundaries that even his most recent predecessors approached more cautiously.

At a time in history when the United States faces constant world-wide threats, the stewardship theory of presidential power as articulated by Theodore Roosevelt can and has been expanded to cover almost any conceivable situation. Presidents exercising prerogative powers, as President Abraham Lincoln once did, have not acted with as much deference to the powers of the coordinated branches as did the sixteenth president, who sought congressional approval for his wide-sweeping actions during the Civil War. Also, some notable scholars have aided the continuing growth of presidential power—some with fanciful notions of a "great man" theory, others by a belief in the virtue of power-seeking leaders, and others with theories purporting to prove the intended supremacy of executive power in our constitutional system.

Definitions of the unitary executive vary,[2] but most versions include some or all of the following features: a belief in a strong president who enjoys various unilateral powers, the ability to oversee and command the entire executive branch, abilities derived from the president's "inherent" authority under the Constitution, and the ability to ignore congressional restraints when exercising executive power. The "weak" version of the unitary executive as endorsed by Steven Calabresi and Christopher Yoo would vest all of the Constitution's executive power in the president and therefore give the chief executive the ability to control the entire executive branch.[3] In contrast, the "strong" version of the unitary executive came out of the George W. Bush administration. Advocates of the "strong" unitary executive theory argue that the president may exercise inherent powers and may act without fear of congressional checks, thereby expanding unlimited executive power from the domestic sphere to include international affairs as well.[4]

The president is but one actor in a separation of powers system.[5] Like the other actors in that system, he is subject to checks on his authority by the others. Moreover, presidents do not have "inherent powers": they have only the express and implied powers provided by the Constitution, nothing more and nothing less. Overall, a theory of the unitary executive that legitimizes presidential power without boundaries is a threat to the constitutional system of checks and balances and does not conform either with the framers' intentions or with how most presidents in US history have viewed their authority. When taking unilateral actions, presidents all claim to be acting only in the public interest. We grant that they sincerely believe in their cause as being synonymous with the national interest. But the power of a one-person-led office to make that determination without constraint is exactly what scared the framers, who put into place many restrictions on the president's ability to act alone. They understood that whether out of sincere motivation or pure power-seeking, presidents, more than any other actors in our system, had the ability to do the most damage to the Republic.

Throughout this study, we have explored numerous examples of presidential power in both domestic and foreign affairs contexts to show the upward trajectory of the unitary executive theory and of the president's ability to exercise unilateral power. Modern presidents, Republicans and Democrats alike, have consistently agreed—implicitly, if not always explicitly—that the president has vast powers. Some have behaved as though the powers of the presidency even lack limits under certain circumstances. President Trump is merely the most recent president to pursue far-reaching executive powers, although he has been the most direct in making the claim that the Article II–based powers of his office allow him to do anything that he wants.

DOMESTIC POWERS

Calabresi and Yoo argue in their study of the unitary executive theory that the president has complete control over every official in the executive branch. This view contradicts the constitutional design whereby Congress is charged with passing laws that structure and fund the various agencies of the executive branch. The comptroller of the Treasury position is one example of an executive branch official whose job description required him to provide an independent check on the Treasury secretary rather than blindly follow the president's orders. Moreover, past presidents often struggled to control the executive branch, to the point that President Franklin D. Roosevelt assembled the Brownlow Committee to recommend changes that would give the president a firm grasp on his subordinates. Still, the offices and bureaus of the executive branch have always been decentralized and remain so even today.

The president's lack of total control over the executive branch is not a flaw in the constitutional system—rather, the framers crafted a system of separated powers and checks and balances to prevent a single government official, or branch of the government, from amassing too much power. To those unitary executive theory proponents who argue that the unitary executive is justified in today's modern world (if not in the past), the evidence substantiates that presidents who have tried to unilaterally command the executive bureaucracy have largely failed, and some have done grave damage.

Some of those who advocate for a strong unitary executive theory maintain that presidents can use executive orders to dictate terms to the executive branch and thereby exert direct influence over the policymaking process. To be sure, presidents have resorted to this tack after being frustrated by a lack of legislative action on their policy priorities. But executive orders can be overturned by successive presidents, hemmed in by a court decision, or overturned by a contrary law passed by Congress. Moreover, presidents who issue executive orders may see their orders carried out, or they may not—these orders are no sure thing despite the aura of finality that they may convey.

Signing statements are another unilateral presidential tool that modern era chief executives have called on. To some unitary executive supporters, signing statements are a long-standing and legitimate way for a president to object to a newly signed law, which may contain provisions that the president believes will interfere with his ability to supervise the executive branch, or may violate constitutional authority lodged in the executive. The Ronald Reagan administration was the first to craft constitutional signing statements as part of a strategy to expand executive influence, and Reagan's successors have followed this practice, to varying degrees. Signing statements threaten the separation of powers system because there is no clear legislative recourse available for Congress to object to one. The proper course of action would be for the president to veto a bill containing such unacceptable provisions, as called for in the Constitution. That is exactly what presidential candidate Barack Obama said in his first run for the office, although once elected he followed established precedents and issued signing statements. As practiced now, signing statements often have the effects of a line-item veto.

Presidential clemency is one of the few areas where the president enjoys a virtually unchecked power. But even the ability to forgive federal offenses is usually informally hemmed in by the two long-standing rationales for using clemency: to show mercy to a specific individual or to serve the public welfare. Recent presidents (namely, George H. W. Bush, Bill Clinton, George W. Bush, and Donald J. Trump) have to varying degrees abused the clemency power. Instead of granting official forgiveness for the traditional reasons, each of these presidents has used clemency to forgive donors or political allies or for some other personal or political reason. Whether a president may "self-pardon," as President Trump has alluded to twice, is an open question that, if undertaken, would be the ultimate culmination of the kind of power apparently envisioned by some unitary executive supporters. Fortunately, in such an extreme case, the system of checks and balances provides for impeachment as a potential remedy to executive power run amok. But even here, with political polarization in full force in Congress, it is not clear that legislators would act in such a case based on long-standing constitutional standards or merely temporary political calculations.

Regarding presidential appointments and removals, a tenet of the unitary executive theory, for some of its advocates, is that Article II of the Constitution gives the president the exclusive power to nominate federal officials and judges, free from meddling by Congress. Moreover, proponents of wide-ranging executive power often interpret vague constitutional language in a manner that favors the president's ability to make recess appointments. But the Constitution requires the Senate's confirmation, and practices such as "senatorial courtesy," "holds," and other mechanisms ensure that Congress will have a say in who ends up holding these positions. On the flip side of appointments is the question of removal from office. Some unitary executive proponents contend that the president may remove any officials he chooses from their positions. But, in fact, Congress may establish statutory qualifications for officials, a practice that presidents have generally acquiesced to.

Some unitary executive theorists argue that the independent counsel statute was unconstitutional because it purportedly took away the president's ability to control an investigation into executive branch misconduct. But the Supreme Court disagreed, holding in *Morrison v. Olson*, a 7–1 decision, that the independent counsel did not usurp executive authority. Despite this finding of constitutionality, Congress allowed the independent counsel statute to lapse, returning full control over special counsel investigations to the attorney general. The lone dissenting opinion in that ruling has gained substantial currency among proponents of unitary executive powers.

Unitary executive supporters argue that the Supreme Court's ruling in the *INS v. Chadha* case in 1983 supports their view that legislative vetoes are unconstitutional. But the legislative veto continues to exist even today because both Congress and the president see the usefulness of the mechanism to lawmaking and are reluctant to abandon the device altogether, even though it provides Congress with a means to exert its own influence over executive branch policymaking.

Unitary executive advocates such as Calabresi and Yoo argue that moves by President Reagan and his successors to control agency-level rulemaking constitute broad-reaching examples of the unitary executive theory in action. But the president's Office of Information and Regulatory Affairs does not actually have the capacity to allow him to proactively direct the actions of executive agencies. Agencies can work around White House oversight, and ultimately Congress alone may define and control an agency's activities.

A White House "czar" is viewed by some unitary executive theorists merely as someone assuming an executive branch role via a legitimate exercise of the president's authority to unilaterally name someone to help him oversee a particular policy, spending, or regulatory area. But czars, though unconfirmed by the Senate, may enjoy authority and exercise powers that can exceed the capacities of officials who have actually earned the Senate's approval to serve. Czars owe their allegiance to the president, are not subject to congressional control, and are therefore a threat to our system of checks and balances. There is a constitutional process for determining who is fit for high-level executive branch service that must be followed for that person to be viewed as legitimate by the public.

Executive privilege is the constitutional principle that the president may keep some executive branch communications secret under certain circumstances. It is subject to a test of political wills that often comes down to whether Congress desires the information enough to push the issue with the president. A unitary executive supporter may argue that Congress holds the burden of proof in its struggle with the president for access to the information in question. But Congress is the branch of the federal government entrusted with oversight responsibilities, and it has the mechanisms available (holding hearings, calling witnesses, issuing subpoenas, etc.) to coax the president into providing confidential information to the legislature. One of Congress's main jobs is to facilitate enough information to allow the public to hold its elected officials accountable for their actions. As such, the burden is properly on the president to show a compelling need to keep information from the legislature.

FOREIGN AFFAIRS POWERS

Regarding foreign affairs, we see some of the starkest examples of the unitary executive theory in action after 9/11 as some unitary executive supporters expanded their goal from just exercising control over domestic affairs to include overseas matters as well. George W. Bush administration official John Yoo argued that, in the context of an uncertain and dangerous new time, the president needed to have extraordinary flexibility that could be delivered by a broad understanding of Article II's Commander-in-Chief Clause. Yoo's efforts to elevate the role of the Commander-in-Chief Clause occurred even as he de-emphasized Article I's Declare War Clause. But Yoo's views are antithetical to what the Constitution actually contains, what its authors wrote about it, and what scholars have debated in the decades following. The Commander-in-Chief Clause was originally merely a title, not a source of presidential power, and Congress—not the president—was given the constitutional responsibility to declare war. The American system under the Constitution reflected the framers' belief that the legislature, not the executive, would be entrusted with decisions over war and peace.

Some unitary executive supporters have injected confusion into the war powers debate by equating the term "inherent" with the separate concept "implied," a move that complicates efforts to determine the proper boundaries of executive power. "Implied powers" are properly drawn from explicit constitutional language, but "inherent" powers may be unlimited and therefore unconstrained by a system of checks and balances. In the context of emergency powers, we believe presidents should exercise implied powers where appropriate, but not inherent power.

The "sole organ" doctrine from *United States v. Curtiss-Wright* (1936) has been cited by some unitary executive advocates as justification for wide-ranging presidential powers on foreign affairs questions. But the "sole organ" concept was based on a mischaracterization of what former chief justice John Marshall had intended, which was that the president was the means through which Congress's policy preferences would be implemented. He did not argue that the president alone should determine what those policies were, as some unitary executive advocates have done.

President George W. Bush tried to exercise "inherent" powers in the context of the war on terror by, for example, repeatedly trying to unilaterally create military commissions for trying accused terrorists. But in the end, Congress passed the Military Commissions Act and took control itself. The Bush administration also claimed the ability to surveil American citizens without following the FISA law created by Congress, a clear statutory violation. Congress later amended FISA in response to prevailing political concerns.

"Enhanced interrogation" or torture was also pursued by the Bush administration to obtain information from suspected terrorists about potential attacks planned on America. A memo by Assistant Attorney General Jay Bybee argued that a law passed by Congress that banned torture could be ignored by the president, a broad understanding of executive power shared by some unitary executive advocates. A similar technique that the Bush administration claimed in the context of the war on terror is "extraordinary rendition," which had traditionally been just "rendition," a responsibility shared by both the president and Congress via a treaty with another country. Both Bush and Obama claimed the right to ship potential terror suspects overseas for questioning.

State secrets privilege is the ability of the president to prevent the disclosure of sensitive national security–related information in court proceedings. Its advocates identify it as inherent in the executive branch, although the phrase itself does not appear in the Constitution. Presidents Bush, Obama, and Trump have all claimed state secrets privilege in cases related to the war on terror.

We have illustrated through these various examples how dangerous the unitary executive can be. It has thrived not only because presidents have aggressively pursued power upgrades wherever they can do so, but also because other American institutions (Congress, the press, the public) have failed to adequately push back against executive power grabs.

We agree with Ryan Barilleaux and Jewerl Maxwell, who forecast ongoing threats to the system of separated powers and checks and balances established by the framers. More specifically, they articulate "three lessons about unilateralism, Obama's legacy, and the future of the presidency."[6] First, they argue that President Obama's own "aggressive unilateralism" following Bush will mean that Obama's successor will feel free to follow suit; second, they contend that even if Congress responds to executive overreach by limiting the president, over the long haul the consequence will be "a bipartisan presidential project to restore and expand executive power,"; finally, Obama's decision to follow rather than repudiate Bush has made "the unitary executive safe for Democrats."[7] They also warn—and indeed, recent history has shown—that "Donald Trump also indicated he would use unilateralism to circumvent Congress."[8]

Given these trends, we urge a return to first governing principles to push back against the threat of executive tyranny. As we noted in the introduction, the time is ripe for democratic controls, as envisioned by the framers, to guide our government forward and restore the system of checks and balances and separated powers as a means to resist the possibility of a presidency run amok, both now and in the future.

OUR MODEL: HOW GOVERNMENT SHOULD FUNCTION

We believe that a fully functional government must be based on representation. In *Federalist* No. 49, James Madison declared, "The people are the only legitimate fountain of power, and it is from them that the constitutional charter, under which the several branches of government hold their power, is derived."[9] Alexander Hamilton agreed, arguing in *Federalist* No. 9 that republican government is maintained through "the representation of the people in the legislature by deputies of their own election."[10] At the time of the founding, even opponents of the Constitution supported this point. Anti-Federalist author "Brutus" wrote that "in a free republic . . . all laws are derived from the consent of the people."[11] Another Anti-Federalist, Melancton Smith of New York, said that "the scheme of representation had been adopted, by which the people deputed others to represent them."[12] Both sides in the ratification controversy agreed that the people were at the heart of government authority, and that their involvement provided energy, direction, and legitimacy.

Equally important to the concept of republicanism is the notion that Congress was the first branch of the national government for good reasons. "In republican government," Madison declared in *Federalist* No. 51, "the legislative authority necessarily predominates."[13] This belief in legislative primacy is the reason the framers devoted Article I of the Constitution to structuring and empowering Congress, and only then turned to the presidency in Article II. The framers viewed Congress as the primary institution for carrying out the will of the people and established a presidency where nearly all executive power required the legislative branch's consent. "The genius of republican liberty seems to demand on one side, not only that all power should be derived from the people," Madison noted in *Federalist* No. 37, "but that those intrusted with it should be kept in dependence on the people, by a short duration of their appointments; and that even during this short period the trust should be placed not in a few, but a number of hands."[14] Congress, not the president, offers the protection of the many over the few as commanded by Madison's republican liberty. Even Hamilton, who was obviously more committed to executive power than Madison, argued in *Federalist* No. 77 that entrusting power to the many was the best protection against executive influence.[15] Republicanism therefore helps guide the actions of the federal government by ensuring that the legislative branch has a significant say in the process of creating offices, laying out their responsibilities, appointing officers, and finally funding both officers and other employees.

Republican government also provides a link between citizens and their elected representatives. Members of Congress have a constitutional duty to express the people's opinions on various matters. This arrangement provides both protection against unworthy candidates from taking office and indirect public support for the unelected officials within the federal government. As an early nineteenth-century US senator once explained, no branch of government "can exist without the affections of the people," and if any are "placed in such a situation as to be independent of the nation," they "will soon lose that affection which is essential to [their] durable existence."[16] A close link between the elected and the unelected helps to assure citizens that their government is responsive to their wishes. This process of accountability is perhaps the most important goal of a republican form of government.

The framers made the people the ultimate source of government authority to guard against the concentration of power, but their concern with providing safeguards against misguided government actions did not stop there. They also wanted to prevent the government from accumulating too much power. "In framing a government which is to be administered by men over men," Madison memorably declared in *Federalist* No. 51, "the great difficulty lies in this: you must first enable the government to control the governed; and in the next place oblige it to control itself." Madison rejected the idea that mere popular control of government would provide sufficient control. Instead, he argued for separation of powers, checks and balances, and federalism, or what he called "auxiliary precautions," to help guard against the concentration of governmental power.[17] These structural safeguards join republicanism as the core principles of democratic controls.

The framers did not create a one-branch government, nor did they design a government with separate parts containing their own unique powers operating entirely independently of the other branches. Rather, they agreed on a system in which the branches shared powers to provide a check on the ambition of the others. As Madison wrote in *Federalist* No. 51, "The great security against a gradual concentration of the several powers in the same department, consists in giving to those who administer each department the necessary constitutional means and personal motives to resist encroachments of the others. The provision for defence must in this, as in all other cases, be made commensurate to the danger of attack. Ambition must be made to counteract ambition. The interest of the man must be connected with the constitutional rights of the place."[18] The Constitution assumes each branch will defend itself against encroachments by the others to protect its own institutional interests.

Unfortunately, the modern Congress has not done very well in upholding its responsibility to check presidential overreaching of authority. It is quite amazing, actually, to read the many vigorous defenses of unilateral executive powers based on the belief that Congress is unduly constraining presidents from being able to fulfill their governing duties. The evidence of presidential overreaching and congressional acquiescence is simply overwhelming. Scholar Graham Dodds puts it well: "Although presidents and their advisors have been the main force behind the rise of the unitary executive, Congress has been complicit in it."[19]

GOING FORWARD

In 2019, the *New York Times* polled Democratic candidates hoping to challenge President Donald J. Trump in 2020 about their own views of executive power. Asked by the *Times* to read the candidates' answers, Jack Goldsmith viewed their responses skeptically, observing that "institutional prerogative often defeats prior reformist pledges."[20] Put slightly differently, candidates might feel comfortable saying they are for changes while they remain candidates, but the president's view of the world from the Oval Office can quickly change one's mind.

Over many years of studying and writing about the presidency, we too have observed the numerous promises of successful presidential candidates to be respectful of limits on executive authority and then seen them move aggressively to expand their powers once in office. It is a natural tendency of those with authority to seek ways to avoid constraints on exercising power. And that is exactly the point of the constitutional framers, who imbued the system of separated powers with all kinds of limits on executive authority and vested powers in the coordinated branches to constrain presidents. Unitary executive theorists portray a presidency and a system of separated powers very different from the principles of the constitutional founding.

It is one thing to argue, as some have, that modern necessities call for flexible constitutional arrangements that enable strong executive powers, but entirely another to claim that the constitutional framers imbued the executive with strong unilateral powers. Our constitutional system is out of balance today. We are discouraged by the many observers who attribute the current state of affairs uniquely to the actions of President Donald J. Trump. He indeed has overreached in the exercise of his powers and has made indefensible claims of absolute authority derived from Article II of the Constitution. But he is not alone among US presidents in doing so, and he and his key advisers have many precedents, as well as some influential academic writings, from which to draw justification.

At the conclusion of a text such as this one in which we have identified a serious constitutional issue and critiqued a theory of executive powers, it is tempting to propose a set of "solutions." We do not. The very word "solution" implies a kind of permanency in fixing a problem, and regarding the evolution of powers in a constitutional system such as ours, there is no permanent solution. Congress cannot legislate a solution, nor can the courts mandate one. The problems we identify have evolved over a long period of time.

It is unfortunately not possible to reboot the presidency and start over again from an earlier period in US history. Rebalancing constitutional powers certainly can happen piecemeal over time, through the collective works of elected leaders in the legislative and executive branches, as well as the decisions of federal courts. Congress can legislate some controls, and it can act more aggressively than it has in oversight and investigations that address the core of constitutional powers of the presidency. Court decisions can narrow presidential powers somewhat. And it is not inconceivable that future presidents would pull back on exercising unilateral powers, as the impeachments of Clinton and Trump may actually provide an impetus for chief executives to recognize that their actions can potentially risk their reputations and even their presidencies. Critics of the impeachments of these two presidents have made the argument that the "bar" for impeaching a president has been lowered substantially. Perhaps. But if presidents perceive that Congress is no longer reluctant to exercise its impeachment power, they are likely to think more carefully about their actions. We would see this as a positive development.

Therefore, the give-and-take of a system of separated powers in which the coordinate branches take seriously the exercise of their prerogatives can begin to rebalance the constitutional system. Finally, the ideas of academic writers, whose works can provide a foundation of legitimacy for the actions of those in power, play an important role as well in rebalancing the system. The unitary executive theorists are the latest in a long trend of scholarship extolling the virtues of "strong" presidencies imbued with unilateral or unfettered powers. We have offered here a very different view of the scope and limits of executive powers in the Constitution—one in which the president is subject to the democratic controls that assure that one person may not unilaterally command the fate of the nation.

Notes

INTRODUCTION: A FLAWED THEORY WITH
DANGEROUS CONSEQUENCES

1. H. Res. 755, Report No. 116-346, 116th Cong., 1st sess., December 15, 2019, https://www.congress.gov/bill/116th-congress/house-resolution/755/text (accessed May 15, 2020); Michael D. Shear and Peter Baker, "Key Moments: The Day the House Impeached Trump," *New York Times*, December 18, 2019, https://www.nytimes.com/2019/12/18/us/politics/impeachment-vote.html (accessed May 15, 2020).

2. Benjamin Kentish, "Trump Slams 'Archaic' US Constitution That Is 'Really Bad' for the Country," *Independent*, April 30, 2017, https://www.independent.co.uk/news/world/americas/us-politics/donald-trump-us-constitution-archaic-really-bad-fox-news-100-days-trump-popularity-ratings-barack-a7710781.html (accessed May 15, 2020).

3. Katelyn Polantz, "Trump Lawyer: 'We're Asking for Temporary Presidential Immunity,'" CNN Politics, May 12, 2020, https://www.cnn.com/2020/05/12/politics/temporary-presidential-immunity-jay-sekulow-supreme-court/index.html (accessed May 15, 2020).

4. *State of New York, et al. v. United States Department of Justice, et al.*, No. 1:2018cv06471—Document 114 (S.D.N.Y. 2018), https://www.documentcloud.org/documents/5347980-New-York-state-et-al-vs-Department-of-Justice-et.html#document/ (accessed May 15, 2020); Lydia Wheeler, "Federal Judge in New York Rules against Trump in Sanctuary Cities Case," *The Hill*, November 30, 2018, https://thehill.com/regulation/court-battles/419146-judge-sides-with-sanctuary-cities-over-trump (accessed May 15, 2020).

5. Citing *City of Chicago v. Sessions*, 888 F.3d 272 (7th Cir. 2018) in *State of New York, et al. v. United States Department of Justice, et al.*, No. 1:2018cv06471—Document 114 (S.D.N.Y. 2018).

6. Donald J. Trump, "Executive Order: Protecting the Nation from Foreign Terrorist Entry into the United States," Office of the Press Secretary, The White House,

January 27, 2017; "Trump's Executive Order on Immigration, Annotated," National Public Radio, January 31, 2017, https://www.npr.org/2017/01/31/512439121 /trumps-executive-order-on-immigration-annotated (accessed May 15, 2020).

7. Jeremy Diamond and Steve Almasy, "Trump's Immigration Ban Sends Shockwaves," CNN, January 30, 2017, https://www.cnn.com/2017/01/28/politics /donald-trump-executive-order-immigration-reaction/index.html (accessed May 15, 2020).

8. William C. Canby, Richard R. Clifton, and Michelle T. Friedland, US Circuit Court Judges. Order in *State of Washington and State of Minnesota v. Trump* 17-35105 (9th Cir. 2017), 4–5, https://cdn.ca9.uscourts.gov/datastore/opinions/2017 /02/09/17-35105.pdf (accessed May 15, 2020).

9. The Economist Explains, "What Is the Scope of a President's Executive Orders?," *The Economist*, January 31, 2017, https://www.economist.com/the-econ omist-explains/2017/01/31/what-is-the-scope-of-a-presidents-executive-orders (accessed May 15, 2020).

10. James L. Robart, US District Court Judge, Order in *State of Washington and State of Minnesota v. Trump*, No. 2:17-cv-00141 (W.D. Wash. 2017).

11. Amy B. Wang, "Trump Lashes Out at 'So-Called' Judge Who Temporarily Blocked Travel Ban," *Washington Post*, February 4, 2017, https://www.washington post.com/news/the-fix/wp/2017/02/04/trump-lashes-out-at-federal-judge-who -temporarily-blocked-travel-ban/?utm_term=.4ba434fffd11 (accessed May 15, 2020).

12. William C. Canby, Richard R. Clifton, and Michelle T. Friedland, US Circuit Court Judges, Order in *State of Washington and State of Minnesota v. Trump* 17-35105 (9th Cir. 2017).

13. William C. Canby, Richard R. Clifton, and Michelle T. Friedland, US Circuit Court Judges, Order in *State of Washington and State of Minnesota v. Trump* 17-35105 (9th Cir. 2017), 13.

14. William C. Canby, Richard R. Clifton, and Michelle T. Friedland, US Circuit Court Judges, Order in *State of Washington and State of Minnesota v. Trump* 17-35105 (9th Cir. 2017), 14.

15. Ariane De Vogue and Laura Jarrett, "Trump Furious after Court Upholds Block on Travel Ban," CNN, February 10, 2017, https://www.cnn.com/2017/02 /09/politics/travel-ban-9th-circuit-ruling-immigration/index.html (accessed May 15, 2020).

16. Donald J. Trump, "Executive Order: Protecting the Nation from Foreign Terrorist Entry into the United States," Office of the Press Secretary, The White House, March 6, 2017.

17. Derrick K. Watson, US District Court Judge, Order in *State of Hawaii, et al. v. Trump*, No. 17-00050-DKW-KSC (D. Haw. 2017), https://www.govinfo.gov/con tent/pkg/USCOURTS-hid-1_17-cv-00050/pdf/USCOURTS-hid-1_17-cv-00050-6 .pdf (accessed May 15, 2020); Theodore D. Chuang, US District Court Judge, Order in *International Refugee Assistance Project v. Trump*, No. TDC-17-0361 (D.

Md. 2017), https://www.mdd.uscourts.gov/sites/mdd/files/TDC-17-0361-Opin ion-03162017.pdf (accessed May 15, 2020).

18. *Trump v. Hawaii*, No. 17-965, 585 U.S. ___ (2018), https://www.supreme court.gov/opinions/17pdf/17-965_h315.pdf (accessed May 15, 2020).

19. John Yoo, "Executive Power Run Amok," *New York Times*, February 6, 2017, https://www.nytimes.com/2017/02/06/opinion/executive-power-run-amok .html (accessed May 15, 2020).

20. Donald J. Trump, "A New National Security Strategy for a New Era," National Security & Defense, The White House, December 18, 2017, https://www .whitehouse.gov/articles/new-national-security-strategy-new-era/ (accessed May 15, 2020). Full report available at https://www.whitehouse.gov/wp-content/up loads/2017/12/NSS-Final-12-18-2017-0905-2.pdf (accessed May 15, 2020).

21. Donald J. Trump, "What You Need to Know: Section 232 Investigations and Tariffs," Statements & Releases, Economy & Jobs, The White House, March 8, 2018, https://www.whitehouse.gov/briefings-statements/need-know-section-232-investi gations-tariffs/ (accessed May 15, 2020). For a description of Section 232 of the Trade Expansion Act, see Rachel F. Fefer and Vivian C. Jones, "Section 232 of the Trade Expansion Act of 1962," In Focus, Congressional Research Service, May 7, 2020, https://fas.org/sgp/crs/misc/IF10667.pdf (accessed May 15, 2020).

22. Senator Rob Portman (R-OH) initiated one legislative challenge; see "Portman to Introduce Bill Aimed at 'Reforming' Section 232 Statute," World Trade Online, July 12, 2018, https://insidetrade.com/daily-news/portman-introduce-bill -aimed-%E2%80%98reforming%E2%80%99-section-232-statute (accessed May 15, 2020).

23. Quoted in Caitlin Owens, "Chuck Grassley Wants to Limit Trump's Trade Authority," Axios, December 3, 2018, https://www.axios.com/chuck-grassley-trump -tariffs-section-232-national-security-613bb759-acac-4a36-9703-9a2ee1958f28.html (accessed May 15, 2020).

24. *American Institute for International Steel, Inc., et al. v. United States, et al.*, Ct. Int'l Trade, March 25, 2019, https://www.cit.uscourts.gov/sites/cit/files/19-37 .pdf (accessed May 15, 2020). For a summary of the court case, see Adam Behsudi, "Trump Victorious in Court Case against Steel Tariffs," *Politico*, March 25, 2019, https://www.politico.com/story/2019/03/25/trump-steel-tariffs-case-1292005 (accessed May 15, 2020).

25. The Supreme Court case cited is *Algonquin SNG Inc. v. Federal Energy Administration*, 426 U.S. 548 (1976). See *American Institute for International Steel, Inc., et al. v. United States, et al.*, Court No. 18-00152, slip op. at 14, Ct. Int'l Trade, March 25, 2019, https://www.cit.uscourts.gov/sites/cit/files/19-37.pdf (accessed May 15, 2020).

26. See *Trump v. Hawaii*, No. 17-965, 585 U.S. ___ (2018), https://www .supremecourt.gov/opinions/17pdf/17-965_h315.pdf (accessed May 15, 2020).

27. "Donald Trump Threatens to Cancel NAFTA Entirely If Congress Interferes with His Plans," *Edmonton Journal*, September 1, 2018, https://edmonton

journal.com/news/canada/trump-warns-congress-not-to-interfere-with-nafta-ne gotiations/wcm/e725fb85-fb5c-46a4-b084-a371882c3ac6 (accessed May 15, 2020).

28. For an overview of some of the different interpretations of the unitary executive theory, see Graham G. Dodds, *The Unitary Presidency* (New York: Routledge, 2020), 2–5.

29. Steven G. Calabresi and Kevin H. Rhodes, "The Structural Constitution: Unitary Executive, Plural Judiciary," *Harvard Law Review* 105 (1992): 1153–1216.

30. Steven G. Calabresi and Saikrishna B. Prakash, "The President's Power to Execute the Laws," *Yale Law Journal* 104 (1994): 541.

31. Steven G. Calabresi and Christopher S. Yoo, *The Unitary Executive* (New Haven, CT: Yale University Press, 2008), 18–19, 35, 223, 245.

32. Saikrishna B. Prakash, "Fragmented Features of the Constitution's Unitary Executive," *Willamette Law Review* 45 (2009): 701–722.

33. Citing Black's *Law Dictionary* in statement by Louis Fisher presented to the Senate Committee on the Judiciary for hearings on "Restoring the Rule of Law," September 16, 2008, 3, http://www.loc.gov/law/help/usconlaw/pdf/senate%20 judiciary%20sept_16_%202008.pdf (accessed May 15, 2020).

34. Calabresi and Yoo, *The Unitary Executive*, 429.

35. Cass Sunstein, "What the 'Unitary Executive' Debate Is and Is Not About," *The University of Chicago Law School Faculty Blog*, August 6, 2007, http://uchicago law.typepad.com/faculty/2007/08/what-the-unitar.html (accessed May 15, 2020).

36. Ilya Somin, "Distinguishing the Scope of Executive Power from Its Distribution," *The Volokh Conspiracy Blog*, August 13, 2007, http://volokh.com/posts/11871 18574.shtml (accessed May 15, 2020).

37. US Congress, Senate Judiciary Committee, *Confirmation Hearing on the Nomination of Samuel A. Alito, Jr. to Be an Associate Justice of the Supreme Court of the United States,* 109th Cong., 2nd sess., January 9–13, 2006, 483.

38. Andrew Rudalevige, *The New Imperial Presidency* (Ann Arbor: University of Michigan Press, 2006), 261.

39. Two of us (Mitchel A. Sollenberger and Mark J. Rozell) advanced the term "democratic controls" in *The President's Czars: Undermining Congress and the Constitution* (Lawrence: University Press of Kansas, 2012), chap. 1.

CHAPTER 1. PRESIDENTIAL POWER AND THE UNITARY EXECUTIVE THEORY

1. Donald Anderson, *William Howard Taft: A Conservative's Conception of the Presidency* (Ithaca: Cornell University Press, 1973), vii.

2. Louis Koenig, *The Chief Executive*, 5th ed. (New York: Harcourt Brace Jovanovich, 1986), 18–19.

3. William Howard Taft, *The President and His Powers* (New York: Columbia University Press, 1967), 139–140. The "Neagle case" refers to the 1890 Supreme Court case of *In re Neagle* (135 U.S. 1) where the Court held that the appointment of

US marshals to guard a Supreme Court justice was an implied power reasonably inferred from the Take Care Clause of the Constitution.

4. Jeffrey Crouch and Mark J. Rozell, "Lincoln and Executive Power: Rebutting the Dictatorship Thesis," in *Lincoln's American Dream: Clashing Political Perspectives*, ed. Kenneth L. Deutsch and Joseph R. Fornieri (Dulles, VA: Potomac Books, 2005), 306–307.

5. Clinton L. Rossiter, *Constitutional Dictatorship: Crisis Government in the Modern Democracies* (New Brunswick, NJ: Transaction Publishers, 2005), 225–227.

6. Brief for the United States and Captors in *The Prize Cases*, *Landmark Briefs and Arguments of the Supreme Court of the United States*, ed. Philip B. Kurland and Gerhard Casper (Washington, DC: University Publications of America, 1978), 3:590.

7. John P. Roche, "Executive Power and Domestic Emergency: The Quest for Prerogative," *Western Political Quarterly* 5, no. 4 (1952): 598.

8. Roche, 598–599.

9. Richard Pious, *The American Presidency* (New York: Basic Books, 1979), 58.

10. *The Prize Cases*, 67 U.S. 635 (1863).

11. James G. Randall, *Constitutional Problems under Lincoln*, rev. ed. (Urbana: University of Illinois Press, 1951), 56.

12. Randall, 57.

13. Roche, "Executive Power and Domestic Emergency," 600.

14. Theodore Roosevelt, *Theodore Roosevelt: An Autobiography* (New York: Macmillan, 1913), 389.

15. Roosevelt, 306.

16. Theodore Roosevelt, Letter to John St. Loe Strachey, February 12, 1906, in *The Letters of Theodore Roosevelt*, ed. Elting E. Morison (Cambridge, MA: Harvard University Press, 1952), 5:151.

17. Steven G. Calabresi and Christopher S. Yoo, *The Unitary Executive: Presidential Power from Washington to Bush* (New Haven, CT: Yale University Press, 2008), 4.

18. Gary L. Gregg II, "Whiggism and Presidentialism: American Ambivalence toward Executive Power," in *The Presidency Then and Now*, ed. Phillip G. Henderson (Lanham, MD: Rowman & Littlefield, 2000), 81.

19. Woodrow Wilson, *Constitutional Government in the United States* (New York: Columbia University Press, 1917), 70.

20. Gregg, "Whiggism and Presidentialism," 83–84.

21. William E. Leuchtenburg, *The FDR Years: On Roosevelt and His Legacy* (New York: Columbia University Press, 1995), 30.

22. Edward S. Corwin, *The President: Office and Powers, 1787–1957*, 4th ed. (New York: New York University Press, 1957), 252.

23. Richard E. Neustadt, *Presidential Power: The Politics of Leadership* (New York: Wiley, 1960), 10.

24. Arthur M. Schlesinger Jr., *The Imperial Presidency* (Boston: Houghton Mifflin, 1973), x.

25. See, generally, Morton Rosenberg, "Congress's Prerogative over Agencies

and Agency Decisionmakers: The Rise and Demise of the Reagan Administration's Theory of the Unitary Executive," *George Washington Law Review* 57 (January 1989): 627–703.

26. Christopher S. Kelley, "To Be (Unitarian) or Not to Be (Unitarian): Presidential Power in the George W. Bush Administration," *White House Studies* 10, no. 2 (2010): 108; Christopher S. Kelley, "The Unitary Executive and the Presidential Signing Statement" (PhD diss., Miami University, 2003), 23; Andrew Rudalevige, *The New Imperial Presidency: Renewing Presidential Power after Watergate* (Ann Arbor: University of Michigan Press, 2006).

27. We acknowledge the important scholarship by Ryan Barilleaux and David Zellers, who contend that the Ford and Carter presidencies developed important practices and precedents that made the Reagan administration's advancement of the unitary executive theory much easier. See Barilleaux and Zellers, "Executive Unilateralism in the Ford and Carter Presidencies," in *The Unitary Executive and the Modern Presidency*, ed. Ryan J. Barilleaux and Christopher S. Kelley (College Station: Texas A&M University Press, 2010), 41–76.

28. Christopher S. Kelley, "Who's at Fault Here? The Bush Administration, Presidential Power, and the Signing Statement," in *Presidential Power in America: The Constitution, the Defense of a Nation, and the National Ethos*, ed. Kurt Olson, Jeffrey Demers, and Lawrence R. Velvel (Andover, MA: Doukathsan Press, 2007), 307–308.

29. Charlie Savage, *Takeover: The Return of the Imperial Presidency and the Subversion of American Democracy* (New York: Little, Brown, 2008), 48.

30. President Reagan established the Office of Information and Regulatory Affairs through Executive Order 12291. See, generally, Rosenberg, "Congress's Prerogative over Agencies and Agency Decisionmakers," 627.

31. L. Gordon Crovitz and Jeremy A. Rabkin, eds., *The Fettered Presidency: Legal Constraints on the Executive Branch* (Washington, DC: American Enterprise Institute, 1989), 1.

32. Crovitz and Rabkin, ix.

33. Gordon S. Jones and John A. Marini, eds., *The Imperial Congress: Crisis in the Separation of Powers* (Washington, DC: Heritage Foundation, 1988), 1.

34. Christopher S. Kelley and Bryan W. Marshall, "Like Father, Like Son? The Presidents' Bush and the Presidential Signing Statement," *White House Studies* 7, no. 1 (2007): 144.

35. Mark Tushnet, "A Political Perspective on the Theory of the Unitary Executive," *Harvard Law School Public Law and Legal Theory Working Paper Series*, Paper No. 09-23 (2009): 2.

36. Calabresi and Yoo, *The Unitary Executive*, 4.

37. Tushnet, "A Political Perspective on the Theory of the Unitary Executive," 7.

38. Louis Fisher, "Invoking Inherent Powers: A Primer," *Presidential Studies Quarterly* 37 (March 2007): 1.

39. John Yoo, "The President's Constitutional Authority to Conduct Military Operations against Terrorists and Nations Supporting Them," September 25, 2001, Office of Legal Counsel memorandum, https://www.thetorturedatabase .org/document/olc-memo-president%E2%80%99s-constitutional-authority-con duct-military-operations-against-terrorist?pdf_page=1 (accessed May 18, 2020).

40. Calabresi quoted in John P. MacKenzie, *Absolute Power: How the Unitary Executive Theory Is Undermining the Constitution* (New York: Century Foundation Press, 2008), 34.

41. Calabresi and Yoo, *The Unitary Executive*, 430.

42. Stephen Skowronek, "The Conservative Insurgency and Presidential Power: A Developmental Perspective on the Unitary Executive," *Harvard Law Review* 122, no. 8 (2009): 2076.

43. Ryan J. Barilleaux and Christopher S. Kelley, "Introduction: What Is the Unitary Executive?," in *The Unitary Executive and the Modern Presidency*, ed. Ryan J. Barilleaux and Christopher S. Kelley (College Station: Texas A&M University Press, 2010), 3–4.

44. For the most prominent example of this type of scholarship, see Calabresi and Yoo, *The Unitary Executive*.

45. Calabresi and Yoo, 55.

46. Pacificus, Letter I, June 29, 1793, https://founders.archives.gov/docu ments/Hamilton/01-15-02-0038 (accessed April 21, 2020).

47. Calabresi and Yoo, *The Unitary Executive*, 55.

48. James P. Pfiffner, *Power Play: The Bush Presidency and the Constitution* (Washington, DC: Brookings Institution Press, 2009), 79.

49. *Morrison v. Olson*, 487 U.S. 654, 705 (1988) (emphasis in original).

50. Edward S. Corwin, "The Steel Seizure Case: A Judicial Brick without Straw," *Columbia Law Review* 53, no. 1 (January 1953): 53.

51. Steven G. Calabresi, "The Vesting Clauses as Power Grants," *Northwestern University Law Review* 88 (1994): 1392–1393.

52. Saikrishna Bangalore Prakash, *Imperial from the Beginning: The Constitution of the Original Executive* (New Haven, CT: Yale University Press, 2015), 83.

53. Barilleaux and Kelley, "Introduction: What Is the Unitary Executive?," 3.

54. Skowronek, "The Conservative Insurgency and Presidential Power," 2076; Kelley, "Who's at Fault Here?," 312–313.

55. Charles Fried, *Order and Law: Arguing the Reagan Revolution* (New York: Simon & Schuster, 1991), 170–171.

56. Steven G. Calabresi, "Some Normative Arguments for the Unitary Executive," *Arkansas Law Review* 48 (1995): 38.

57. Niels Bjerre-Poulsen, "The Bush Administration and the Theory of 'The Unitary Executive,'" in *Projections of Power in the Americas*, ed. Niels Bjerre-Poulsen, Helene Balslev Clausen, and Jan Gustafsson (New York: Routledge, 2012), 17.

58. MacKenzie, *Absolute Power*, 7.

59. MacKenzie, 7.

60. Cass R. Sunstein, "The Myth of the Unitary Executive," *American University Administrative Law Journal* 7 (Summer 1993): 305.

CHAPTER 2. DOMESTIC POWERS: PART I

1. Steven G. Calabresi and Christopher S. Yoo, *The Unitary Executive: Presidential Power from Washington to Bush* (New Haven, CT: Yale University Press, 2008), 3.

2. Calabresi and Yoo, 4.

3. Donald R. Brand, "Progressivism, the Brownlow Commission, and the Rise of the Administrative State," in *Modern America and the Legacy of the Founding*, ed. Ronald J. Pestritto and Thomas G. West (Lanham, MD: Lexington Books, 2006), 160.

4. Leonard D. White, *The Federalists: A Study in Administrative History* (New York: Macmillan, 1964), 434.

5. White, 425.

6. 1 Annals of Congress 604 (June 22, 1789).

7. 17 U.S. 316 (1819).

8. 1 Ops. Att'y Gen. 624, 625 (1823).

9. 272 U.S. 52, 129 (1926).

10. This aspect of presidential control is covered more fully in the removal power section.

11. *Marbury v. Madison*, 5 U.S. 137, 158 (1803).

12. *Marbury v. Madison*, 165–166.

13. *Marbury v. Madison*, 166.

14. *Kendall v. United States*, 37 U.S. 524, 610 (1838).

15. *Kendall v. United States*, 610.

16. *Kendall v. United States*, 612–613.

17. *Kendall v. United States*, 613.

18. 6 Ops. Att'y Gen. 326, 341 (1854).

19. 25 Ops. Att'y Gen. 320, 322 (1905).

20. William Howard Taft, *The President and His Powers* (New York: Columbia University Press, 1967), 125.

21. Robert E. Cushman, *The Independent Regulatory Commissions* (New York: Oxford University Press, 1941), 453.

22. 1 Stat. 65 (September 2, 1789).

23. Alexander Hamilton, "Explanation," November 11, 1795, in *The Works of Alexander Hamilton*, ed. Henry Cabot Lodge (New York: Haskell House, 1904), 8:150.

24. 1 Annals of Congress 636 (June 29, 1789).

25. 1 Ops. Att'y Gen. 678, 679 (1824). See also, 1 Ops. Att'y Gen. 624 (1823); 1 Ops. Att'y Gen. 636 (1824); 1 Ops. Att'y Gen. 705 (1825); 1 Ops. Att'y Gen. 706 (1825).

26. 1 Ops. Att'y Gen. 624, 625 (1823).

27. 4 Ops. Att'y Gen. 515, 516 (1846).

28. Leonard D. White, *The Jacksonians: 1829–1861* (New York: Macmillan, 1954), 84.

29. Jerry L. Mashaw, "Governmental Practice and Presidential Direction: Lessons from the Antebellum Republic?," *Willamette Law Review* 45 (2009): 695.

30. Leonard D. White, *The Republican Era: 1869–1901* (New York: Macmillan, 1958), 47.

31. See, generally, Jerry L. Mashaw, *Creating the Administrative Constitution: The Lost 100 Years of American Administrative Law* (New Haven, CT: Yale University Press, 2012).

32. William F. Willoughby, *Principles of Public Administration* (Baltimore, MD: Johns Hopkins University Press, 1927), 11.

33. *The President's Committee on Administrative Management* (Washington, DC: GPO, 1937), 5 [hereinafter Brownlow Committee Report].

34. Brownlow Committee Report, 43.

35. *Commission on Organization of the Executive Branch of the Government* (Washington, DC: GPO, 1949), 8 [hereinafter Hoover Commission Report].

36. "Report of the President's Task Force on Government Reorganization," November 6, 1964, container 1, Task Force Reports (Lyndon Baines Johnson Library), 7.

37. White, *The Federalists*, 454–455.

38. See, generally, White, *The Jacksonians*, 534–540.

39. White, 538.

40. Department of Commerce and Labor, *Organization and Law of the Department of Commerce and Labor* (Washington, DC: Government Printing Office, 1904), 519.

41. Hoover Commission Report, 23.

42. Richard E. Neustadt, *Presidential Power: The Politics of Leadership* (New York: Wiley, 1960), 39.

43. Richard Nixon, "Proposals for the Reorganization of the Executive Branch of the Government," March 25, 1971, House of Representatives, 92nd Cong., 1st sess., Document No. 92-75, p. 3.

44. Harold Seidman and Robert Gilmour, *Politics, Position, and Power: From the Positive to the Regulatory State*, 4th ed. (New York: Oxford University Press, 1986), 169.

45. Andrew Rudalevige, *Managing the President's Program* (Princeton, NJ: Princeton University Press, 2002), 21.

46. Herbert Kaufman, *The Administrative Behavior of Federal Bureau Chiefs* (Washington, DC: Brookings, 1981), 182.

47. For a useful example of the committee-bureau level interactions, see Louis Fisher, "Congress and the President in the Administrative Process: The Uneasy Alliance," in *The Illusion of Presidential Government*, ed. Hugh Heclo and Lester M. Salamon (Boulder, CO: Westview Press, 1981), 25–26.

48. Louis Fisher, *The Constitution between Friends: Congress, the President, and the Law* (New York: St. Martin's Press, 1978), 247.

49. Loren A. Smith, "Administration: An Idea Whose Time May Have Passed," in *The Fettered Presidency: Legal Constraints on the Executive Branch*, ed. L. Gordon Crovitz and Jeremy A. Rabkin (Washington, DC: American Enterprise Institute, 1989), 165.

50. Kaufman, *Administrative Behavior*, 167.

51. Kaufman, 168.

52. Francis E. Rourke, "Whose Bureaucracy Is This, Anyway? Congress, the President, and Public Administration," *PS: Political Science and Politics* 26 (1993): 690.

53. Thomas H. Hammond and Jack H. Knott, "Who Controls the Bureaucracy? Presidential Power, Congressional Dominance, Legal Constraints, and Bureaucratic Autonomy in a Model of Multi-Institutional Policy-Making," *Journal of Law, Economics, and Organization* 12 (April 1996): 163.

54. Chris Edelson, *Power without Constraint: The Post-9/11 Presidency and National Security*, 6th ed. (Madison: University of Wisconsin Press, 2016), 14.

55. 44 USC 1505 (2016).

56. Louis Fisher, *Constitutional Conflicts between Congress and the President* (Lawrence: University Press of Kansas, 2014), 119.

57. 66 FR 49079 (September 25, 2001).

58. 74 FR 4897 (January 22, 2009).

59. 82 FR 20429 (April 26, 2017).

60. Harold J. Krent, *Presidential Powers* (New York: New York University Press, 2005), 51.

61. Fisher, *Constitutional Conflicts*, 123. See also Krent, *Presidential Powers*, 52.

62. Adam L. Warber, *Executive Orders and the Modern Presidency* (Boulder, CO: Lynne Rienner, 2006), 129; Fisher, *Constitutional Conflicts*, 123.

63. *Youngstown Sheet & Tube Co. v. Sawyer*, 343 U.S. 579 (1952).

64. William G. Howell, *Power without Persuasion: The Politics of Direct Presidential Action* (Princeton, NJ: Princeton University Press, 2003), 153.

65. Howell, 155.

66. *United States v. Midwest Oil Company*, 236 U.S. 459 (1915).

67. *United States v. Midwest Oil Company*, 471.

68. *United States v. Midwest Oil Company*, 481.

69. 36 Stat. 847. The Midwest Oil case dealt with an executive order issued by President William Howard Taft on September 27, 1909. The Supreme Court explicitly acknowledged that the Pickett Act did not retroactively impact the president's order.

70. William A. Wilcox Jr., *The Modern Military and the Environment: The Laws of Peace and War* (Lanham, MD: Rowman & Littlefield, 2007), 61–62.

71. 74 FR 4897 (January 22, 2009).

72. Louis Fisher, "Don't Act Unilaterally to Close Guantanamo," *National Law Journal*, December 7, 2015.

73. Charlie Savage, "Guantanamo Is Leaving Obama with Choices, Neither of Them Simple," *New York Times*, October 31, 2015.

74. Missy Ryan and Julie Tate, "With Final Detainee Transfer, Obama's Guantanamo Policy Takes Its Last Breath," *Washington Post*, December 28, 2016, https://www.washingtonpost.com/world/national-security/with-final-detainee-transfer-obamas-guantanamo-policy-takes-its-last-breath/2016/12/28/dfdf8cb2-cd0f-11e6-a747-d03044780a02_story.html?utm_term=.d2cb89ce8ff5 (accessed April 29, 2020).

75. Harold Koh, "After the NDAA Veto: Now What?," *Just Security*, October 23, 2015, https://www.justsecurity.org/27028/ndaa-veto-what/ (accessed April 29, 2020).

76. Deborah Pearlstein, "Constitutionality of Congressional Restrictions on Guantanamo Prisoner Transfers," *Opinio Juris*, October 27, 2015, http://opiniojuris.org/2015/10/27/constitutionality-of-congressional-restrictions-on-guantanamo-prisoner-transfers/ (accessed April 29, 2020); see also Savage, "Guantanamo Is Leaving Obama with Choices."

77. Chris Edelson and Robert J. Spitzer, "Obama's Guantanamo Paradox," *US News*, November 30, 2015, https://www.usnews.com/opinion/blogs/world-report/2015/11/30/obama-should-not-try-to-close-guantanamo-bay-with-an-executive-order?int=a39d09&int=a55a09 (accessed April 29, 2020).

78. Joshua B. Kennedy, "'Do This! Do That!' and Nothing Will Happen: Executive Orders and Bureaucratic Responsiveness," *American Politics Research* 43 (January 2014): 59–82.

79. See, generally, Howell, *Power without Persuasion*.

80. Kennedy, "'Do This! Do That!' and Nothing Will Happen," 76.

81. Gregory Korte, "Trump's Executive Actions Come Faster and in Different Forms Than Before," *USA Today*, January 30, 2017, https://www.usatoday.com/story/news/politics/2017/01/30/trumps-executive-actions-come-faster-and-different-forms-than-before/97255592/ (accessed April 29, 2020).

82. Howell quoted in Korte, "Trump's Executive Actions Come Faster."

83. John Woolley and Gerhard Peters, "Minimizing the Economic Burden the Patient Protection and Affordable Care Act Pending Repeal," The American Presidency Project, UC Santa Barbara, https://www.presidency.ucsb.edu/documents/executive-order-13765-minimizing-the-economic-burden-the-patient-protection-and-affordable (accessed April 29, 2020).

84. John Woolley and Gerhard Peters, "Border Security and Immigration Enforcement Improvements," The American Presidency Project, UC Santa Barbara, https://www.presidency.ucsb.edu/documents/executive-order-13767-border-security-and-immigration-enforcement-improvements (accessed April 29, 2020).

85. John Woolley and Gerhard Peters, "Protecting the Nation from Foreign

Terrorist Entry Into the United States," The American Presidency Project, UC Santa Barbara, https://www.presidency.ucsb.edu/documents/executive-order -13769-protecting-the-nation-from-foreign-terrorist-entry-into-the-united (accessed April 29, 2020).

86. Grace Panetta and Michelle Mark, "How 11 of Trump's Most Controversial Actions Have Fared in Court," *Business Insider,* April 15, 2019, https://www.busi nessinsider.sg/trump-administration-court-cases-policy-outcomes-2019-4 (accessed April 29, 2020).

87. Richard W. Waterman, "The Administrative Presidency, Unilateral Power, and the Unitary Executive Theory," *Presidential Studies Quarterly* 39 (March 2009): 6.

88. Christopher S. Kelley, "The Unitary Executive and the Presidential Signing Statement" (PhD diss., Miami University, 2003), 45–50.

89. Calabresi and Yoo, *The Unitary Executive,* 86, 104.

90. Neil Kinkopf cited by American Bar Association Report on the Task Force on Presidential Signing Statements and the Separation of Powers Doctrine (2006), https://www.americanbar.org/content/dam/aba/publishing/abanews /1273179616signstatereport.authcheckdam.pdf (accessed April 29, 2020); Philip J. Cooper, "George W. Bush, Edgar Allan Poe, and the Use and Abuse of Presidential Signing Statements," *Presidential Studies Quarterly* 35 (September 2005): 517.

91. Rebecca H. Byrum and Cheryl Truesdell, "The Unitary Executive and Presidential Signing Statements," *Documents to the People* 36 (Fall 2008): 29–30.

92. Kelley, "The Unitary Executive," 102.

93. Cooper, "George W. Bush, Edgar Allan Poe," 520.

94. American Bar Association Report on the Task Force on Presidential Signing Statements and the Separation of Powers Doctrine (2006), https://www.ameri canbar.org/content/dam/aba/publishing/abanews/1273179616signstatereport .authcheckdam.pdf (accessed April 29, 2020).

95. According to Joyce Green's Presidential Signing Statements: 2001–Present Blog, coherentbabble.com, in his two terms as president, Bush "issued 161 signing statements affecting over 1,100 provisions of federal law"; http://www.coherent babble.com/faqs.htm (accessed April 29, 2020).

96. Gene Healy, *The Cult of the Presidency: America's Dangerous Devotion to Executive Power* (Washington, DC: Cato Institute, 2008).

97. Ian Ostrander and Joel Sievert, "What's So Sinister about Presidential Signing Statements?," *Presidential Studies Quarterly* 43 (March 2013): 58–80.

98. Ostrander and Sievert, 60.

99. Christopher S. Kelley, "Rhetoric and Reality? Unilateralism and the Obama Administration," *Social Science Quarterly* 93 (December 2012): 1156–1157.

100. George Washington, *The Writings of George Washington,* ed. Worthington Chauncey Ford (New York: G. P. Putnam's Sons, 1891), 12:327.

101. Charlie Savage, "Obama Takes New Route to Opposing Parts of Laws," *New York Times,* January 8, 2010, https://www.nytimes.com/2010/01/09/us/pol

itics/09signing.html?mtrref=www.google.com&gwh=7385EEAC8568E979078DC 8D8552CDA58&gwt=pay&assetType=REGIWALL (accessed April 29, 2020).

102. Louis Fisher, "Signing Statements: Constitutional and Practical Limits," *William and Mary Bill of Rights Journal* 16 (October 2007): 210.

103. Fisher, 210.

104. Kelley, "Rhetoric and Reality?," 1155.

105. Robert J. Spitzer, "Comparing the Constitutional Presidencies of George W. Bush and Barack Obama: War Powers, Signing Statements, Vetoes." *White House Studies* 12 (October 2013): 135.

106. Mitchel A. Sollenberger and Mark J. Rozell, "Prerogative Power and Executive Branch Czars: President Obama's Signing Statement," *Presidential Studies Quarterly* 41 (December 2011): 819.

107. See Joyce Green's coherentbabble.com, http://www.coherentbabble.com /faqs.htm (accessed April 29, 2020). Trump's predecessor, Barack Obama, "issued 37 signing statements affecting 114 specified provisions and making eight mentions of unspecified provisions of law in 37 Congressional enactments. Obama issued 13 rhetorical signing statements, 23 constitutional signing statements, and one statement remarking on an 'inadvertent technical drafting error' in the affected bill."

108. Donald J. Trump, "Statement by President Donald J. Trump on the Signing of H.R. 3364," https://www.whitehouse.gov/the-press-office/2017/08/02 /statement-president-donald-j-trump-signing-hr-3364 (August 2, 2017) (accessed April 29, 2020).

109. See Charlie Savage, "Trump's Signing Statement on the Russia Sanctions Bill, Explained," *New York Times*, August 2, 2017, https://www.nytimes.com /2017/08/02/us/politics/trump-signing-statement-russia-sanctions.html (accessed April 29, 2020).

110. See Jeffrey Crouch, *The Presidential Pardon Power* (Lawrence: University Press of Kansas, 2009), chap. 2.

111. Crouch, 25–26.

112. Crouch, 18–19, 29–31, 55–56.

113. Crouch, 107–117.

114. Crouch, 101–107, 117–126.

115. See Jeffrey Crouch, "President Donald J. Trump and the Clemency Power: Is Claiming 'Unfair' Treatment for Pardon Recipients the New 'Fake News'?," in *Presidential Leadership and the Trump Presidency: Executive Power and Democratic Government*, ed. Charles M. Lamb and Jacob R. Neiheisel (New York: Palgrave Macmillan, 2019).

116. Crouch.

117. Donald J. Trump, Twitter, July 22, 2017, https://twitter.com/realdon aldtrump/status/888724194820857857?lang=en (accessed April 29, 2020); Donald J. Trump, Twitter, June 4, 2018, https://twitter.com/realDonaldTrump/status

/1003616210922147841?ref_src=twsrc%5Etfw%7Ctwcamp%5Etweetembed%
7Ctwterm%5E1003616210922147841&ref_url=https%3A%2F%2Fwww.cnn.com%
2F2018%2F06%2F04%2Fpolitics%2Fdonald-trump-pardon-tweet%2Findex.html.
(accessed April 29, 2020).

CHAPTER 3. DOMESTIC POWERS: PART II

1. Saikrishna Prakash, "Regulating Presidential Powers," *Cornell Law Review* 91 (November 2005): 238; John C. Eastman, "The Limited Nature of the Senate's Advice and Consent Role," *U.C. Davis Law Review* 36 (February 2003): 657; John C. Yoo, "The New Sovereignty and the Old Constitution: The Chemical Weapons Convention and the Appointments Clause," *Constitutional Commentary* 15 (Spring 1998): 109; Felix A. Nigro, "Senate Confirmation," *Georgetown Law Journal* 42 (January 1954): 260; William D. Mitchell, "Appointment of Federal Judges," *ABA Journal* 17 (September 1931): 569.

2. US Constitution, Art. II, Sec. 2.

3. *Federalist* No. 66, in *The Federalist Papers*, ed. Clinton Rossiter (New York: Mentor, 1999), 373 (emphasis in original).

4. Mitchel A. Sollenberger, *The President Shall Nominate: How Congress Trumps Executive Power* (Lawrence: University Press of Kansas, 2008).

5. Mitchel A. Sollenberger, "Georgia's Influence on the U.S. Senate: A Reassessment of the Rejection of Benjamin Fishbourn and the Origin of Senatorial Courtesy," *Georgia Historical Quarterly* 93 (Summer 2009): 183.

6. G. Calvin Mackenzie, *The Politics of Presidential Appointments* (New York: Free Press, 1981), xix.

7. Mike Allen, "Bush Again Bypasses Senate to Seat Judge," *Washington Post*, February 21, 2004, https://www.washingtonpost.com/archive/politics/2004/02/21 /bush-again-bypasses-senate-to-seat-judge/de6c73ef-77a9-4d66-812d-48c dff4bdc11/ (accessed April 29, 2020).

8. Louis Fisher, *Constitutional Conflicts between Congress and the President*, 5th ed., rev. (Lawrence: University Press of Kansas, 2007), 45.

9. Paul Kane, "Senate Stays in Session to Block Recess Appointments," *Washington Post*, November 17, 2007, A4; Editorial, "Recess Abuse," *Washington Post*, April 6, 2007.

10. Peter Baker, "During Recess, Democrats Push Back," *Washington Post*, December 24, 2007.

11. Office of Legal Counsel, "Lawfulness of Recess Appointments during a Recess of the Senate Notwithstanding Periodic Pro Forma Sessions," January 6, 2012, http://www.justice.gov/sites/default/files/olc/opinions/2012/01/31 /pro-forma-sessions-opinion.pdf (accessed April 29, 2020); https://obamawhite house.archives.gov/the-press-office/2012/01/04/president-obama-announc es-recess-appointments-key-administration-posts (accessed September 16, 2020).

12. *National Labor Relations Board v. Noel Canning*, slip opinion, No. 12-1281,

6 (June 26, 2014), https://www.supremecourt.gov/opinions/13pdf/12-1281_mc
8p.pdf (accessed April 29, 2020).

13. *National Labor Relations Board v. Noel Canning*, 20.

14. *National Labor Relations Board v. Noel Canning*, 34–36.

15. 12 Stat. 646 (1863).

16. 54 Stat. 751 (1940); 5 U.S.C. § 5503 (2006).

17. 5 U.S.C. § 5503(a) (1–3) (2006).

18. 5 U.S.C. § 5503(b) (2006).

19. Mitchel A. Sollenberger, "The Blue Slip: A Theory of Unified and Divided
Government, 1979–2009," *Congress and the Presidency* 37 (May–August 2010): 125–
156; Mitchel A. Sollenberger, "The History of the Blue Slip in the Senate Committee on the Judiciary, 1917–Present," *CRS Report*, October 22, 2003, https://fas
.org/sgp/crs/misc/RL32013.pdf (accessed April 29, 2020).

20. Paul Kane, "Reid, Democrats Trigger 'Nuclear' Option, Eliminate Most
Filibusters on Nominees," *Washington Post*, November 22, 2013.

21. Michael Catalini, "How Long until Senate Leadership Resorts to the Nuclear
Option?," *National Journal*, November 7, 2013, http://www.nationaljournal .com/mag
azine/how-long-until-senate-leadership-resorts-to-the-nuclear-option-20131107
(accessed April 29, 2020).

22. Kane, "Reid, Democrats Trigger 'Nuclear' Option."

23. Donald J. Trump, "The U.S. Senate should switch to 51 votes . . . ," Twitter,
May 30, 2017, 9:59 a.m., https://twitter.com/realdonaldtrump/status/8695538
53750013953?lang=en (accessed April 29, 2020).

24. Emily Knapp, Brent Griffiths, and Jon McClure, "Kavanaugh Confirmed:
Here's How Senators Voted," *Politico*, October 6, 2018, https://www.politico.com
/interactives/2018/brett-kavanaugh-senate-confirmation-vote-count/ (accessed
April 29, 2020).

25. See Matt Flegenheimer, "Senate Republicans Deploy 'Nuclear Option' to
Clear Path for Gorsuch," *New York Times*, April 7, 2017, https://www.nytimes.com
/2017/04/06/us/politics/neil-gorsuch-supreme-court-senate.html (accessed
April 29, 2020).

26. Niels Lesniewski, "How the Nuclear Option Changed the Judiciary," *Roll
Call Blog*, December 19, 2014, https://www.rollcall.com/2014/12/19/how-the-nu
clear-option-changed-the-judiciary/ (accessed April 29, 2020).

27. Erin Kelly, "'Nuclear Option' Could Blow Up Senate Far beyond Gorsuch Vote," *USA Today*, April 5, 2017, https://www.usatoday.com/story/news
/politics/2017/04/05/nuclear-option-could-blow-up-senate-far-beyond-gorsuch
-vote/100038856/ (accessed April 29, 2020).

28. See Clare Foran, "The 'Nuclear Option' Won't Dramatically Change the
Senate," *The Atlantic*, April 4, 2017, https://www.theatlantic.com/politics/archive
/2017/04/nuclear-option-senate-mcconnell-gorsuch-trump/521760/ (accessed
April 29, 2020).

29. Charles Krauthammer, "Abolish the Filibuster," *National Review*, February

20, 2015, https://www.nationalreview.com/2015/02/abolish-filibuster-charles-krauthammer/ (accessed April 29, 2020).

30. Mike Lee, "Lee Welcomes Simple-Majority Threshold for Obamacare Repeal," press release, July 24, 2015, https://www.lee.senate.gov/public/index.cfm/2015/7/lee-welcomes-simple-majority-threshold-for-obamacare-repeal (accessed April 29, 2020).

31. Robert C. Byrd, "The Filibuster and Its Consequences," Statement before the Senate Rules and Administration Committee, May 19, 2010, https://www.byrdcenter.org/byrd-center-blog/senator-byrd-the-nuclear-option-and-the-fate-of-the-senate (accessed April 29, 2020).

32. Steven G. Calabresi and Christopher S. Yoo, *The Unitary Executive: Presidential Power from Washington to Bush* (New Haven, CT: Yale University Press, 2008), 4.

33. Calabresi and Yoo, 248.

34. 19 Stat. 80, 81 (July 12, 1876).

35. Calabresi and Yoo, *The Unitary Executive*, 248, citing Taft in *Myers v. United States*, 272 U.S. 52, 117 (1926).

36. *Myers v. United States*, 161.

37. *Myers v. United States*, 135.

38. See chapter 1 for a discussion and analysis of the comptroller of the Treasury under President George Washington.

39. *Humphrey's Executor v. United States*, 295 U.S. 602, 626 (1935).

40. *Humphrey's Executor v. United States*, 627.

41. *Humphrey's Executor v. United States*, 629.

42. Saikrishna Prakash, "Regulating Presidential Powers," *Cornell Law Review* 91 (November 2005): 238.

43. *Myers v. United States*, 129 (1926).

44. Edward S. Corwin, *The President: Office and Powers, 1787–1957* (New York: New York University Press, 1957), 74.

45. Calabresi and Yoo, *The Unitary Executive*, 16.

46. Supreme Court justice Louis Brandeis in *Myers v. United States*, 265.

47. 42 U.S.C. § 2000e-4(a) (2012).

48. 47 U.S.C. § 154(b) (2012); 2 U.S.C. § 437(c)(a)(3) (2012); 15 U.S.C. § 78(d)(a) (2012).

49. 5 U.S.C. App. § 3(a) (2012).

50. 13 U.S.C. § 22 (2012); 35 U.S.C. § 3 (2012); 12 U.S.C. § 1462(a)(c)(1) (2012).

51. 28 U.S.C. § 545(a) (2012); 28 U.S.C. § 561(e) (2012).

52. 29 U.S.C. § 12 (2012).

53. Sollenberger, *The President Shall Nominate*, 179.

54. US House, Committee on the Judiciary, *Presidential Signing Statements under the Bush Administration: A Threat to Checks and Balances and the Rule of Law?*, 110th Cong., 1st sess. January 31, 2007, 12.

55. Pub. L. No. 81-788, 64 Stat. 853 (1950).

56. Paul Blustein, "Clinton Seeks Waiver for Barshefsky," *Washington Post*, January 9, 1997, https://www.washingtonpost.com/archive/business/1997/01/09/clinton-seeks-waiver-for-barshefsky/ab388aec-3740-4bb0-9fc1-cf5b7aeead26/ (accessed April 29, 2020).

57. Christopher Schroeder, "Constitutionality of Statute Governing Appointment of United States Trade Representative," Office of Legal Counsel Opinion, July 1, 1997, https://www.justice.gov/sites/default/files/olc/opinions/1996/07/31/op-olc-v020-p0279_0.pdf (accessed April 29, 2020).

58. Pub. L. No. 105-5, 111 Stat. 11 (1997); David Stout, "Hearings on Lake's Appointment Delayed," *New York Times*, January 31, 1997, https://www.nytimes.com/1997/01/31/us/hearings-on-lake-s-appointment-delayed.html (accessed April 29, 2020).

59. Paul Blustein, "Barshefsky Confirmed by Senate: Vote on Trade Official Spurs Angry Debate," *Washington Post*, March 6, 1997.

60. Calabresi and Yoo, *The Unitary Executive*, 426.

61. 92 Stat. 1072 (1978).

62. Charles A. Johnson and Danette Brickman, *Independent Counsel: The Law and the Investigations* (Washington, DC: CQ Press, 2001), 43.

63. 38 FR 14688 (May 31, 1973); Louis Fisher, *The Law of the Executive Branch: Presidential Power* (New York: Oxford University Press, 2014), 144, citing 38 Fed. Reg. 14688 (1973).

64. Johnson and Brickman, *Independent Counsel*, 43.

65. Katy Harriger, *The Special Prosecutor in American Politics*, 2nd ed. (Lawrence: University Press of Kansas, 2000), 43.

66. Terry Eastland, *Ethics, Politics and the Independent Counsel: Executive Power, Executive Vice, 1789–1989* (Washington, DC: National Legal Center for the Public Interest, 1989), 20.

67. Johnson and Brickman, *Independent Counsel*, 43.

68. Eastland, *Ethics, Politics and the Independent Counsel*, xii; Johnson and Brickman, *Independent Counsel*, 79.

69. Eastland, *Ethics, Politics and the Independent Counsel*, 35.

70. Eastland, 46.

71. The Ethics in Government Act of 1978, Pub. L. No. 95-521, 92 Stat. 1824; Ken Gormley, "An Original Model of the Independent Counsel Statute," *Michigan Law Review* 97 (1998): 604.

72. 92 Stat. 1824, 1867–1874 (1978).

73. Harriger, *The Special Prosecutor*, 70.

74. Calabresi and Yoo, *The Unitary Executive*, 365.

75. Jimmy Carter, "Ethics in Government Act of 1978 Remarks on Signing S. 555 into Law," October 26, 1978, The American Presidency Project, https://www.presidency.ucsb.edu/documents/ethics-government-act-1978-remarks-signing-s-555-into-law (accessed April 29, 2020).

76. Fisher, *The Law of the Executive Branch*, 145.

77. Ronald Reagan, "Statement on Signing the Independent Counsel Reauthorization Act of 1987," December 15, 1987, The American Presidency Project, https://www.presidency.ucsb.edu/documents/statement-signing-the-independent-counsel-reauthorization-act-1987 (accessed April 29, 2020).

78. *Morrison v. Olson*, 487 U.S. 654, 671–672 (1988).

79. *Morrison v. Olson*, 676.

80. *Morrison v. Olson*, 678–679.

81. *Morrison v. Olson*, 680.

82. *Morrison v. Olson*, 681.

83. *Morrison v. Olson*, 682–683.

84. *Morrison v. Olson*, 689.

85. *Morrison v. Olson*, 689–690.

86. *Morrison v. Olson*, 691.

87. *Morrison v. Olson*, 692.

88. *Morrison v. Olson*, 701–702; 28 U.S.C. § 592 (b)(1).

89. See Gormley, "An Original Model of the Independent Counsel Statute," 644.

90. *Morrison v. Olson*, 705.

91. *Morrison v. Olson*, 706.

92. Calabresi and Yoo, *The Unitary Executive*, 378.

93. Charles Fried, *Order and Law: Arguing the Reagan Revolution—A Firsthand Account* (New York: Simon & Schuster, 1991), 160.

94. William J. Clinton, "Statement on Signing the Independent Counsel Reauthorization Act of 1994," June 30, 1994, The American Presidency Project, https://www.presidency.ucsb.edu/documents/statement-signing-the-independent-counsel-reauthorization-act-1994 (accessed April 29, 2020).

95. Stephen Wolf, "In the Pursuit of Power without Accountability: How the Independent Counsel Statute Is Designed and Used to Undermine the Energy and Independence of the Presidency," *South Dakota Law Review* 35 (1990): 3.

96. Wolf, 21.

97. Fisher, *The Law of the Executive Branch*, 148.

98. 64 FR 37042 (July 9, 1999).

99. 28 CFR §600.7.

100. Attorney General Jeff Sessions recused himself from the case. See Tessa Berenson, "Jeff Sessions Is Recusing Himself. What Does That Mean?," *Time*, March 3, 2017, https://time.com/4689877/recuses-meaning-jeff-sessions-donald-trump/ (accessed April 29, 2020).

101. Phil Helsel, "'Special Counsel' Less Independent Than under Expired Watergate-Era Law," NBC News, May 17, 2017, http://www.nbcnews.com/news/us-news/special-counsel-less-independent-under-expired-watergate-era-law-n761311 (last accessed by author on September 15, 2018); see Neal Katyal, "Trump or Congress Can Still Block Robert Mueller. I Know. I Wrote the Rules," *Washington Post*, May 19, 2017, https://www.washingtonpost.com/posteverything/wp

/2017/05/19/politics-could-still-block-muellers-investigation-i-know-i-wrote-the -rules/?utm_term=.ddfca4453d28 (last accessed by author on September 15, 2019).

102. Emily Tillett, "Here's Everyone Who Was Charged in the Mueller Probe," CBS News, July 23, 2019, https://www.cbsnews.com/news/mueller-testimon-who -was-charged-in-special-counsel-robert-mueller-russia-probe-2019-07-23/ (accessed on September 15, 2019).

103. Reuters, "Timeline: Big Moments in Mueller Investigation of Russian Meddling in 2016 U.S. Election," July 23, 2019, https://www.reuters.com/article /us-usa-trump-russia-timeline/timeline-big-moments-in-mueller-investigation-of -russian-meddling-in-2016-us-election-idUSKCN1UI278 (accessed April 29, 2020).

104. Reuters, "Timeline: Big Moments in Mueller Investigation of Russian Meddling in 2016 U.S. Election."

105. Ramsey Touchberry, "OLC Opinion Explained: Why Robert Mueller Couldn't Indict Trump, Despite 10 Obstruction Incidents," *Newsweek*, July 24, 2019, https://www.newsweek.com/olc-opinion-mueller-doj-memo-indict-trump-sitting -president-1450896 (accessed April 29, 2020).

106. Hannah Gilberstadt, "For the First Time, Majority of Republicans Express Confidence in the Fairness of Mueller's Investigation," Pew Research Center, FactTank: News in the Numbers, July 23, 2019, https://www.pewresearch.org /fact-tank/2019/07/23/majority-republicans-express-confidence-fairness-muel ler-investigation/ (accessed April 29, 2020).

107. Donald J. Trump, "The Greatest Witch Hunt in U.S. history," Twitter, July 24, 2019, 7:03 a.m., https://twitter.com/realDonaldTrump/status/1153984090712 018950 (accessed April 29, 2020).

CHAPTER 4. DOMESTIC POWERS: PART III

1. *Immigration and Naturalization Service v. Chadha*, 462 U.S. 919 (1983), https:// supreme.justia.com/cases/federal/us/462/919/ (accessed April 30, 2020) (hereinafter *INS v. Chadha*).

2. Daniel E. Lungren and Mark L. Krotoski, "The War Powers Resolution after the Chadha Decision," 17 *Loyola L.A. Law Review* (1984): 767.

3. See Barbara Hinkson Craig, *The Legislative Veto: Congressional Control of Regulation* (Boulder, CO: Westview Press, 1983).

4. A finely detailed book-length treatment of this constitutional case is Barbara Hinkson Craig, *Chadha: The Story of an Epic Constitutional Struggle* (Berkeley: University of California Press, 1990).

5. Steven G. Calabresi and Christopher S. Yoo, *The Unitary Executive: Presidential Power from Washington to Bush* (New Haven, CT: Yale University Press, 2008), 12.

6. Calabresi and Yoo, 300.

7. Calabresi and Yoo, 16.

8. Louis Fisher, "The Unitary Executive and Inherent Executive Power," *Journal of Constitutional Law* 12 (February 2010): 581.

9. Louis Fisher, *Constitutional Conflicts between Congress and the President*, 6th ed. (Lawrence: University Press of Kansas, 2014), 156.

10. 6 Op. Att'y Gen. 680, 682 (1854).

11. 6 Op. Att'y Gen. 683.

12. H. Lee Watson, "Congress Steps Out: A Look at Congressional Control of the Executive," *California Law Review* 63 (July 1975): 996. For a discussion of why reporting requirements have been classified as legislative vetoes, see Michael J. Berry, *The Modern Legislative Veto: Macropolitical Conflict and the Legacy of* Chadha (Ann Arbor: University of Michigan Press, 2016), 30.

13. Watson, "Congress Steps Out," 998.

14. Louis Fisher, "The Legislative Veto: Invalidated, It Survives," *Law and Contemporary Problems* 56 (Autumn 1993): 273.

15. See, generally, Watson, "Congress Steps Out."

16. Watson, 1006, 1007–1009.

17. Louis Fisher, *The Law of the Executive Branch: Presidential Power* (New York: Oxford University Press, 2014), 198–199.

18. Herbert Hoover, "Annual Message to Congress on the State of the Union," December 3, 1929, https://www.presidency.ucsb.edu/documents/annual-message -congress-the-state-the-union-0 (accessed April 30, 2020).

19. Fisher, *The Law of the Executive Branch*, 199.

20. Fisher, *Constitutional Conflicts between Congress and the President*, 160.

21. Calabresi and Yoo, *The Unitary Executive*, 389.

22. Calabresi and Yoo, 12.

23. *INS v. Chadha*, 946–958.

24. *INS v. Chadha*, 948.

25. *INS v. Chadha*, 946–948.

26. Fisher, *Constitutional Conflicts between Congress and the President*, 168–170.

27. Fisher, 169–170.

28. This is a view held by Louis Fisher well before the Supreme Court decided *Chadha*. See Louis Fisher, "Congress Can't Lose on Its Veto Power," *Washington Post*, February 21, 1982, http://www.loufisher.org/docs/lv/legveto82.pdf (accessed April 30, 2020).

29. Fisher, "The Legislative Veto," 273–292.

30. Fisher, 289–290.

31. Berry, *The Modern Legislative Veto*.

32. Fisher, *Constitutional Conflicts between Congress and the President*, 173–174.

33. Fisher, 174.

34. Fisher, 171.

35. Fisher, "The Unitary Executive and Inherent Executive Power," 579.

36. Before this time, most presidents were disinterested in dealing with rulemaking. See William L. Cary, *Politics and the Regulatory Agencies* (New York: McGraw-Hill, 1967), 5–9.

37. Kenneth R. Mayer, *With the Stroke of a Pen: Executive Orders and Presidential Power* (Princeton, NJ: Princeton University Press, 2001), 124.

38. Gary C. Bryner, *Bureaucratic Discretion: Law and Policy in Federal Regulatory Agencies* (New York: Pergamon Press, 1987), 70–71.

39. 46 FR 13193 (1981).

40. Fisher, *The Law of the Executive Branch*, 106–107.

41. 58 FR 51735 (1993), Section 3(f).

42. 58 FR 51735 (1993), Section 1(b)(6).

43. Calabresi and Yoo, *The Unitary Executive*, 381.

44. Calabresi and Yoo, 427.

45. Calabresi and Yoo, 428.

46. William F. West, "Presidential Leadership and Administrative Coordination: Examining the Theory of a Unified Executive," *Presidential Studies Quarterly* 36 (September 2006): 433.

47. West, 440.

48. West, 442.

49. West, 446.

50. West, 446–447. See also William F. West, "The Administrative Presidency as Reactive Oversight: Implications for Positive and Normative Theory," *Public Administration Review* 75 (July 2015): 531.

51. West, "Presidential Leadership and Administrative Coordination," 447.

52. Elena Kagan, "Presidential Administration," *Harvard Law Review* 114 (2001): 2345.

53. Kagan, 2308.

54. Kagan, 2356.

55. Morton Rosenberg, "Beyond the Limits of Executive Power: Presidential Control of Agency Rulemaking under Executive Order 12,291," *Michigan Law Review* 80 (December 1981): 212.

56. West, "Presidential Leadership and Administrative Coordination," 454.

57. Jennifer Nou, "Agency Self-Insulation under Presidential Review," *Harvard Law Review* 126 (May 2013): 1783.

58. Curtis W. Copeland, "Federal Rulemaking: The Role of the Office of Information and Regulatory Affairs," *Congressional Research Service*, RL32397, June 9, 2009, 17, https://fas.org/sgp/crs/misc/RL32397.pdf (accessed September 15, 2019).

59. Nou, "Agency Self-Insulation under Presidential Review," 1783.

60. Kirti Datla and Richard L. Revesz, "Deconstructing Independent Agencies (and Executive Agencies)," *Cornell Law Review* 98 (May 2013): 810.

61. Datla and Revesz, 810.

62. Datla and Revesz, 800.

63. Neal Devins, "Political Will and the Unitary Executive: What Makes an Independent Agency Independent?," *Cardozo Law Review* 15 (1993): 276.

64. Devins, 298.

65. Nou, "Agency Self-Insulation under Presidential Review," 1784.

66. Jack M. Beermann, *Inside Administrative Law: What Matters and Why* (New York: Aspen, 2011), 190.

67. Nou, "Agency Self-Insulation under Presidential Review," 1785.

68. Nou, 1785–1786.

69. Nou, 1786.

70. For a useful list and descriptions, see Nou, 1786–1796.

71. Nou, 1787.

72. We acknowledge President Clinton's 1993 executive order, which requires independent regulatory agencies to submit to the regulatory review process but does not require them to adhere to the White House dispute resolution process. See Executive Order 12866, 58 FR 51735 (1993), https://www.archives.gov/files/federal-register/executive-orders/pdf/12866.pdf (accessed September 15, 2019).

73. Fisher, *The Law of the Executive Branch*, 162. For additional features that make an agency independent, see Devins, "Political Will and the Unitary Executive," and Jennifer L. Selin, "What Makes an Agency Independent?," *American Journal of Political Science* 59 (October 2015).

74. Harold J. Krent, *Presidential Powers* (New York: New York University Press, 2005), 56.

75. Christopher D. Ahlers, "Presidential Authority over EPA Rulemaking under the Clean Air Act," *Environmental Law* 44 (2014): 69.

76. *PHH Corp. v. Consumer Financial Protection Bureau*, October 11, 2016, D.C. Court of Appeals, No. 15-1177, 16, https://www.cadc.uscourts.gov/internet/opinions.nsf/AAC6BFFC4C42614C852580490053C38B/$file/15-1177-1640101.pdf (accessed April 30, 2020).

77. *PHH Corp. v. Consumer Financial Protection Bureau*, January 31, 2018, D.C. Court of Appeals, No. 15-1177, 6, https://www.cadc.uscourts.gov/internet/opinions.nsf/B7623651686D60D585258226005405AC/$file/15-1177.pdf (accessed April 30, 2020).

78. Greg Iacurci, "The Supreme Court Could Upend Consumer Financial Protection as We Know It," CNBC, January 24, 2020, https://www.cnbc.com/2020/01/24/the-supreme-court-has-the-power-to-upend-consumer-financial-protection.html (accessed April 30, 2020).

79. Justice Department Amicus Curiae Brief, *PHH Corp. v. Consumer Financial Protection Bureau*, May 17, 2017, D.C. Court of Appeals, https://buckleyfirm.com/sites/default/files/Buckley%20Sandler%20InfoBytes%20-%202017.03.17%20-%20PHH%20v%20CFPB%20-%20Brief%20for%20the%20United%20States%20as%20Amicus%20Curiae%20%28Doc%20No.%201666553%29.pdf, 19 (accessed April 30, 2020).

80. Justice Department Amicus Curiae Brief, *PHH Corp. v. Consumer Financial Protection Bureau*, May 17, 2017, D.C. Court of Appeals, https://www.housingwire.com/ext/resources/files/Editorial/Documents/3-17-17-US-Amicus-Brief-PHH.pdf, 2.

81. See especially James P. Pfiffner, *Power Play: The Bush Presidency and the Constitution* (Washington, DC: Brookings Institution Press, 2009). Also see John W. Dean, *Worse Than Watergate: The Secret Presidency of George W. Bush* (New York: Little, Brown, 2004); Andrew Rudalevige, "George W. Bush and the Imperial Presidency,"

in *Testing the Limits: George W. Bush and the Imperial Presidency*, ed. Mark J. Rozell and Gleaves Whitney (Lanham, MD: Rowman & Littlefield, 2009), 243–268; Charlie Savage, *Takeover: The Return of the Imperial Presidency and the Subversion of American Democracy* (New York: Little, Brown, 2007); Peter M. Shane, *Madison's Nightmare: How Executive Power Threatens American Democracy* (Chicago: University of Chicago Press, 2009). Different perspectives are offered by Jack Goldsmith, *Power and Constraint: The Accountable President after 9/11* (New York: W. W. Norton, 2012); and Alasdair Roberts, *The Collapse of Fortress Bush: The Crisis of Authority in American Government* (New York: New York University Press, 2008).

82. Hans Sperber and Travis Trittschuh, *Dictionary of American Political Terms* (Detroit: Wayne State University Press, 1964), 111.

83. Mitchel A. Sollenberger and Mark J. Rozell, *The President's Czars: Undermining Congress and the Constitution* (Lawrence: University Press of Kansas, 2012).

84. For example, all top-level officials within the Department of the Treasury receive Senate confirmation. See 31 U.S.C. § 301 (2006).

85. Barack Obama, "Remarks at a Campaign Event," *Congressional Quarterly Transcriptions*, March 31, 2008.

86. Steve Fishman, "Exit the Czar," *New York*, July 31, 2009, http://nymag .com/news/features/58193/ (accessed April 30, 2020). For additional background on the firing of Wagoner, see Steven Rattner, *Overhaul: An Insider's Account of the Obama Administration's Emergency Rescue of the Auto Industry* (Boston: Houghton Mifflin Harcourt, 2010), 111, 134.

87. Congressional Oversight Panel, "The Use of TARP Funds in the Support and Reorganization of the Domestic Automotive Industry," September 9, 2009, 56, https://fraser.stlouisfed.org/title/5016 (accessed April 30, 2020).

88. Rattner, *Overhaul*, 57.

89. Rattner, 301.

90. Peter Lattman, "Rattner Settles Pension Inquiry for $10 Million: Feud with Cuomo Ends; Kickback Case Dogged Financier Who Led U.S. Auto Rescue," *New York Times*, December 31, 2010; Joshua Gallu, "Steven Rattner Will Pay $6.2 Million to Settle SEC Claims," *Bloomberg*, November 18, 2010, https://www.bloomberg .com/news/articles/2010-11-18/rattner-to-pay-6-2-million-to-settle-sec-new-york -pension-kickback-claim.

91. Gabriel Nelson, "Energy and Climate Czar Browner's Resignation Seen as the End of an Era," *New York Times*, January 25, 2011, at http://www.nytimes .com/gwire/2011/01/25/25greenwire-energy-and-climate-czar-browners -resignation-s-34804.html (accessed April 30, 2020).

92. Sollenberger and Rozell, *The President's Czars*, chap. 7.

93. Letter from Senator Robert Byrd (D-WV) to President Barack Obama, February 23, 2009, https://lawprofessors.typepad.com/conlaw/2009/10/do-white -house-czars-violate-the-appointments-clause.html (accessed April 30, 2020).

94. Richard M. Pious, *Why Presidents Fail: White House Decision Making from Eisenhower to Bush II* (Lanham, MD: Rowman & Littlefield, 2008), 280.

95. Pious, 285.

96. Pious, 292.

97. "The Vice President Appears on ABC's This Week," January 27, 2002, https://georgewbush-whitehouse.archives.gov/vicepresident/news-speeches/speeches/vp20020127.html (accessed April 30, 2020).

98. Louis Fisher, "Obama's Executive Privilege and Holder's Contempt: 'Operation Fast and Furious,'" *Presidential Studies Quarterly* 43 (March 2013).

99. Fisher, 178.

100. Fisher, 179.

101. Fisher, 181.

102. Mitchel A. Sollenberger and Mark J. Rozell, "Obama Administration Needs to Renew Its Pledge to Greater Transparency," *The Hill*, November 21, 2013, https://thehill.com/opinion/op-ed/191077-obama-administration-needs-to-renew-its-pledge-to-greater-transparency (accessed April 30, 2020).

103. Kevin Johnson, "Judge Rejects Privilege Claim in 'Fast and Furious' Inquiry," *USA Today*, January 19, 2016, https://www.usatoday.com/story/news/politics/2016/01/19/judge-fast-and-furious-atf/79012328/ (accessed April 30, 2020).

104. Stephen Dinan, "Obama Relents on Fast & Furious Executive Privilege, Turns Records Over to Congress," *Washington Times*, April 8, 2016, http://www.washingtontimes.com/news/2016/apr/8/obama-relents-fast-furious-turns-records-congress/ (accessed April 30, 2020).

105. Assistant Attorney General Peter Kadzik's letter to House Oversight Chairman Jason Chaffetz (R-UT), US Department of Justice, April 8, 2016, http://www.politico.com/f/?id=00000153-f7ab-d0e4-af73-ffbb91c90001 (accessed April 30, 2020).

106. During Supreme Court nominee confirmation hearings, the Trump administration also refused to provide to the Senate Judiciary Committee more than one hundred thousand pages of records regarding Brett Kavanaugh's prior service in the George W. Bush administration. Although there was no formal claim of executive privilege, the bases for withholding the records dovetailed with the reasons typically cited for asserting that power, including protecting a president's right to receive candid, confidential advice. Mark J. Rozell, "The Trump Administration Is Exercising Executive Privilege without Saying So," *Washington Post*, September 4, 2018, https://www.washingtonpost.com/opinions/the-trump-administration-is-exercising-executive-privilege-without-saying-so/2018/09/04/4301954e-b05b-11e8-9a6a-565d92a3585d_story.html?utm_term=.db964ba2b1c3 (accessed April 30, 2020).

107. Politico Staff, "Transcript: Jeff Sessions' Testimony on Trump and Russia," *Politico*, June 13, 2017, https://www.politico.com/story/2017/06/13/full-text-jeff-session-trump-russia-testimony-239503 (accessed April 29, 2020).

108. Politico Staff, "Transcript: Jeff Sessions' Testimony on Trump and Russia."

109. Nicholas Fandos, "House Panel Approves Contempt for Barr after Trump Claims Privilege over Full Mueller Report," *New York Times*, May 8, 2019, https://

www.nytimes.com/2019/05/08/us/politics/trump-executive-privilege-muel ler-report.html (accessed April 29, 2020).

110. Letter from Assistant Attorney General Stephen Boyd to House Judiciary Committee Chair Jerry Nadler (D-NY), Department of Justice, Office of Legislative Affairs, May 8, 2019, https://assets.documentcloud.org/documents/5993531/5-8 -19-Boyd-Letter-Nadler.pdf (accessed April 29, 2020). See also Letter from William Barr to Donald Trump, May 8, 2019, Attorney General, https://assets.document cloud.org/documents/5993580/5-8-19-Barr-Letter-to-President-Re-Protective.pdf (accessed April 29, 2020).

111. *Protective Assertion of Executive Privilege Regarding White House Counsel's Office Documents*, 20 Op. O.L.C. 1 (1996), https://www.justice.gov/file/20031/down load (accessed April 29, 2020).

112. Mark J. Rozell, *Executive Privilege: Presidential Power, Secrecy, and Accountability*, 4th ed. (Lawrence: University Press of Kansas, 2010), 200.

113. US House of Representatives Committee on the Judiciary, Jerrold Nadler to William Barr and Pat Cipollone, May 24, 2019, 2, https://judiciary.house.gov /sites/democrats.judiciary.house.gov/files/documents/5.24.2019%20letter%20 to%20ag%20barr%20and%20mr.%20cipollone.pdf (accessed April 30, 2020). See also Nicholas Fandos, "Justice Department Agrees to Turn Over Key Mueller Evidence to House," *New York Times*, June 10, 2019, https://www.nytimes.com /2019/06/10/us/politics/mueller-judiciary-committee.html (accessed April 30, 2020).

114. "Remarks by President Trump and Prime Minister Pellegrini of the Slovak Republic before Bilateral Meeting," The White House, https://www.white house.gov/briefings-statements/remarks-president-trump-prime-minister-pel legrini-slovak-republic-bilateral-meeting/ (accessed April 30, 2020); see also Tamara Keith, "Trump Threatens to Use Executive Privilege to Block Testimonies on Capitol Hill," NPR, All Things Considered, May 3, 2019, https:// www.npr.org/2019/05/03/720097342/trump-threatens-to-use-executive-privi lege-to-block-testimonies-on-capitol-hill (accessed April 30, 2020).

CHAPTER 5. FOREIGN AFFAIRS POWERS: PART I

1. David J. Bodenhamer, *The Revolutionary Constitution* (New York: Oxford University Press, 2012), 234.

2. Dick Cheney, "Vice President's Remarks to the Traveling Press," December 20, 2005, found in George W. Bush's archived White House webpage, https:// georgewbush-whitehouse.archives.gov/news/releases/2005/12/20051220-9.html (accessed May 1, 2020).

3. *Report of the Congressional Committees Investigating the Iran-Contra Affair, with Supplemental, Minority, and Additional Views*, S. Rep. No. 100-216, H. Rep. No. 100-433 (Washington, DC: Government Printing Office, 1987), 457 (hereafter Minority Report).

4. Minority Report, 459.

5. Minority Report, 460.

6. Minority Report, 465 (emphasis in original).

7. Minority Report, 469.

8. Frederick A. O. Schwarz Jr. and Aziz Z. Huq, *Unchecked and Unbalanced: Presidential Power in a Time of Terror* (New York: New Press, 2008), 159.

9. Memorandum for Alberto R. Gonzales, Counsel to the President, "Standards of Conduct for Interrogation under 18 U.S.C. Sc. 2340-2340A," August 1, 2002, 33. The memo was signed by Assistant Attorney General Jay Bybee but ghostwritten by John Yoo. See Scott Shane, "Two Testify on Memo Spelling Out Interrogation," *New York Times*, June 27, 2008, https://www.nytimes.com/2008/06/27/washing ton/27hearing.html?mtrref=www.google.com&gwh=29A5D71CFEC32F6F8B5D 8E8D486EE8D8&gwt=pay&assetType=REGIWALL (accessed May 1, 2020).

10. John C. Yoo, "The President's Constitutional Authority to Conduct Military Operations against Terrorists and Nations Supporting Them," Memorandum Opinion for the Deputy Counsel to the President, Office of Legal Counsel, September 25, 2001, https://fas.org/irp/agency/doj/olc092501.html (accessed May 1, 2020).

11. Yoo (emphasis added).

12. Yoo.

13. In fact, footnote 4 of Yoo's September 25, 2001, memorandum cites his own *California Law Review* article as the only source of evidence to claim that "during the period leading up to the Constitution's ratification, the power to initiate hostilities and to control the escalation of conflict had been long understood to rest in the hands of the executive branch." This claim misses the mark given that there was no executive branch under the Articles of Confederation.

14. See footnote 1 in John C. Yoo, "The Continuation of Politics by Other Means: The Original Understanding of War Powers," *California Law Review* 84 (March 1996): 170–171. Yoo's assessment of the consensus among scholars has been confirmed elsewhere. See Louis Fisher, "Unchecked Presidential Wars," *University of Pennsylvania Law Review* 148 (2000), 1657–1658.

15. James P. Pfiffner, *Power Play: The Bush Presidency and the Constitution* (Washington, DC: Brookings Institution Press, 2008), 75.

16. Yoo, "The Continuation of Politics by Other Means," 242.

17. Yoo, 252.

18. David Gray Adler, "*The Law*: George Bush as Commander in Chief: Toward the Nether World of Constitutionalism," *Presidential Studies Quarterly* 36 (September 2006): 526.

19. Pfiffner, *Power Play*, 72.

20. David J. Barron and Martin S. Lederman, "The Commander in Chief at the Lowest Ebb: Framing the Problem, Doctrine, and Original Understanding," *Harvard Law Review* 121 (January 2008): 773.

21. Adler, "*The Law*: George Bush as Commander in Chief," 527.

22. *Little v. Barreme*, 6 U.S. (2 Cranch) 170, 177 (1804).

23. Barron and Lederman, "The Commander in Chief at the Lowest Ebb," 696.

24. Yoo, "The President's Constitutional Authority to Conduct Military Operations."

25. *Prize Cases*, 67 U.S. 635, 650, 660 (1862).

26. *Prize Cases*, 660.

27. *Prize Cases*, 660–661.

28. Yoo, "The President's Constitutional Authority to Conduct Military Operations."

29. Yoo, "The Continuation of Politics by Other Means," 295.

30. Louis Fisher, "*The Law*: John Yoo and the Republic," *Presidential Studies Quarterly* 41 (March 2011): 185.

31. Max Farrand, ed., *The Records of the Federal Convention of 1787* (New Haven, CT: Yale University Press, 1966), 1:65. 2:318.

32. Farrand, 2:318–319.

33. Jonathan Elliot, ed., *The Debates in the Several State Conventions on the Adoption of the Federal Constitution, as Recommended by the General Convention at Philadelphia, in 1787* (Washington, DC: Author, 1836), 2:488.

34. *Federalist* No. 69, in *The Federalist Papers*, ed. Clinton Rossiter (New York: Mentor, 1999), 385–386.

35. Louis Fisher, *Presidential War Power* (Lawrence: University Press of Kansas, 1995), 1.

36. Pfiffner, *Power Play*, 77.

37. Adler, "*The Law*: George Bush as Commander in Chief," 530.

38. Charlie Savage, "2 Top Lawyers Lost to Obama in Libya War Policy Debate," *New York Times*, June 17, 2011, https://www.nytimes.com/2011/06/18/world/africa/18powers.html (accessed May 1, 2020). See also Caroline Krass, "Authority to Use Military Force in Libya," Office of Legal Counsel, April 1, 2011, https://fas.org/irp/agency/doj/olc/libya.pdf (accessed May 1, 2020).

39. Jack Balkin, "George W. Obama and the OLC," *Balkinization*, June 18, 2011, https://balkin.blogspot.com/2011/06/george-w-obama-and-olc.html (accessed May 1, 2020).

40. Harold Koh, "Testimony before the Senate Foreign Relations Committee," June 28, 2011, https://2009-2017.state.gov/documents/organization/167452.pdf (accessed May 1, 2020).

41. War Powers Resolution, Section 5(b).

42. Charlie Savage, "Barack Obama's Q&A," Boston.com, December 20, 2007, http://archive.boston.com/news/politics/2008/specials/CandidateQA/ObamaQA/ (accessed May 1, 2020).

43. "House Rejects Measure Backing Libya War," CBS News, June 24, 2011, https://www.cbsnews.com/news/house-rejects-measure-backing-libya-war/ (accessed May 1, 2020).

44. Alan J. Kuperman, "Obama's Libya Debacle: How a Well-Meaning Inter-

vention Ended in Failure," *Foreign Affairs*, March/April 2015, https://www.foreign affairs.com/articles/libya/2019–02–18/obamas-libya-debacle (accessed May 1, 2020).

45. Ilya Somin, "Obama Admits That His Handling of the Libya War Was His Worst Mistake—but Not That It Was Unconstitutional," *Washington Post*, April 13, 2016, https://www.washingtonpost.com/news/volokh-conspiracy/wp/2016 /04/13/obama-admits-that-his-handling-of-the-libya-war-was-his-worst-mistake -but-not-that-it-was-unconstitutional/ (accessed May 1, 2020).

46. Courtney Kube, Alex Johnson, Hallie Jackson, and Alexander Smith, "U.S. Launches Missiles at Syrian Base over Chemical Weapons Attack," NBC News, April 6, 2017, https://www.nbcnews.com/news/us-news/u-s-launches-missiles-syrian -base-after-chemical-weapons-attack-n743636 (accessed May 1, 2020).

47. Steven Engel, "April 2018 Airstrikes against Syrian Chemical-Weapons Facilities," Office of Legal Counsel, May 31, 2018, https://www.justice.gov/sites /default/files/opinions/attachments/2018/05/31/2018-05-31-syrian-air strikes_1.pdf (accessed May 1, 2020).

48. Barack Obama, "Statement by the President on Syria," August 31, 2013, https://obamawhitehouse.archives.gov/the-press-office/2013/08/31/state ment-president-syria (accessed May 1, 2020).

49. Saagar Enjeti and Jordan Fabian, "Trump: I Do Not Need Congressional Approval to Strike Iran," *The Hill*, June 24, 2019, https://thehill.com/homenews /administration/450117-trump-i-do-not-need-congressional-approval-to-strike -iran (accessed May 1, 2020).

50. Luke Johnson, "The Trump Administration Thinks It Can Ignore Congress on Iran Because of 9/11," *Fortune*, June 18, 2019, https://fortune .com/2019/06/18/trump-congress-war-on-iran/ (accessed May 1, 2020).

51. Fred Kaplan, "Congress Needs to Take Responsibility for America's Wars," *Slate*, May 23, 2019, https://slate.com/news-and-politics/2019/05/aumf-con gress-syria-barbara-lee.html (accessed May 1, 2020). See also Matthew Weed, "Pres- idential Reference to the 2001 Authorization for Use of Military Force in Publicly Available Executive Actions and Reports to Congress," Congressional Research Service, May 11, 2016, https://fas.org/sgp/crs/natsec/pres-aumf.pdf (accessed May 1, 2020); Curtis A. Bradley and Jack L. Goldsmith, "Obama's AUMF Legacy," *American Journal of International Law* 110 (October 2016): 628–645.

52. Charlie Savage, "Is the U.S. Now at War with the Shabab? Not Exactly," *New York Times*, March 14, 2016, https://www.nytimes.com/2016/03/15/us/poli tics/is-the-us-now-at-war-with-the-shabab-not-exactly.html?rref=collection%2F byline%2Fcharlie-savage&action=click&contentCollection=undefined&region =stream&module=stream_unit&version=search&contentPlacement=3&pgtype =collection (accessed May 1, 2020).

53. Johnson, "The Trump Administration Thinks It Can Ignore Congress."

54. Chris Edelson, "Trump Is Wrong about Iran. He Needs Approval from Congress for a Military Strike," *USA Today*, June 28, 2019, https://www.usatoday

.com/story/opinion/2019/06/28/trump-wrong-iran-attack-requires-approval-from-congress-column/1564107001/ (accessed May 1, 2020).

55. John Nichols, "Trump Cannot Declare War—Especially on Iran—Without Congress," *The Nation*, July 23, 2019, https://www.thenation.com/article/khanna-trump-war-iran-congress/ (accessed May 1, 2020).

56. On December 29, 2019, the US military launched airstrikes against Iranian assets in Iraq and Syria. US Department of Defense, "Statement from Assistant to the Secretary of Defense Jonathan Hoffman," December 29, 2019, https://www.defense.gov/Newsroom/Releases/Release/Article/2047960/statement-from-assistant-to-the-secretary-of-defense-jonathan-hoffman/ (accessed May 1, 2020).

57. US Department of Defense, "Immediate Release: Statement by the Department of Defense," January 2, 2020, https://www.defense.gov/Newsroom/Releases/Release/Article/2049534/statement-by-the-department-of-defense/ (accessed May 1, 2020).

58. Zachary B. Wolf and Veronica Stracqualursi, "The Evolving US Justification for Killing Iran's Top General," CNN, January 8, 2020, https://edition.cnn.com/2020/01/07/politics/qasem-soleimani-reasons-justifications/index.html (accessed May 1, 2020); Andrew P. Napolitano, "Shifting Justification for the Killing of Soleimani Persists," *Washington Times*, January 15, 2020, https://www.washingtontimes.com/news/2020/jan/15/shifting-justification-for-the-killing-of-soleiman/ (accessed May 1, 2020).

59. Rachel Frazin, "Pelosi Says Trump Launched Strike Killing Iranian General without Authorization," *The Hill*, January 3, 2020, https://thehill.com/policy/defense/476626-pelosi-says-trump-launched-strike-killing-iranian-general-without (accessed May 1, 2020).

60. Catie Edmondson and Charlie Savage, "House Votes to Restrain Trump's Iran War Powers," *New York Times*, January 9, 2020, https://www.nytimes.com/2020/01/09/us/politics/trump-iran-war-powers.html (accessed May 1, 2020).

61. 462 U.S. 919 (1983).

62. Roll Call Vote on S.J. Res. 68, February 13, 2020, https://www.senate.gov/legislative/LIS/roll_call_lists/roll_call_vote_cfm.cfm?congress=116&session=2&vote=00052 (accessed May 1, 2020).

63. S.J. Res. 68, Congress.gov, https://www.congress.gov/bill/116th-congress/senate-joint-resolution/68/text (accessed May 1, 2020).

64. Donald J. Trump "It is very important . . . ," Twitter, February 12, 2020, https://twitter.com/realdonaldtrump/status/1227661700264013826?lang=en (accessed May 1, 2020).

65. Roll call vote on S.J. Res. 68, March 11, 2020, http://clerk.house.gov/evs/2020/roll101.xml (accessed May 1, 2020).

66. Patricia Zengerie, "U.S. Senate Upholds Trump Veto of 'Insulting' Iran War Powers Resolution," Reuters, May 7, 2020, https://www.reuters.com/article/us-mideast-crisis-congress/us-senate-upholds-trump-veto-of-insulting-iran-war-powers-resolution-idUSKBN22J30A (accessed May 8, 2020).

67. Lisa Hagen, "Senate Falls Short of Overriding Trump's Veto of Iran War Powers Resolution," *U.S. News*, May 7, 2020, https://www.usnews.com/news/pol itics/articles/2020-05-07/senate-falls-short-of-overriding-trumps-veto-of-iran-war -powers-resolution (accessed May 8, 2020).

68. See, generally, Fisher, *Presidential War Power*, chaps. 2 and 3.

69. Yoo, "The President's Constitutional Authority to Conduct Military Operations."

70. Alberto R. Gonzales, "Advising the President: The Growing Scope of Executive Power to Protect America," *Harvard Journal of Law and Public Policy* 38 (Spring 2015): 456.

71. Steven G. Calabresi and Christopher S. Yoo, *The Unitary Executive: Presidential Power from Washington to Bush* (New Haven, CT: Yale University Press, 2008).

72. *Youngstown Sheet & Tube Company v. Sawyer*, 343 U.S. 579, 646–647 (1952).

73. *Youngstown Sheet & Tube Company v. Sawyer*, 652.

74. Louis Fisher, "Invoking Inherent Powers: A Primer," *Presidential Studies Quarterly* 37 (March 2007): 2; see also Louis Fisher, "The Unitary Executive and Inherent Executive Power," *University of Pennsylvania Journal of Constitutional Law* 12 (February 2010): 569–591.

75. Alpheus Todd, *On Parliamentary Government in England: Its Origin, Development, and Practical Operation* (London: Longmans, Green, 1867), 1:244; and George Burton Adams, *Constitutional History of England* (New York: Holt, 1921), 78.

76. John Locke, *Second Treatise of Government*, ed. C. B. Macpherson (Indianapolis: Hackett, 1980), 84.

77. Todd, *On Parliamentary Government in England*, 244; Adams, *Constitutional History of England*, 78–79.

78. William Blackstone, *Commentaries on the Laws of England* (Oxford: Clarendon Press, 1765), 1:232.

79. See, generally, Marc W. Kruman, *Between Authority and Liberty: State Constitution Making in Revolutionary America* (Chapel Hill: University of North Carolina Press, 1997).

80. Farrand, 1:65–66.

81. Theodore Roosevelt, *Theodore Roosevelt: An Autobiography* (New York: Macmillan, 1913), 388–389.

82. Gary L. Gregg II, "Whiggism and Presidentialism: American Ambivalence toward Executive Power," in *The Presidency Then and Now*, ed. Phillip G. Henderson (Lanham, MD: Rowman & Littlefield, 2000), 82.

83. Woodrow Wilson, *Constitutional Government in the United States* (New Brunswick, NJ: Transaction Publishers, 2004), 14, 68.

84. 135 U.S. 1 (1890).

85. 67 U.S. 635, 668 (1863).

86. 71 U.S. 2, 121 (1866).

87. See, for example, *Korematsu v. United States*, 323 U.S. 214 (1944).

88. *Youngstown Sheet & Tube Company v. Sawyer*, 343 U.S. 579 (1952).

89. *Youngstown Sheet & Tube Company v. Sawyer*, 582.

90. *Youngstown Sheet & Tube Company v. Sawyer*, 587.

91. *Youngstown Sheet & Tube Company v. Sawyer*, 642.

92. *Youngstown Sheet & Tube Company v. Sawyer*, 643–644 (emphasis in original).

93. *Youngstown Sheet & Tube Company v. Sawyer*, 645.

94. One of the significant drawbacks to the current system is the fact that national emergencies may not ever officially end. For example, President Jimmy Carter's Executive Order 12170, issued during the Iranian hostage crisis and intended to prevent the Iranian government from accessing funds held in US banks, was issued on November 14, 1979, and remains in effect more than forty years later.

95. 50 U.S.C. 1621.

96. 40 Stat. 411 (1917) and 91 Stat. 1626 (1977).

97. *Dames & Moore v. Regan*, 453 U.S. 654, 686 (1981).

98. *Dames & Moore v. Regan*, 678.

99. 299 U.S. 304 (1936).

100. See Yoo, "The President's Constitutional Authority to Conduct Military Operations"; and Office of Legal Counsel, "Legal Authorities Supporting the Activities of the National Security Agency Described by the President," January 19, 2006, https://www.justice.gov/sites/default/files/olc/opinions/attach ments/2015/05/29/op-olc-v030-p0001.pdf (accessed May 1, 2020).

101. 299 U.S. 304, 320 (1936).

102. 10 Annals of Cong. 613 (1800).

103. Edward S. Corwin, *The President: Office and Powers, 1787–1957* (New York: New York University Press, 1957), 178 (emphasis in original).

104. Louis Fisher, *The Constitution and 9/11* (Lawrence: University Press of Kansas, 2008), 296 (emphasis in original).

105. 576 U.S. ___ (2015).

106. 576 U.S. slip op. at 11 (2015).

107. 576 U.S. slip op. at 8 (2015).

108. 576 U.S. slip op. at 11 (2015).

109. 576 U.S. slip op. at 14 (2015) (citing Antonin Scalia's dissent).

110. 576 U.S. slip op. at 14 (2015).

111. *Federalist* No. 51, in Rossiter, *The Federalist Papers*, 290.

112. *Federalist* No. 51, in Rossiter, *The Federalist Papers*, 289–290.

CHAPTER 6. FOREIGN AFFAIRS POWERS: PART II

1. John C. Yoo, "The President's Constitutional Authority to Conduct Military Operations against Terrorists and Nations Supporting Them," Memorandum Opinion for the Deputy Counsel to the President, US Department of Justice, Office of Legal Counsel, September 25, 2001, https://www.thetorturedatabase .org/document/olc-memo-president%E2%80%99s-constitutional-authority-con duct-military-operations-against-terrorist?search_url=search/apachesolr_search&

search_args=filters=sm_cck_field_doc_from:522%26author_name=John%20 C.%20Yoo%26advsearch=1 (accessed May 2, 2020).

2. 115 Stat. 224 (September 18, 2001).

3. George W. Bush, Military Order of November 13, 2001, 66 FR 57833.

4. Patrick F. Philbin, "Legality of the Use of Military Commissions to Try Terrorists," Memorandum Opinion for the Counsel to the President, US Department of Justice, Office of Legal Counsel, November 6, 2001, https://nsarchive2.gwu .edu/torturingdemocracy/documents/20011106.pdf (accessed May 2, 2020).

5. For a review of the incident, see Louis Fisher, *Military Tribunals and Presidential Power* (Lawrence: University Press of Kansas, 2005), 32–33.

6. 147 Cong. Rec. S13277 (December 14, 2001).

7. Task Force on Terrorism and the Law, "Report and Recommendations on Military Commissions," American Bar Association, January 4, 2002, 6, https:// www.americanbar.org/content/dam/aba/migrated/leadership/military.auth checkdam.pdf (accessed May 2, 2020).

8. 317 U.S. 1 (1942).

9. William P. Barr and Andrew G. McBride, "Military Justice for al Qaeda," *Washington Post*, November 18, 2001, https://www.washingtonpost.com/archive /opinions/2001/11/18/military-justice-for-al-qaeda/ee8ea2b7–3e59–499a-b962 –5f1b63836f62/ (accessed September 29, 2019).

10. *Ex parte Milligan*, 71 U.S. 2 (1866).

11. 317 U.S. 1, 45 (1942).

12. *Hamdi v. Rumsfeld*, 542 U.S. 507, 523 (2004).

13. *Hamdi v. Rumsfeld*, 533, 539.

14. Patrick F. Philbin and John C. Yoo, "Possible Habeas Jurisdiction over Aliens Held in Guantanamo Bay, Cuba," US Department of Justice, Office of Legal Counsel, December 28, 2001, https://nsarchive2.gwu.edu/torturingdemocracy /documents/20011228.pdf (accessed May 2, 2020).

15. 542 U.S. 466 (2004).

16. 339 U.S. 763 (1950).

17. 542 U.S. 466, 475–476 (2004).

18. Paul Wolfowitz, "Order Establishing Combatant Status Review Tribunal," US Department of Defense, July 7, 2004, https://www.law.utoronto.ca/docu ments/Mackin/MuneerAhmad_ExhibitV.pdf (accessed May 2, 2020).

19. Louis Fisher, *The Constitution and 9/11: Recurring Threats to America's Freedoms* (Lawrence: University Press of Kansas, 2008), 235.

20. 542 U.S. 466, 487–488 (2004).

21. 119 Stat. 2739, sec. 1003(a) (2005).

22. 119 Stat. 2741–2742, sec. 1005(e).

23. 41 Weekly Comp. of Pres. Doc. 1919 (2005).

24. Dianne Feinstein, "Senator Feinstein Warns against the Bush Administration's Efforts to Vastly Expand Executive Powers," Office of US Senator Dianne Feinstein, Press Release, June 1, 2006, https://www.feinstein.senate.gov/public

/index.cfm/press-releases?ID=792A0663-7E9C-9AF9-7572-3ACABBA1D402 (accessed May 2, 2020).

25. *Hamdan v. Rumsfeld*, 548, 567 U.S. 557 (2006).

26. *Hamdan v. Rumsfeld*, 635.

27. 120 Stat. 2600, 2608, sec. 3 (2006).

28. 553 U.S. 723 (2008).

29. William Glaberson, "Judge Declares Five Detainees Held Illegally," *New York Times*, November 20, 2008, https://www.nytimes.com/2008/11/21/us/21guanta namo.html (accessed May 2, 2020).

30. Barack Obama, "Statement of President Barack Obama on Military Commissions," Office of the Press Secretary, The White House, May 15, 2009, https:// obamawhitehouse.archives.gov/the-press-office/statement-president-barack -obama-military-commissions (accessed May 2, 2020).

31. Barack Obama, "Remarks by the President on National Security at the National Archives and Records Administration," cited in Jack Goldsmith, *Power and Constraint: The Accountable Presidency after 9/11* (New York: W. W. Norton, 2012), 8–9.

32. Goldsmith, 9.

33. 123 Stat. 2190 (2009).

34. Quinta Jurecic, "The Legality of Donald Trump's Proposal to Try US Citizens by Military Commission," *Lawfare*, August 12, 2016, https://www.lawfareblog .com/legality-donald-trumps-proposal-try-us-citizens-military-commission (accessed May 2, 2020).

35. Donald J. Trump, "Presidential Executive Order on Protecting America through Lawful Detention of Terrorists," The White House, January 30, 2018, https://www.whitehouse.gov/presidential-actions/presidential-executive-or der-protecting-america-lawful-detention-terrorists/ (accessed May 2, 2020).

36. James P. Pfiffner, *Power Play: The Bush Presidency and the Constitution* (Washington, DC: Brookings Institution Press, 2009), 171, 174–175.

37. 41 Weekly Comp. of Pres. Doc. 1885 (2005).

38. William Moschella, "Letter to Congressional Leaders," US Department of Justice, Office of Legislative Affairs, December 22, 2005, https://fas.org/irp /agency/doj/fisa/doj122205.pdf (accessed May 2, 2020).

39. Alberto R. Gonzalez, "Legal Authorities Supporting the Activities of the National Security Agency Described by the President," US Department of Justice, Office of Legal Counsel, January 19, 2006, https://www.justice.gov/olc/opinion /legal-authorities-supporting-activities-national-security-agency-described-presi dent (accessed May 2, 2020).

40. Gonzalez, 3.

41. 121 Stat. 552 (2007).

42. 122 Stat. 2436 (2008).

43. Erin Kelly, "Senate Approves USA Freedom Act," *USA Today*, June 2, 2015, https://www.usatoday.com/story/news/politics/2015/06/02/patriot-act-usa -freedom-act-senate-vote/28345747/ (accessed May 2, 2020).

44. 129 Stat. 268 (2015).

45. Rand Paul, Ron Wyden, Michael S. Lee, and Patrick Leahy, "Bipartisan FISA Reform Letter," Office of US Senator Rand Paul, January 12, 2018, https://www.paul.senate.gov/bipartisan-fisa-reform-letter (accessed May 2, 2020).

46. "CIA Tactics: What Is Enhanced Interrogation?," BBC News, December 10, 2014, https://www.bbc.com/news/world-us-canada-11723189 (accessed July 20, 2019).

47. Robert M. Pallitto, ed., *Torture and State Violence in the United States: A Short Documentary History* (Baltimore: Johns Hopkins University Press, 2011), 184–185.

48. George W. Bush, "Memo on the Humane Treatment of Taliban and Al Qaeda Detainees," The White House, February 7, 2002, https://www.pegc.us/ar chive/White_House/bush_memo_20020207_ed.pdf (accessed May 2, 2020).

49. Jay S. Bybee, "Memorandum for Alberto R. Gonzales, Counsel to the President," US Department of Justice, Office of Legal Counsel, August 1, 2002, 31, https://www.justice.gov/olc/file/886061/download (accessed May 2, 2020).

50. Bybee, 34.

51. Pallitto, *Torture and State Violence in the United States*, 186–188.

52. Pallitto, 211–212.

53. Pallitto, 189–193.

54. Pallitto, 189–193.

55. Pallitto, 212–213.

56. Pallitto, 215.

57. George W. Bush, "Executive Order 13440," The American Presidency Project, July 20, 2007, https://www.presidency.ucsb.edu/documents/executive -order-13440-interpretation-the-geneva-conventions-common-article-3-applied (accessed May 2, 2020).

58. Barack Obama, "Executive Order 13491—Ensuring Lawful Interrogations," The White House, January 22, 2009, https://obamawhitehouse.archives.gov /the-press-office/ensuring-lawful-interrogations (accessed May 2, 2020).

59. Adam Withnall, "Donald Trump Says Torture 'Absolutely Works' in First Major Interview as President," *Independent*, January 26, 2017, https://www.inde pendent.co.uk/news/world/americas/donald-trump-abc-news-interview-presi dent-torture-works-a7546616.html (accessed May 2, 2020).

60. Margaret L. Satterthwaite, "Rendered Meaningless: Extraordinary Rendition and the Rule of Law" *George Washington Law Review* 75 (August 2007): 1336.

61. Louis Fisher, "Extraordinary Rendition: The Price of Secrecy," *American University Law Review* 57, no. 5 (June 2008): 1407–1408.

62. Fisher, 1408.

63. Fisher, 1409.

64. William G. Weaver and Robert M. Pallitto, "*The Law:* 'Extraordinary Rendition' and Presidential Fiat," *Presidential Studies Quarterly* 36, no. 1 (March 2006): 105.

65. Fisher, "Extraordinary Rendition," 1410.

66. Fisher, 1411.

67. Weaver and Pallitto, "*The Law*: Extraordinary Rendition," 104.

68. *Holmes v. Jennison*, 39 U.S. 540, 569 (1840).

69. *Holmes v. Jennison*, 583.

70. *Valentine, Police Commissioner of New York City, et al. v. United States ex rel. B. Coles Neidecker*, 299 U.S. 5, 6 (1936).

71. *Valentine, Police Commissioner of New York City, et al. v. United States ex rel. B. Coles Neidecker*, 9.

72. Fisher, "Extraordinary Rendition," 1415.

73. Mark J. Rozell, *Executive Privilege: Presidential Power, Secrecy, and Accountability*, 3rd ed. (Lawrence: University Press of Kansas, 2010), 119.

74. James D. Boys, "What's So Extraordinary about Rendition?," *International Journal of Human Rights* 15, no. 4 (2011): 594.

75. Boys, 595.

76. Executive Order 13491, "Ensuring Lawful Interrogations," January 22, 2009, https://obamawhitehouse.archives.gov/the-press-office/ensuring-lawful-in terrogations (accessed May 2, 2020).

77. Executive Order 13492, "Review and Disposition of Individuals Detained at the Guantanamo Bay Naval Base and Closure of Detention Facilities," January 22, 2009, https://www.govinfo.gov/content/pkg/CFR-2010-title3-vol1/pdf/CFR -2010-title3-vol1-eo13492.pdf (accessed September 16, 2020).

78. Executive Order 13493, "Review of Detention Policy Options," January 22, 2009, https://obamawhitehouse.archives.gov/the-press-office/2009/01/22/ex ecutive-order-13493-review-detention-policy-options (accessed May 2, 2020).

79. Boys, "What's So Extraordinary about Rendition?," 598–599.

80. Boys, 599.

81. Katherine Hawkins, "Enhanced Evasion Techniques," Just Security, May 21, 2018, https://www.justsecurity.org/56574/enhanced-evasion-techniques/ (ac cessed May 2, 2020).

82. William G. Weaver and Robert M. Pallitto, "State Secrets and Executive Power," *Political Science Quarterly* 120, no. 1 (Spring 2005): 92.

83. 345 U.S. 1 (1953).

84. Weaver and Pallitto, "State Secrets and Executive Power," 98.

85. Lee Tien, "Litigating the State Secrets Privilege," *Case Western Reserve Journal of International Law* 42 (2010): 677, https://scholarlycommons.law.case.edu /jil/vol42/iss3/8/ (accessed May 2, 2020).

86. Erin M. Stilp, "The Military and State-Secrets Privilege: The Quietly Expanding Power," *Catholic University Law Review* 55 (Spring 2006): 836, https:// scholarship.law.edu/lawreview/vol55/iss3/11/ (accessed May 2, 2020).

87. Louis Fisher, *In the Name of National Security: Unchecked Presidential Power and the* Reynolds *Case* (Lawrence: University Press of Kansas, 2006), 246.

88. Fisher, 247.

89. Todd Garvey and Edward C. Liu, "The State Secrets Privilege: Preventing

the Disclosure of Sensitive National Security Information during Civil Litigation," Congressional Research Service, August 16, 2011, 8–9, https://fas.org/sgp/crs /secrecy/R41741.pdf (accessed May 2, 2020).

90. James Risen, Sheri Fink, and Charlie Savage, "State Secrets Privilege Invoked to Block Testimony in C.I.A. Torture Case," *New York Times,* March 8, 2017, https://www.nytimes.com/2017/03/08/us/justice-department-cia-psychol ogists-interrogation-program.html (accessed May 2, 2020).

91. Risen, Fink, and Savage.

92. Frank Thorp V, "Barack Obama Signs 'USA Freedom Act' to Reform NSA Surveillance," NBC News, June 2, 2015, https://www.nbcnews.com/storyline/nsa -snooping/senate-vote-measure-reform-nsa-surveillance-n368341 (accessed May 2, 2020).

93. Bush, "Memo on the Humane Treatment of Taliban and Al Qaeda Detainees."

94. Bybee, "Memorandum for Alberto R. Gonzales."

95. David Welna, "Trump Presidency Casts Doubt over Declassification of CIA Torture Report," NPR, November 28, 2016, https://www.npr.org/2016/11/28 /503632423/trump-presidency-casts-doubt-over-declassification-of-cia-torture-re port (accessed May 2, 2020).

96. Fisher, "Extraordinary Rendition," 1416.

CONCLUSION

1. See Charlie Savage, *Power Wars: Inside Obama's Post-9/11 Presidency* (Boston: Little, Brown, 2015), 659.

2. In his study of the theory, Graham G. Dodds observes, "For a theory that values unity, there is surprisingly little unity among unitarians about a strict defi-nition of the unitary executive theory." Graham G. Dodds, *The Unitary Presidency* (New York: Routledge, 2020), 2.

3. See Mark Tushnet, "A Political Perspective on the Theory of the Unitary Ex-ecutive," *University of Pennsylvania Journal of Constitutional Law* 12 (February 2010): 313; Steven G. Calabresi and Christopher S. Yoo, *The Unitary Executive: Presidential Power from Washington to Bush* (New Haven, CT: Yale University Press, 2008), 4.

4. See Tushnet, "A Political Perspective on the Theory of the Unitary Execu-tive"; Louis Fisher, "Invoking Inherent Powers: A Primer," *Presidential Studies Quar-terly* 37, no. 1 (March 2007):1–22, https://www.loc.gov/law/help/usconlaw/pdf /Inherent-March07.pdf (accessed May 3, 2020).

5. Charles O. Jones, *The Presidency in a Separated System* (Washington, DC: Brookings Institution Press, 1994).

6. Ryan J. Barilleaux and Jewerl Maxwell, "Has Barack Obama Embraced the Unitary Executive?," *PS,* January 2017, 33.

7. Barilleaux and Maxwell, 33–34.

8. Barilleaux and Maxwell, 34.

9. *Federalist* No. 49, in *The Federalist Papers*, ed. Clinton Rossiter (New York: Mentor, 1999), 281–282.

10. *Federalist* No. 9, in Rossiter, *The Federalist Papers*, 40. For a detailed account of Hamilton's views on republican government, see Gerald Stourzh, *Alexander Hamilton and the Idea of Republican Government* (Stanford, CA: Stanford University Press, 1970).

11. Brutus, October 18, 1787, in *The Anti-Federalist Papers*, ed. Ralph Ketcham (New York: New American Library, 1986), 276.

12. Speeches of Melancton Smith, June 20–27, 1788, in Ketcham, *The Anti-Federalist Papers*, 341.

13. *Federalist* No. 51, in Rossiter, *The Federalist Papers*, 290.

14. *Federalist* No. 37, in Rossiter, *The Federalist Papers*, 195.

15. *Federalist* No. 77, in Rossiter, *The Federalist Papers*, 427–432.

16. Virginia senator Stevens Thomas Mason quoted in Larry D. Kramer, *The People Themselves: Popular Constitutionalism and Judicial Review* (New York: Oxford University Press, 2004), 107.

17. *Federalist* No. 51, in Rossiter, *The Federalist Papers*, 290.

18. *Federalist* No. 51, in Rossiter, *The Federalist Papers*, 289–290.

19. Dodds, *The Unitary Presidency*, 101.

20. Charlie Savage, "Presidential Power Must Be Curbed after Trump, 2020 Candidates Say," *New York Times*, September 12, 2019, https://www.nytimes.com/2019/09/10/us/politics/executive-power-survey-2020.html (accessed May 3, 2020).

Index

Abu Ghraib prison, 131
Adams, John, 122
Adams, John Quincy, 141
Adler, David Gray, 107, 111
administrative powers, 29
agencies: use of litigation authority, 85
agency-level adjudication, 85
agency-level regulations
 guidance documents as, 85–86
 OIRA review of, 82–83, 85, 86
 presidential control over, 82–87, 156
Ahlers, Christopher, 86
Algonquin SNG Inc. v. Federal Energy Administration, 8
Alito, Samuel, 11, 20
American Bar Association Task Force on Presidential Signing Statements, 45, 129
American colonies: governing structure of, 117–118
appointments
 constitutional provisions on, 53–54, 55, 65, 69, 155
 evolution of the process of, 54
 intersession vs. intrasession, 56, 57
 nuclear option, 59, 60–61
 power to reject, 54
 Senate's review of, 57–59, 60
 "senatorial courtesy" practice, 54
 statutory restrictions of, 64–65
 waiver-seeking process, 65–66
 See also recess appointments
Arpaio, Joe, 51
Articles of Confederation, 111, 117, 190n13

attorney general
 contempt of Congress, 99–100
 powers of, 73
Authorization for Use of Military Force (AUMF), 113, 128, 136
Awlaki, Nasser al-, 147

Balkin, Jack, 112
Barilleaux, Ryan, 158
Barlow, Richard, 146
Barlow v. United States, 146
Barr, William, 73, 99
Barron, David, 107
Barshefsky, Charlene, 65, 66
Baruch, Bernard, 94
Bas v. Tingy, 108
Bauer, Robert, 112
Berry, Michael, 81
bicameralism: concept of, 78
Biddle v. Perovich, 50
Biden, Hunter, 1
Bjerre-Poulsen, Niels, 27
Black, Hugo, 120
Blackstone, William, 117
Bodenhamer, David, 103
Boehner, John, 96, 148
Bork, Robert, 21, 67
Boumediene v. Bush, 132
Boyd, Stephen, 100
Bradbury, Steven, 139
Brand, Donald, 29
British Monarch: prerogative powers of, 117–118
Broomfield, William, 104
Browner, Carol, 92

Brownlow Committee, 35–36, 153
bureaus, 36–37, 38, 39
Bush, George H. W., 72, 80, 81, 89,
    143, 154
Bush, George W.
    clemency decisions, 50, 154
    control of military commissions,
        147–148
    criticism of, 47–48, 129
    czar appointments, 87–88, 89–90, 94
    executive orders of, 40, 139
    executive privilege claims, 95–96
    exercise of inherent powers, 157–158
    foreign policy of, 128
    memo on Geneva Convention, 148
    practice of extraordinary rendition,
        140, 143, 148, 158
    recess appointments, 55, 56
    signing statements of, 44, 45, 47–48
    on treatment of terrorists, 138
    unilateral actions of, 3, 22
    use of state secrets privilege, 145,
        147, 158
    use of war powers, 127, 129, 131–132
    view of presidential power, 10, 11, 118,
        125, 135–136, 151, 152
Bush administration
    claim for broader presidential power,
        108, 136
    surveillance program, 134, 135–136
    unitary executive theory and, 103
    war on terror, 130, 158
Butler, Pierce, 110
Bybee, Jay, 138, 139, 148, 158
"Bybee memo," 148
Byrd, Robert C., 61, 93

Calabresi, Steven
    on control of agency-level rulemaking,
        82–83, 156
    on independent counsel bill, 68
    on inherent powers, 116
    on legislative veto, 78–79
    on presidential control of the execu-
        tive branch, 35, 152
    on removal power, 61–62
    on signing statements, 44
    study of the unitary executive theory,
        11, 18, 20, 23, 24, 26, 64, 71, 152, 153
    on Vesting Clause, 25
Carter, Jimmy
    executive orders of, 195n94

review of agency-level rulemaking
        process, 82
    special prosecutor bill, 68
    surveillance policies of, 134
Census Bureau, 64
Chaffetz, Jason, 97
checks and balances, 61, 124–125,
    144–145, 155, 158, 160
Cheney, Richard, 22, 103–104, 105,
    125, 127
clemency power
    congressional check on, 49–50
    evaluation of appropriateness of, 51
    presidential use of, 49, 50–51, 154–155
Clinton, Bill
    clemency decisions, 50, 154
    control of agency-level rules, 84
    executive orders of, 82, 86, 186n72
    executive privilege claims, 95, 100
    impeachment of, 163
    investigation of, 72
    nominations by, 65, 66
    practice of extraordinary rendition, 143
    signing statements of, 71–72
Cohen, Michael, 73
Cole, James, 96
Combatant Status Review Tribunal, 131
Commander-in-Chief Clause, 106–108,
    109, 118, 120–121, 125, 157
comptroller of the Treasury, 33–34
Congressional Budget and Impound-
        ment Control Act, 20
Consumer Financial Protection Bureau
    (CFPB), 87
Continental Congress, 107, 117
Cooper, Phillip, 45
Corwin, Edward, 19, 24, 64, 122
Courter, Jim, 104
Cox, Archibald, 67
Crovitz, L. Gordon, 21
crown privilege, 145–146
Cuomo, Andrew, 91
Cushing, Caleb, 32, 78–79
Cushman, Robert, 33
czars
    accountability of, 93
    appointments of, 87–88, 89, 90, 92,
        102, 156
    authority of, 156
    faith-based, 89
    features of, 88–89
    governing concerns, 90, 92

incompetence of, 94
power of, 90–91, 92

Dames & Moore v. Regan, 121, 122
Declare War Clause, 109–111, 115,
 125, 157
Department of Commerce and Labor, 37
Department of Justice (DOJ), 5, 66–67,
 75, 81, 87
Department of the Treasury, 33–34
departments, 36–37, 38
Detainee Treatment Act (DTA), 131–132
Devins, Neal, 85
DeWine, Michael, 104
discretionary duties, 30–31, 33–36
Dodds, Graham, 161
D'Souza, Dinesh, 51
Duncan v. Cammell Laird & Co. Ltd., 145

Edelson, Chris, 40
Elwood, John P., 65
Emergency Economic Stabilization Act
 (EESA), 90–91
emergency presidential power
 claims for, 115–116
 limits of, 120–121
 rationale for, 119, 121–122
 roots of, 118
 statutorily granted, 121
 views of, 118–119
Emergency Price Control Act, 19
Engle Act, 42
enumerated powers, 116
Equal Employment Opportunity Commission (EEOC), 64
Ethics in Government Act, 20, 66, 68
executive branch
 arguments for unitary control of, 52
 checks on, 74–75
 control over, 31–32, 35, 38, 39–40,
 153–154
 discretionary powers of, 33–34
 function of, 38–39
 hierarchical model of, 39
 nominations, 58, 59–60
 supporters of, 72
Executive Office of the President, 37
executive orders
 congressional pushback against, 42–43
 court challenges of, 41–42
 versus law, 41
 limits of, 41

presidents' use of, 5–6, 40–43, 82, 86,
 139, 154, 170n30, 186n72, 195n94
executive power
 constitutional provisions on, 23, 24, 27
 presidential power and, 19–20, 21, 36,
 161–162
executive privilege, 95, 101–102, 156
Ex parte Milligan, 119–120, 130
Ex parte Quirin, 129–130
extraordinary rendition, 140, 142–143,
 144, 148, 158

Fast and Furious investigation, 96–98, 100
Federal Bureau of Investigation (FBI)
 apprehension of fugitives, 143
 review of judiciary nominees, 58
Federal Communications Commission
 (FCC), 64
federal court system, 8
Federal Election Commission (FEC), 64
Federal Land Policy and Management
 Act, 42
Feinberg, Kenneth, 90
Feinstein, Dianne, 132
Fettered Presidency, The, 21
Field, Stephen, 119
FISA Amendments Reauthorization Act,
 137, 148
Fishbourn, Benjamin, 54
Fisher, Louis
 on abuse of state secrets privilege, 146
 on *Chadha* case, 81
 on claim of inherent powers, 117
 on executive privilege, 97
 on implied powers, 10, 38
 on intersession appointments, 56
 on Iran-Contra affair, 72
 on legislative veto, 78
 on power in foreign affairs, 122
 on rendition, 148
 on signing statements, 47
 on war powers, 110, 111
Flynn, Michael, 73
"for cause" provision, 86–87
Ford, Gerald R., 82, 103
foreign affairs powers, 13, 103, 105,
 122–123, 125–126, 127, 157–159
Foreign Intelligence Surveillance Act
 (FISA), 134–135, 137, 148, 158
Franco-American Extradition Treaty of
 1909, 142
Frank, Barney, 46, 47

Fried, Charles, 26, 71
Fuerzas Armadas de Liberación Nacional (FALN), 50

Gaddafi, Muammar, 112
Geithner, Timothy, 90
Genêt, Edmond-Charles, 140
Geneva Convention Relative to the Treatment of Prisoners of War, 138, 139
Gerry, Elbridge, 110
Gilmour, Robert, 37
Goldsmith, Jack, 133, 161
Gonzales, Alberto, 116, 138
Gorsuch, Neil, 59
Grassley, Chuck, 8
Gregg, Gary L., 19
Guantanamo Bay detention camp, 40, 42–43, 130, 132, 133–134, 148

habeas corpus
    military commissions and, 128–134
    suspension of, 15, 17
Hamdan v. Rumsfeld, 132
Hamdi, Yaser, 129
Hamdi v. Rumsfeld, 130
Hamilton, Alexander
    on administrative powers, 29
    on "energy" of the executive, 104–105
    justification of clemency decisions, 50
    Pacificus-Helvidius debates and, 23–24
    on power of the comptroller, 33
    on presidential power, 54, 123
    on republican government, 159, 160
    as secretary of the Treasury, 36
    on the unity of the executive, 26–27
    on war powers, 111
Hammond, Thomas, 40
Haspel, Gina, 144
Hatch, Orrin, 104
Haupt, Herbert Hans, 130
Healy, Gene, 45
Holder, Eric, 96, 100
Holmes, George, 141
Holmes v. Jennison, 141
Hoover, Herbert, 36, 79
Hoover Commission, 36, 37
Howell, William, 41, 43
Humphrey, William, 63
Humphrey's Executor v. United States, 62, 70
Huq, Aziz, 105
Hyde, Henry, 104

impeachments, 1–2, 162–163
implied powers, 116
independent counsel
    appointment of, 69
    court challenge of statute of, 70, 71, 72
    critics of, 72
    investigations of executive branch by, 72
    legislation on, 73, 75
    power of, 69
    removal of, 70
independent regulatory agencies, 86
inherent powers, 10–11, 116–117, 157–158
In re Neagle, 119
INS v. Chadha, 77, 78, 80–81, 114, 155–156
International Emergency Economic Powers Act, 121
interrogation techniques. *See* torture
intrasession recess appointments, 56, 57
Iran-Contra scandal, 104–105, 125
Iran nuclear deal, 9
Issa, Darrell, 96

Jackson, Amy Berman, 97
Jackson, Andrew, 44
Jackson, Lisa, 92
Jackson, Robert, 116, 120–121
Jaworski, Leon, 67
Jefferson, Thomas, 105, 140
Johnson, Alice Marie, 51
Johnson, Jack, 51
Johnson, Jeh, 112
Johnson, Lyndon B., 134
Johnson v. Eisentrager, 131
Jones, Gordon: *The Imperial Congress*, 21
Justice Department. *See* Department of Justice (DOJ)

Kadzik, Peter, 97
Kagan, Elena, 83, 84
Kaine, Tim, 115
Kardashian, Kim, 51
Kaufman, Herbert, 37, 39
Kavanaugh, Brett, 59, 188n106
Kelley, Christopher, 44, 48
Kendall, Amos, 31, 32
Kendall v. United States, 31–32
Kennedy, Anthony, 69, 123–124
Kennedy, Joshua, 43
Kinkopf, Neil, 44
Knott, Jack, 40
Koenig, Louis: *The Chief Executive*, 14

Koh, Harold, 42, 112, 125
Korean War, 115
Krass, Caroline, 112
Krauthammer, Charles, 60
Krent, Harold, 41

Leahy, Patrick, 129, 137
Lederman, Martin, 107
Lee, Mike, 60, 137
legislative veto
    criticism of, 77–78
    formal recognition of, 77
    presidents and mechanism of, 78–79,
        80, 81
    Supreme Court decision on, 77–78,
        80–81
    of US Congress, 76–77, 79, 81–82
    as vehicle for balancing the powers, 102
"Levin memo," 139, 148
Libby, I. Lewis "Scooter," 50, 51
"life and limb" theory. *See* presidential
    prerogative
Lincoln, Abraham
    Congress and, 17
    legislative acts of, 16–17
    prerogative power of, 15–17, 152
    reputation of, 3
    Supreme Court and, 17, 109
    war powers of, 118, 119
literalist theory, 14–15
Little v. Barreme, 25, 108

Mackenzie, G. Calvin, 55
Madison, James, 30, 33, 124, 125, 159,
    160–161
Manafort, Paul, 73
Manchin, Joe, 59
Marbury v. Madison, 31
Marini, John: *The Imperial Congress*, 21
Marshall, George C., 65, 66
Marshall, John, 30, 31, 108, 116,
    122–123, 157
Mason, George, 110
Mason, John, 34
Masri, Khaled al-, 147
Maxwell, Jewerl, 158
McCain, John, 60
McClure, James, 104
McCollum, Bill, 104
McCulloch v. Maryland, 30, 116
McCumber, Porter, 37

McGahn, Don, 100, 101
Meese, Edwin, 20, 45
Merkley, Jeff, 59
military commissions, 129, 132,
    133–134, 148
military tribunals, 128–129, 131
ministerial duties, 30, 31
Monroe, James, 44
Moody, William, 32
Morrison v. Olson, 24, 69, 155
Moschella, William, 136
Mueller, Robert
    restriction of access to Report of, 100
    Russian interference investigation, 51,
        73–74, 98, 99, 101
    testimony before Congress, 73
Murkowski, Lisa, 59
Myers, Frank, 61
Myers v. United States, 30, 61, 63, 70

Nadler, Jerry, 99
national emergencies, 195n94
National Security Agency (NSA), 134, 135
National Security Strategy, 7
Neustadt, Richard: *Presidential Power*,
    19, 37
Niles, John, 36–37
9/11 terrorist attacks, 103, 127, 130,
    133, 157
Nixon, Richard M.
    assessment of offices and bureaus, 37
    control over agency-level rulemaking,
        84
    creation of Quality of Life review
        process, 82
    criticism of independent counsel, 72
    czars of, 94
    domestic surveillance policies of, 134
    executive privilege claims of, 95
    removal power of, 67
    vision of president power, 1
    Watergate scandal, 67
Noriega, Manuel, 143
North American Free Trade Agreement
    (NAFTA), 9

Obama, Barack
    cooperation with Congress, 46
    criticism of Bush administration, 147
    czar appointments, 87–88, 90
    executive orders of, 40, 42–43, 139

Obama, Barack (*continued*)
  executive privilege claims, 95, 96–97
  "Fast and Furious" case, 96–98
  legislative process and, 46–47
  military commissions, plan for, 132–133
  military strikes in Libya, 112–113
  objections to committee-level vetoes, 81
  recess appointments of, 56, 58
  review of practice of rendition, 143–144
  signing statements of, 46, 48, 154, 177n107
  state secrets privilege claims, 158
  unilateral actions of, 3, 112–113, 125, 158–159
  USA Freedom Act, 148
  view of presidential powers, 3, 9, 12, 151–152
Obamacare, 43
O'Connor, Sandra Day, 130
Office of Information and Regulatory Affairs (OIRA), 21, 170n30
Office of Legal Counsel, Department of Justice, 65–66
Office of Legal Counsel (OLC) memorandum, 128
Office of Management and Budget (OMB), 82
Office of the Pardon Attorney, 51
Office of Watergate Special Counsel, 67
Olson, Theodore, 69

Pacificus-Helvidius debates, 23
Padilla, Jose, 129
Paris Climate Accord, 9
Paul, Rand, 137
Pearlstein, Deborah, 43
Petraeus, David, 139
Pfiffner, James, 24, 106, 111, 135
Philbin, Patrick, 128, 129, 130
Pickering, Charles W., 55
Pickering, Timothy, 36
Pickett Act, 42
Pinckney, Charles, 110
Pious, Richard: *Why Presidents Fail*, 93
Plame, Valerie, 50
Polk, James, 34
Post Office Department, 54
Prakash, Saikrishna, 63
prerogative powers, 117–118, 151, 152, 161, 163
presidential aides, 37–38

presidential power
  authority of Congress vs., 12
  of clemency, 49–51
  constitutional provisions on, 10, 20–21, 28, 38, 123, 152–153, 162
  court decisions and, 162
  of czar appointments, 87–94
  decline of, 20, 103
  definitions of, 10
  as discretionary duty, 31
  in domestic affairs, 76–102, 153–156
  effect of 9/11 attack on, 130
  in foreign affairs, 13, 103–126, 127–149, 157–159
  justification for expansion of, 11–12, 18, 20, 93–94, 108–109
  limits of, 2, 5, 21, 34–36, 51–52, 74–75, 102, 119
  to make appointments, 53–61, 155
  national security concerns and, 9, 125
  to order extraordinary rendition, 140–144
  over agency-level rulemaking process, 82–87
  over executive branch, 31–32, 38, 39–40, 52, 152, 153–154
  over trade policy, 8
  of removal from office, 61–66, 155
  Senate's check on, 74
  "sole organ" doctrine of, 122–125
  theories of, 14, 19, 22–23, 151
  of veto, 47, 49
presidential prerogative ("life and limb" theory), 14, 15–17
Prize Cases, 17, 119
Pryor, William H., 55
Public Papers of the Presidents of the United States, 45

Quality of Life review process, 82
Quasi-War, 115

Rabkin, Jeremy, 21
Rasul v. Bush, 130–131
Rattner, Steven, 90, 91–92
Reagan, Nancy, 94
Reagan, Ronald
  agency-level rulemaking, 156
  criticism of independent counsel, 72
  election as president, 20
  executive orders of, 82, 170n30
  Iran-Contra affair, 105
  legislative vetoes signed by, 80

objection of appropriation bill, 81
"rendition to justice" technique, 143
signing statements of, 68–69, 71, 154
use of Oath Clause, 25
use of Vesting Clause, 23
view of presidential power, 3, 11,
    20–21, 22, 45
recess appointments, 55, 57, 58
Rehnquist, William, 69, 70, 121
Reid, Harry, 59
removal power
    criticism of, 66
    independent counsel and, 66–74
    limits of, 63–64, 75
    Taft's opinion about, 61–62, 63–64
rendition, 140, 148. *See also* extraordinary
    rendition
Reno, Janet, 100
republican government
    democratic control of, 160–161
    function of, 159–160
    source of authority of, 160
Rice, Condoleezza, 143
Rich, Marc, 50
Richardson, Elliot, 67
Ridge, Tom, 94
Ritchie, Donald A., 56
Robart, James, 6
Roosevelt, Franklin D.
    appointments of, 58
    Brownlow Committee of, 35–36, 153
    control of executive branch, 36
    court-packing plan of, 58
    dispute between Congress and, 19
    legislative vetoes signed by, 80
    military commission system of, 129
    prerogative power of, 16
    removal power of, 62
    reputation of, 3
Roosevelt, Theodore
    model of the presidency of, 3, 19
    "stewardship" theory of, 14, 16, 17–18
    view of presidential power, 118, 152
Rosenberg, Morton, 84
Rosenstein, Rod, 73
Rourke, Francis, 39
Ruckelshaus, William, 67
Rudalevige, Andrew, 12, 37
Rumsfeld, Donald, 139

sanctuary cities, 4
"Saturday Night Massacre," 66–67

Savage, Charlie, 20, 21
Scalia, Antonin, 24, 69, 70–71, 124
Schlesinger, Arthur, Jr., 19–20
    The Imperial Presidency, 19
Schwarz, Frederick, Jr, 105
Scott, Winfield, 128–129
Securities and Exchange Commission
    (SEC), 64
Sedition Act, 36
Seidman, Harold, 37
Sekulow, Jay, 4
senatorial courtesy, 54, 74
separation of powers: principle of, 2, 127,
    152, 158, 160–161, 162, 163
Sessions, Jeff, 98–99
signing statements
    categories of, 44
    ceremonial function of, 44–45
    congressional reaction to, 46
    Constitution and, 44–46, 47, 48
    definition of, 44
    language of, 48
    as objecting tool to provisions of a law,
        48–49
    presidents' use of, 45, 46, 154
    publication of, 45
Smith, Loren, 37, 38
Smith, Melancton, 159
Smith, William French, 68
Snowden, Edward, 137
Soleimani, Qasem, 114
"sole organ" doctrine, 122–125, 157
Somin, Ilya, 11
special counsel, 73, 75
special prosecutor, 67–68
Spitzer, Robert, 48
Stallone, Sylvester, 51
Starr, Kenneth, 72
state secrets privilege, 144–147, 149, 158
"Steel Seizure" case, 41
stewardship theory, 14, 17–18
Sunstein, Cass, 11, 27
surveillance programs, 134, 135–136
Sutherland, George, 63, 122, 123

Taft, William Howard
    on functions of Congress, 30, 32–33
    on legislative control of the executive
        branch, 32
    opinion in *Myers* case, 63–64
    view of presidential power, 14, 61–62
Take Care Clause, 25–26

Talbot v. Seeman, 108
Taney, Roger, 141–142
Terrorist Surveillance Program (TSP),
 134, 135, 136–137
Thompson, Smith, 31, 32, 142
Tien, Lee, 146
torture, 138–140, 158
Trade Expansion Act, 7, 8
Trading with the Enemy Act, 121
Trans-Pacific Partnership, 9
travel ban, 5–6, 7
Troubled Asset Relief Program, 90–91
Truman, Harry, 25, 41, 115, 120
Trump, Donald J.
 absolute authority claims, 162
 appointments by, 58, 59
 business background of, 4
 clemency decisions of, 50–51, 154–155
 criticism of Obama policy, 139
 emphasis on national security, 6
 executive orders of, 5–6, 40, 43, 134
 executive privilege claims, 95, 98, 100,
  101, 188n106
 fight with sanctuary cities, 4–5
 foreign policy of, 9
 governing style of, 3, 4
 immigration policy of, 5, 7, 151
 impeachment of, 1, 2, 163
 military commissions debate and,
  133–134, 148
 Mueller's investigation and, 73–74, 75
 opinion about torture, 140
 rendition policies of, 144
 self-pardon claims of, 51
 signing statements of, 48–49
 state secrets privilege claims, 147, 158
 trade policy of, 7–8
 travel ban of, 5–6
 tweets of, 6
 unilateral actions of, 5, 9, 159
 use of military force, 113–115, 125
 view of presidential power, 1, 8, 151
Trump v. Hawaii, 7

Uniform Code of Military Justice, 128, 129
unitary executive: definitions of, 152
unitary executive theory
 advancement of, 170n27
 arguments for, 150, 154
 complexity of, 10
 constitutional issues of, 162
 critics of, 26–27

 democratic governance and, 13
 features of, 2, 3, 28, 76, 150, 152–153
 foreign affairs and, 103, 106, 127
 9/11 attack and, 127
 origin of, 3, 18–22
 presidential power and, 11–13,
  14–27, 29
 revisionist view of, 11
 supporters of, 20–21, 26–27, 39
 textual elements of, 23–26
 weak and strong versions of, 22–23, 152
unitary military actions
 justification of, 113–114
 legal obfuscation for taking, 112–113
 national interest and, 113
 restrictions of, 114–115
United Nations Human Rights Council, 9
United States Code, 121
United States v. Midwest Oil Company, 41
United States v. Reynolds, 145, 146, 149
USA Freedom Act, 137, 148
*US Code Congressional and Administrative
 News*, 45
US Congress
 appointment of special prosecutors,
  67–68
 approach to signing statements, 49
 constitutional provisions on power of,
  23, 150–151, 159
 government powers of, 51–52,
  150–151, 159–160, 161
 implied authority of, 116
 legislative powers of, 23, 32–33
 legislative vetoes, 76–77, 79, 81–82
 nomination of federal officials and
  judges, 155, 156
 policy direction of departments and
  bureaus, 38
 power over executive clemency,
  49–50
 presidential authority vs. power of, 5,
  11, 12, 21–22, 37–38, 79–80
 pushback against executive orders,
  42–43
 reaction to signing statements, 46, 47
 removal power of, 63
 rendition power of, 141
 rulemaking power of, 84
 as source of administrative authority, 35
 Trump's impeachment by, 2, 3
 war powers of, 107, 108, 110, 113,
  114–115, 157

US Constitution
  Appointments Clause, 54, 65, 69–70
  Commander-in-Chief Clause,
    106–107, 157
  Declare War Clause, 157
  enumerated powers of, 116
  on executive power, 23, 24, 27
  Necessary and Proper Clause, 27
  Oath Clause, 23, 25
  Opinions Clause, 27
  Pardon Clause, 49
  on powers of Congress, 23, 150–151,
    159
  principle of separation of powers of,
    5, 13
  provisions on presidential power, 10,
    20–21, 28, 38, 123, 152–153, 162
  Take Care Clause, 23, 25–26
  Vesting Clause, 23, 24–25
  on veto authority, 47
US Court of Appeals for the District of
    Columbia, 56, 87
US Court of International Trade, 8–9
US House of Representatives, 1, 8
US Office of Thrift Supervision, 64
US Patent and Trademark Office, 64
US Postal Service, 85
US Refugee Admissions Program, 6
US Senate
  confirmation power of, 74
  impeachment vote against Donald J.
    Trump, 1
  pro forma sessions, 56
  review of Supreme Court nominations,
    58, 60
US Supreme Court
  on discretionary vs. ministerial duties,
    30–31
  interpretation of administrative law, 32
  interpretation of Pardon Clause, 49
  limits on president's emergency
    powers, 120–121
  nominee confirmation hearings,
    188n106
  opinion on president's use of
    executive orders, 41–42
  ruling on military courts, 119–120
  ruling on travel ban, 7, 9
  rulings on rendition questions,
    141–142
  See also individual cases and lawsuits
United States v. Alvarez-Machain, 143

United States v. Curtiss-Wright Export Corp.,
    122, 157
United States v. Wilson, 50

Valentine v. United States, 142
Vattel, Emer de, 123
Vesting Clause, 23, 24–26

Walsh, Lawrence, 50
War Industries Board (WIB), 94
Warner, Mark, 144
"war on terror," 128, 158–159
war powers
  of Congress, 107, 108, 113, 114–115,
    157
  presidents' use of, 118, 119, 127, 129,
    131–132
  theoretical debates on, 110, 111
War Powers Resolution (WPR), 20, 77,
    112, 114
Washington, George, 36, 47, 50, 54, 107
Watergate scandal, 67
Waterman, Richard, 44
Watt, Mel, 59
*Weekly Compilation of Presidential
    Documents*, 45
Weinberger, Caspar, 50
West, William, 83
Whiskey Rebels, 50
White, Leonard, 29, 34, 35
White House Office of Faith-Based and
    Community Initiatives, 89
White House security clearances
    investigation, 98
Willoughby, William, 35
Wilson, James, 111, 118
Wilson, Woodrow, 3, 19, 61–62, 94,
    118–119
Wirt, William, 30, 34, 141
World Trade Organization (WTO), 9
Wyden, Ron, 137

Yoo, Christopher
  on control agency-level rulemaking,
    82–83, 156
  on independent counsel bill, 68
  on inherent powers, 116
  on legislative veto, 78, 79
  on limits of presidential control, 35
  on signing statements, 44
  study of unitary executive theory, 11,
    18, 22, 23, 24, 61, 64, 71, 152, 153

Yoo, John
  analysis of war power, 106–107, 109,
    111
  on executive privilege, 190n13
  on jurisdiction of federal courts, 130
  September 25, 2001 memorandum,
    115–116, 127, 190n13

  view of presidential power, 7, 108–109,
    125, 157
*Youngstown Sheet & Tube Company v.
  Sawyer*, 25, 120

Zivotofsky v. Kerry, 123, 124–125